D0938935

The French Socialists
in Power,
1981–1986

The French Socialists in Power, 1981–1986

From Autogestion to Cohabitation

Thomas R. Christofferson

DELAWARE

Newark: University of Delaware Press
London and Toronto: Associated University Presses

Associated University Presses
440 Forsgate Drive
Cranbury, NJ 08512

Associated University Presses
25 Sicilian Avenue
London WC1A 2QH, England

Associated University Presses
P.O. Box 39, Clarkson Pstl. Stn.
Mississauga, Ontario,
L5J 3X9 Canada

The paper used in this publication meets the requirements
of the American National Standard for Permanence of Paper
for Printed Library Materials Z39.48-1984.

Library of Congress Cataloging-in-Publication Data

Christofferson, Thomas Rodney, 1939–
    The French Socialists in power, 1981–1986: from autogestion to cohabitation / Thomas R. Christofferson.
        p.   cm.
    Includes bibliographical references and index.
    ISBN 0-87413-403-X (alk. paper)
    1. Parti socialiste (France) 2. Socialism—France. 3. France—Politics and government—1981– I. Title.
JN3007.S6C47   1991
324.244'074—dc20   89-40765
                                                                            CIP

PRINTED IN THE UNITED STATES OF AMERICA

To Ramona

Contents

Abbreviations

CERES   *Centre d'Etudes, de Recherches et d'Education Socialistes*

CFDT   *Confedération Français et Démocratique du Travail*

CGT   *Confedération Générale du Travail*

CNPF   *Conseil National du Patronat Français*

FO   *Force Ouvrière*

OECD   Organization for European Cooperation and Development

PCF   *Parti Communiste Français*

PS   *Parti Socialiste*

RPR   *Rassemblement pour la République*

SFIO   *Section Française de l'Internationale Ouvrière*

UDF   *Union pour la Démocratie Française*

Preface

The thesis behind this book is quite simple, but first allow me to clarify what it is not. This is not a history of the Socialist party in the 1980s or of the role of François Mitterrand as the first Socialist president of the Fifth Republic or of the Socialist government from 1981 to 1986. All of those objectives would be too ambitious an undertaking at this time. Instead, I have begun with a problem, or what I have conceived to be a problem: why did the Socialists move so rapidly from espousing an ideological program prior to taking office to the position of implementing a very limited agenda of reforms once they had gained power? Or, to put the question in a slightly different way, why did the Socialists become pragmatists, realists, modernizers by 1986, if not before?

The solution to this problem, I think, lies in an analysis of Socialist ideology and the consequences of the 1981 electoral successes. In order to win election, the party needed to play down such radical policies as *autogestion* and its ties to the Communists, which it did in the 1981 presidential and legislative contests. Once that had been done, the party became partial prisoner to its electoral victories, incapable of or unwilling to adopt the bold policies contained in the *Projet socialiste* or the Common Program. But this alone does not explain the shift. On a different level, I argue that the party may have made the shift before winning the 1981 elections. The much-talked-about, but vague, ideology of *autogestion* allowed every current within the party to interpret what it thought that ideology meant, to the point where mass confusion existed over what socialism stood for. In the course of the 1970s the party was challenged by numerous "new" movements that often appropriated dearly held Socialist beliefs, but interpreted them in ways that challenged the Socialist party's strategy of *union de la gauche, front de classe*, and *autogestion*. This was especially true of the new philosophers and the new left. Increasingly, the party attempted to confront these movements, but it failed to develop an ideology that successfully identified socialism in light of their critiques. Although *autogestion* became the primary concept for distinguishing socialism from the Communist left, the "new" movements, and the right, it remained a confused metaphor, incapable of providing the party with a clear definition or mission, dividing the party as much as it united it. As a consequence, when the Socialists came to power they had a loose set of propositions to implement, but no clearly defined method for carrying out the much-vaunted rupture with capitalism. As events developed—in particular, the economic crisis of 1981–82—the new government rapidly found itself accepting such concepts as "rigor" and the "pause" in reforms, in place of the concepts of revolution and change that had spurred on the rank and file in the party. By 1984, after three devaluations of the franc and the collapse of the government's educational program, the newly installed Fabius government officially inaugurated the *après-socialisme*, which had been struggling to emerge since at least 1981. With the final breakdown of the union of the left, the Socialists moved to embrace the center, abandoning all hope for the "rupture with capitalism," giving up the class struggle, and adopting the goal of a Modern Republic with the slogan *"moderniser et rassembler."* As a result, by 1986 the basis for *cohabitation* between a Socialist president and a rightist prime minister had been established, as the Fabius government's policies had completed the party's transition from the archaic leftist hangovers of the post-1968 period to a form of social democracy or radical reformism, which was essentially another form of archaicism, but one that the Socialists now accepted as a more appropriate response to the challenge of the late twentieth century and the party's role as a hegemonic, electoral force.

To put the argument in such bold outlines is to do injustice to large parts of it. Clearly, the individual actors played significant roles in transforming French socialism in the 1980s. The experience of ruling for five years, longer than any previous Socialist government had been able to muster, no doubt played a major part in the eventual shift to "realism." The mere fact that the Socialists were an electoral party, intent upon winning votes and elections, helped steer its warring factions in the final pragmatic direction that Laurent Fabius outlined after becoming prime minister in 1984. All of these arguments—and many others like them—have to be given their place in the hierarchy of reasons for the transformation of the Socialists, but this work contends that preceding and helping to determine these was the post-1968 climate of opinion that totally condemned the state, communism, the "gulag," and such "totalitarian" excesses in favor of liberty, civil society, decentralization of power, and other basically libertarian concepts. This climate, or hegemonic situation if you will, shaped the Socialists, gradually making them reformists who emphasized liberty as much as if not more than equality and who accepted the continued existence of capitalism, sometimes even with enthusiasm. As a party that had come to accept its dominant position in French politics—the consequence of the post-Epinay period—the Socialists could not resist shifting to the "right." Of course, the party had a choice: it could have refused to shift rightward and been relegated to the role of a second or third force in French politics or it could have adjusted its ideology to circumstances in order to continue to play a key role in electoral politics. It chose the latter and in so doing brought a profound transformation to French politics. After March 1986, the French political system will never be the same again. The prognostications of the intellectuals, contained in such provocative titles as *Adieux au prolétariat* or *Après-socialisme*, have become political reality. How and why that occurred is what this book attempts to reveal.

One final note: Many books have appeared on the Socialist experience. Virtually all of them have been either journalistic accounts or edited works written, primarily, by political scientists. In the first instance scholarship is often forsaken for polemics or factual outlines; in the second instance the uneven quality of the essays and the ahistorical analyses contained in many of them leaves the reader with a very uneven account of what occurred. This work attempts to provide a historical framework for understanding the Socialist domestic political experience, even though it does not pretend to be a total history of that experience. Its success or failure depends on the degree to which it succeeds in providing such a framework.

Acknowledgments

I would like to thank Drew University for its generous support in funding research for this book. I would also like to acknowledge the computer for its sometimes generous support in writing this work. And I would like to thank my mentor, Hans Schmitt, for his continuing support. Most of all, however, in the spirit of the petit bourgeois gnome that infests all of these acknowledgments, I would like to thank my wife for her patience, her support, and her excellent cooking.

The French Socialists
in Power,
1981–1986

1

Victory! *Pour quoi faire?*

On 10 May 1981, François Mitterrand defeated Valéry Giscard d'Estaing in the second round of the French presidential elections to become the first socialist head of state in the history of the Fifth Republic. Slightly more than one month later, the electorate gave the Socialist party an absolute majority of seats in the lower house of the French parliament, virtually guaranteeing five years of Socialist control over the nation's central governmental institutions. Never before in the history of France had the left obtained such extensive powers. Unlike the fragility of the Popular Front's 1936 victory, 1981 promised the *longue durée* in which the Common Program of the left could be implemented and the much-awaited transition phase of the socialist takeover of power would become reality. Yet, unlike 1936, the left's triumph was greeted with muted enthusiasm by the vast majority of French men and women. No massive unrest occurred, no summer of strikes, little working-class rejoicing. Had France matured? Or was this victory less revolutionary than it seemed? Why, and to what extent, had the French voted for change in May and June of 1981?

To comprehend the reasons for the triumph of Mitterrand and the Socialist party in 1981 is no easy task, yet it is essential for understanding whether the left possessed a mandate to rule, what that mandate consisted of, and the degree to which the nation was ready and willing to accept and implement the left's program. Although short-term electoral analysis is an important part of any answer to this problem, it is not sufficient. The 1981 victory has to be understood in terms of the changes that had taken place within the Socialist party since the Epinay congress of 1971, especially the ideological changes that had helped make the party into the largest force on the left by 1978, a position that it reaffirmed in 1981. This chapter, consequently, will examine the immediate reasons for victory in 1981 and the long-term ideological underpinnings of that victory, in order to answer the question of what the Socialists were ready to do with power once they had gained it in the spring and summer of 1981.

Was the Socialist victory of 1981 the triumph of a new hegemonic force in French society? Was it the political manifestation of the sociological changes that had transformed archaic, rural, and Catholic France into modern, urban, and agnostic France in the course of the 1970s? To what degree did a permanent or at least significant shift occur in French electoral geography in 1981? The answer to these questions is both simple and complex: although many observers interpreted 1981 as a cataclysmic change, a watershed of sorts, the evidence is ambiguous, tending to favor the thesis of a moderate shift toward the left.[1] The most significant change that emerged from the elections may be the collapse of the Communist party as an electoral force and a power, ideological or otherwise, on the left. The weak showing of Georges Marchais, who received only 15.3 percent of the vote on the first round of the presidential elections, was confirmed in the June parliamentary elections when the Communists obtained only 16 percent of the vote on the first ballot. Not since 1958 had the party fallen below the 20 percent mark on the first round of a legislative election. In contrast, the Socialist party and its Radical party allies obtained 37.5 percent of the vote on the first ballot, which surpassed by far their previous 1978 record of 24.5 percent. If a hegemonic force for radical change existed, these electoral statistics indicated clearly that it had to be Socialist, not Communist.[2]

Yet the evidence for Socialist hegemony is sketchy at best. At the end of 1980, the conservative government of Giscard d'Estaing carried out a poll to determine the mood of the nation. By an astounding margin, three-quarters of those polled indicated that they wanted a profound transformation of French society; however, two-thirds of this group wanted this transformation to take place in the form of "progressive reforms" rather than "radical changes." This mood for reform was clearly related to the increased pessimism that the French expressed about their standard of living. Between 1978 and 1980, those who believed that they were worse off than ten years before increased from 24.4 percent of the population to 33.6 percent.[3] What the government discovered was also reflected in numerous polls taken by private polling organizations during the winter and spring of 1980–81. They revealed massive discontent with the government among the supporters of Jacques Chirac, the Gaullist candidate for president. A SOFRES poll taken in April 1981 showed that Chirac's followers differed profoundly in attitude, but not in ideology, from Giscard's backers. For example, 67 percent of those who said that they would vote for Chirac claimed that they wanted profound political change in France, compared with only 42 percent of Giscard's potential voters. These disaffected rightists tended to have a "good opinion of the Socialist party'' (47 percent of them versus only 34 percent of the Giscardian UDF voters) and a very negative opinion of Giscard's presidency (56 percent negative compared with 9 percent of the UDF voters). They also viewed the possibility of a Mitterrand victory in a more positive light: 26 percent said that they would be satisfied if he won, whereas only 14 percent of Giscard's electorate made such a claim.[4] This deeply felt political antagonism to Giscard was translated into important defections to the Socialists on the second round of the presidential election: 16 percent of Chirac's voters cast ballots for Mitterrand and an additional 11 percent abstained. Earlier, in an April IFOP poll, 23 percent of Chirac's supporters had claimed that they would vote for Mitterrand on the second ballot if Giscard were running against him.[5]

The attitudes and actions of these disenchanted rightists played an important part in the election of François Mitterrand, going far beyond what the Gaullist electorate had done in 1974, when a total of 17 percent either abstained or voted Socialist on the second ballot in the presidential election. The Communists, in contrast, remained loyal to the left in 1981, as 92 percent of those who voted for Georges Marchais cast their ballots for Mitterrand in May. But these important developments do not totally answer the question of whether 1981 granted the left a mandate for sweeping change, although the move to the Socialists by Chirac's supporters, which helped Mitterrand win election by a margin of 52 to 48 percent, would seem to indicate that the left's claims to a radical mandate must be qualified seriously. Public opinion polls taken after the elections offer more support for the thesis of moderate change over radical innovation. Although 70 percent or more of the electorate supported such Socialist conjunctural reforms as early retirement, five weeks of paid holidays, the implementation of a wealth tax, an increase in the minimum wage, and decreases in wage differentials between the poorest and the richest, far fewer backed such ideological, long-term policies as nationalization, which received the approval of only 43 percent of the electorate, with 32 percent opposing nationalization and 25 percent expressing no opinion. However, even this plurality of approval has to be qualified. Polls indicated that support for nationalization was based almost exclusively on the pragmatic hope that it would lead to increased employment or, at least, to the preservation of endangered jobs. Very few thought of nationalization in ideological terms such as the "rupture" with capitalism.[6]

The relatively moderate, short-term attitudes of the French electorate were further revealed in a SOFRES poll that asked voters to furnish reasons why Mitterrand won and Giscard lost. Although 42 percent of the respondents cited Mitterrand's will to carry out major reforms in French society as the main reason why he won, this group must be balanced carefully against the 44 percent who thought Giscard lost the election because he did not solve the problem of unemployment. It is conceivable that those polled thought that "major reforms" meant combating unemployment rather than implementing the Common Program. This interpretation is borne out partly by two other reasons given by the voters to explain Mitterrand's triumph: 29 percent said he won because it was the only way to get rid of Giscard, while 20 percent claimed that Mitterrand was "the most capable of diminishing unemployment." The unpopularity of Giscard was a factor in all of the other reasons people provided to explain why he had lost: 27 percent said he lost because of Chirac's opposition to him; 26 percent claimed that two terms in office would have given him power for too many years; 25 percent thought he kept Raymond Barre too long as prime minister; and 13 percent mentioned his ties to the African dictator Boukassa and his monarchical style of governing. In short, radical change very often meant ousting Giscard from office.[7]

If the Mitterrand victory offered no clear sense of hegemonic change or a mandate for radical structural reform, possibly the legislative elections told a different story. In them, the Socialists won an overwhelming victory, obtaining an absolute majority of the seats in the National Assembly. Furthermore, the party's strength was uniform throughout the nation, as it gained the largest percentage of the vote in all but one of the twenty-two regions and emerged as the leading vote-getter in every social category except the rural farmers and the upper-middle- and upper-class elite. The party's hegemonic implantation in the social and political structure of France seemed assured by the results. But the election probably exaggerated the extent of the Socialist victory. With only 37.5 percent of the vote, the Socialists gained well over a majority of seats in the legislature due to the nature of the electoral system, which greatly favored any party that could dominate one of the two electoral blocks. In turn, the high level of abstentions in the first round of the election—30.14 percent as opposed to only 18.29 percent in 1978—seemed to indicate that many right-wing voters stayed home, probably because they did not want to create a constitutional crisis by electing a right-wing legislature to challenge the legitimacy of the newly elected Socialist president. Furthermore, the total percentage of the electorate that voted for the left in 1981 was below the 1978 level—39.81 percent versus 40.35 percent with abstentions included—while the right's percentage dropped percipitously from 37.75 percent to 29.85 percent, due it seems to the high rate of abstentions by rightist voters.[8] On the other hand, the abstainers expressed widespread satisfaction with the election results, with 62 percent responding favorably to the Socialist victory against 20 percent who were dissatisfied, according to one opinion poll. Furthermore, in June the French gave the Mitterrand–Mauroy government an overwhelming vote of confidence, a 75 percent favorable rating.[9]

The will for change was real, even if the evidence for Socialist hegemony was problematic. Again, however, the issue is what kind of change. Some political observers, such as the rightist politician Alain Peyrefitte, would later criticize the Socialists for not being honest with the electorate in 1981. Peyrefitte accused Mitterrand of not publishing his 110 propositions until after the elections so that the public would not realize how radical the left's positions were. Although such accusations must be carefully qualified, for the left's program had been known since at least the signing of the Common Program in 1981, there is some truth in what Peyrefitte claimed. Even though there was a Common Program with the Communist party, the Socialists did not run on it in 1981, given the breakdown of the union of the left in 1977. In fact, the Socialist party and Mitterrand distanced themselves as much as possible from any indication that a Socialist victory would bring the Communists into the government. In his first speech as a candidate for the party's nomination, François Mitterrand set the tone that would prevail throughout the campaign: "I am a free man in regard to both the Communists and the ruling class. I owe nothing to anyone, not to Washington, not to Moscow." Electoral alliance with the Communists, such as the one formed for the June legislative elections, was acceptable, even necessary, but the Socialists refused to discuss the inclusion of Communists in a post-June government. The first Mauroy administration, which was set up after the presidential but before the legislative elections, had no Communists in its ranks.[10]

If Peyrefitte was partly correct in claiming that the 110 propositions were not widely known and if the Common Program was not the basis of the 1981 Socialist campaigns, where could the electorate go to find out what the Socialist party's program of radical reform included? The *Projet socialiste,* drawn up in 1980, was one possibility, but not a very likely one. François Mitterrand paid no attention to the *Projet* in his electoral campaign and it was hardly mentioned by anyone in the elections. Most likely, the average voter gained his or her idea of the Socialist program from two major sources: what François Mitterrand said about it prior to 10 May and the actions of the Mauroy government after that. Overwhelmingly, the message that these two sources provided was one of moderate reform and not the ideological program of the *Projet socialiste.*

François Mitterrand's campaign for the presidency in 1981 contrasted sharply with his 1974 effort. Although in both cases he distanced himself from the Socialist party by resigning the post of first secretary, in 1981 that resignation was permanent rather than temporary and it occurred in the context of the continuing breakdown of relations with the Communist party and the Common Program, both of which were prominent factors in 1974, when the Communists supported Mitterrand on the first ballot rather than presenting their own candidate. In the tradition of the Gaullist Fifth Republic, in 1981 François Mitterrand was free to run his own, totally independent presidential campaign. This did not mean, however, that he divorced himself completely from the forces within the Socialist party. His *conseil politique* included representatives from every faction in the party: Michel Rocard, Gaston Defferre, Pierre Mauroy, Jean-Pierre Chevènement, Lionel Jospin, and Véronique Neiertz. But they would remain subservient to the candidate rather than determining the direction and ideology of the campaign.[11]

In retrospect, many observers would emphasize the imagery used by Mitterrand during the campaign, especially the *force tranquille* poster that depicted the candidate standing in front of a peaceful French village. Lionel Stoleru, one of Giscard's ministers, would translate this poster into the essential meaning of the 1981 election, which he interpreted as a struggle between two conceptions of France: "It [the election] was the choice between the emotional France of Freud and the rational France of Descartes, between *la France tranquille* and industrial France."[12] To Stoleru, Mitterrand's electoral mandate was for tranquillity rather than change, Freud rather than Marx. Clearly, the evidence does not support such a categorical, impressionistic conclusion, but it is certain that the *force tranquille* theme was intended to make Mitterrand's image more "positive," which could be interpreted as more Gaullist and less Socialist.[13]

This positive, almost asocialist image was reinforced by the issues Mitterrand chose to address during the campaign. With the exception of the early phase of the race for president, such as Mitterrand's speech before the party faithful in January 1981 after he had been officially nominated as their candidate, the rhetoric of class struggle and socialism was toned down throughout the campaign. As one close observer of Mitterrand's discourse has stated, the vision he portrays in virtually all of his writings and speeches is basically aristocratic.[14] Be that as it may, in the spring of 1981, Mitterrand addressed primarily the immediate issues, paramount among them being unemployment. In speech after speech he hit upon the need to unite the French people behind a "redressement national" to solve the "crise." He made no secret of his Gaullist position on the matter. He wrote in the *Courrier de l'Oise* on 27 March: "But that which counts today is to unite French men and women behind a great work of *redressement national*, to call them to the national resistance against the fatality of the *crise*, as General

De Gaulle did in his time, in other circumstances that posed difficulties for the independence of the nation." In the declaration of Nevers, which was issued on 28 April after the first round of the election, Mitterrand made unemployment the key issue, claiming that those opposed to Giscard "wish to obtain the liberty to live free from the agony of unemployment in a nation that is reconciled with itself" and concluding with a pointed attack on his opponent: "My choice for society is employment. His is unemployment. That's the basic difference. France does not need for President this Mr. Super-Unemployment who offers himself for its votes."[15]

From the beginning of the campaign, unemployment had been the key issue. Every political observer commented on it and every candidate offered a solution to it. Mitterrand's solution was one of the least radical. Whereas Chirac called for a massive *relance* of the economy, with 6 percent growth of the gross national product per year, and Marchais advocated 4.5 percent growth, Mitterrand talked in terms of 3 percent. Although Giscard did not engage in such mundane matters at first, but instead delegated Barre to inagurate a *relance* that would help him win the election, he soon realized that he was losing ground on the issue. On 8 April, he announced that France would borrow 15 billion francs in international markets to finance projects that would increase employment in key areas of the economy, ranging from construction to high technology. François Mitterand's response was to sound a note of caution and moderation: "I do not believe that it was truly necessary to increase French external debt, which is already enormous."[16] The program that Mitterrand had announced earlier in April to achieve full employment and social justice called only for a selective *relance* of the economy, mainly through raising the minimum wage and various social security benefits such as pensions, combined with aid to ailing industries such as construction, the creation of 210,000 jobs, training programs to help the unemployed, and a series of tax increases on the rich and tax cuts for the poor to achieve social justice. In comparison with Giscard's loan proposal and Barre's election year *relance*, Mitterrand's program was modest at best, especially since new taxes were scheduled to help pay for part of the increased expenditures.[17]

The climax of the entire campaign, the event that most French men and women witnessed, was, appropriately, the television debate between Giscard and Mitterrand. In preparation for it, Giscard attacked on three main fronts: he accused Mitterrand of advocating electoral chaos by promising to dissolve the National Assembly if he were elected; he claimed that the Socialist economic program would lead to disaster, namely higher taxes, unemployment, and a decline in the nation's status in Europe; and he argued that the prestige and influence of France in world affairs would decline if the Socialists won, since Communists would be included in the government. None of these accusations bore fruit for Giscard: few people thought chaos would arise from another round of democratic elections; the unemployment issue was one that Giscard had to address, not Mitterrand; and there was no sign yet that Communists would play a role in a future Socialist government. The debate did not improve Giscard's standing. The issue of political chaos was turned against the outgoing president with the first question on whether Chirac's party, the RPR, would accept his government. Giscard dismissed the issue abruptly, claiming that no one was interested in it, but Mitterrand used the opportunity to quote a number of Chirac's statements on Giscard's presidency, such as that of 9 March 1981: "We are in an extremely disquieting situation which requires a complete change of policy and one does not change policy with the same men," or that of 4 March 1981, when Chirac said that he had "a negative opinion of Giscard's presidency [le septennat]." Adroitly, Mitterrand made the Gaullist candidate the radical opponent of Giscard, a tactic that had come close to failing on the first round when the "radical" Chirac gained rapidly on Mitterrand during the last week of the contest. Giscard persisted, however, in claiming that a Mitterrand victory would bring electoral, institutional, and political chaos, but Mitterrand stood his ground, pointing out that the constitution allowed the president to dissolve the assembly when he deemed it necessary and responding to the issue of Communist ministers in the next government by claiming that he did not know whether Communists would join his cabinet and adding that if they did it would only mean that finally Communists were allowed full rights of citizenship rather than being restricted to the limited rights that Giscard offered them to work, fight, and die for France. The main thrust, the greatest part of the debate, however, entailed the issues of unemployment and the economy. On those, the two candidates reiterated old stands: Mitterrand repeated his program to *relance* the economy, promote social justice, and reduce umemployment, pointing to the disaster of Giscard's administration and quoting Chirac once more in order to rally the disaffected Gaullists to his cause; in contrast, Giscard pointed to the success of his *septennat* in achieving higher economic growth than any other industrial nation, argued that exogenous factors, such as the two oil crises, had caused increases in unemployment, and accused Mitterrand of offering an economic program that would end in total disaster if it were implemented. But Mitterrand continued to insist that unemployment was the most important issue facing the nation: "the principal axis of a policy," he insisted, "must revolve around solutions to unemployment." Over and over, Mitterrand reiterated what he would do to solve this mounting, hideous problem. No doubt Giscard realized that he was losing this point badly, for he tired desperately to regain the initiative by trying to trap Mitterrand on the technical point of what the value of the franc was in relation to the Deutschemark. In what became the most famous and most often retold incident in the debate, Mitterrand at first refused to respond to Giscard—"I am not your pupil," he claimed—and then proceeded to quote the exchange rate precisely, reversing in one dramatic moment the doubts that many had about his grasp of economic matters, a moment made more dramatic by the fact that it came at the end of a lengthy discussion of the most crucial issue in the campaign.

With the exception of the issue of nationalization—an exception that would prove the rule—the more radical parts of the Socialist economic program were not raised during the debate. Mitterrand responded to questions on nationalization by arguing that the state had to intervene in the economy to support vital areas, such as exports and investments, and to control monopolies for the public interest. When Giscard responded that these Socialist policies would destroy private enterprise, Mitterrand replied that De Gaulle, not the Socialists, had carried out the greatest wave of nationalizations in the history of France. Appropriately enough, he added a Gaullist justification for nationalization: "to defend the interests of small and medium-sized enterprises, as well as markets and a competitive environment, against the overwhelming power of certain national and international conglomerates." Not once did he offer a purely Socialist justification for nationalization.

In the final summation, Mitterrand the republican spoke. He brought up those subjects that he would have liked to talk about, but could not during the debate, subjects such as Central America and the Third World, the impact of high technology on industry and employment, and, most of all, the idea of liberty. Liberty was the key word in Mitterrand's final speech, not equality. Every struggle of the left—for better education, free time, better jobs, Third World rights—was part of the grand scheme to achieve liberty in this world. Class struggle, Marxism, the rupture with capitalism, all of which were part of the standard rhetoric of the *Projet socialiste*, were totally absent from Mitterrand's discourse. Only the vague idea of "changement" remained: "Le changement pour quoi faire? Pour essayer de rassembler." And, of course, *rassembler* to achieve liberty. If a hegemonic force existed on the left it was the force of this man's rhetoric, his ability to *rassembler* Gaullism, republicanism, and socialism under one common discourse.[18]

François Mitterrand concluded his campaign with a speech before the television cameras on Friday 8 May. Virtually certain of victory by then, he named five objectives that he wanted to accomplish as president: "To conquer unemployment; to *relance* the economy; to construct a juster, freer, more responsible society; to restore the vigor and independence of France; to defend peace in the world." He claimed that all of these objectives would be carried out in the context of unity, "in a great *élan* of national renaissance."[19]

With victory on 10 May, Mitterrand proceeded to select the members of his government on the basis of the same cautious, pragmatic, Gaullist combination that won him the presidency. He offered important positions in the government to the leaders of the major factions within the party. The two leading party notables, Pierre Mauroy from the department of the Nord and Gaston Defferre from Marseille and the Bouches-du-Rhône, received the key positions of prime minister and minister of the interior and decentralization, while the leader of the CERES current in the party, Jean-Pierre Chevènement, and the *deuxième gauche* figurehead, Michel Rocard, received important posts as ministers of state. The president also appointed to his first government two leaders of the Radical party allies of the Socialists: Maurice Faure became minister of justice and Michel Crépeau obtained the post of minister of the environment. But Mitterrand's most intriguing non-Socialist appointment was Michel Jobert, the former Gaullist, who became one of five ministers of state, as minister of foreign trade, a key post for implementing any future *relance* of the economy. The choice of Jobert was a reward to those Gaullists who had deserted Giscard and a signal to them and the nation that the new government would only go so far in pursuing change. In line with this moderate image of change, no Communists became part of this first government, even though one of the principles for the selection of non-Socialists seems to have been the degree to which they represented groups that contributed to Mitterrand's victory. In this instance, however, the *force tranquille* image seemed to prevail over that principle.

In the pursuit of moderate change, probably the most dramatic appointment was that of Nicole Questiaux as a minister of state in charge of the new ministry of national solidarity with three secretaries of state for social security, the elderly, and the family. The total of four major positions made this ministry one of the most important in the government. In the pecking order of ministers of state, Questiaux's post came second to Gaston Defferre's Ministry of the Interior and Decentralization, even though Questiaux was not one of the major leaders within the party. Clearly, this meant that all of the policies on employment and social justice that had been at the heart of the presidential election campaign would occupy a central position in the new government. And, these popular policies would be carried out by the first woman to achieve such high ministerial rank, a point that might help the Socialists capture a significant proportion of the female vote in the legislative elections.[20]

This new government proved to be unique in the history of the Fifth Republic. First, it was the shortest government, lasting only thirty days, from 22 May until the legislative elections had been decided in June. Second, it never presented its program before parliament; its first act was the dissolution of the National Assembly and the call for new elections. Yet, in one way it was not unique at all: like numerous predecessors dating back at least to the days of François Guizot, it had one main objective, to win the parliamentary elections for the head of state so that he could rule effectively. As François Mitterrand informed his Council of Ministers on 27 May: "While remaining loyal to your common obligations, you cease to be the representatives of your parties, you are the representatives of France."[21]

But what did it mean to be "the representatives of France"? Was this not another Napoleonic-Gaullist mystification of power for narrow political purposes, in this case the victory of the Socialist party? Paul Fabra's analysis of the first Mauroy government in a 7 July 1981 *Le Monde* editorial, entitled "Une politique d'exceptions," provides us with a clue. Fabra pointed out that the government had accomplished a great deal since 22 May, but almost everything it had done fell under the category of pragmatic, piecemeal economic reforms rather than under the aegis of a coherent, rational program. He feared that even though the Socialists had established programs to defend jobs and promote employment, those efforts could be jeopardized if, for example, the franc needed to be protected. Such heavy reliance upon short-term solutions to economic problems, he argued, could end up undermining employment in the long run.

Fabra both understood and missed the point. The first Mauroy government had no coherent long-term economic policy; it was created to win the election by implementing the sorts of piecemeal reforms that Fabra found disconcerting rather than offering a vision of a future that many potential voters might not want. Therefore, that government decreed massive increases in the minimum wage, family allowances, housing subsidies, and old-age pensions while announcing that it would create 55,000 new jobs in the public sector by the end of 1981, that it would implement a program to employ 650,000 young people, that it would begin negotiations on 12 June to reduce the work week to thirty-nine hours, that it would reduce the retirement age to sixty, that it would provide funds to build 50,000 new public housing units, that it would inject new funds into education and training for young people, that it would aid industries in difficulty, and that it would finance these programs primarily by increasing taxes on the highest-paid stratum of the population. Public opinion polls had revealed that all of these measures had massive support among the French people, no matter what their party affiliation might be. By implementing them, the Socialists could claim that they were promoting the general will, the national interest, above particular interests. Pierre Mauroy promised that "this action of *relance*, this will for solidarity, shall never be undertaken at the expense of the economic equilibrium of the nation," thereby reassuring the country that the government represented a higher, national interest beyond the particular groups that composed it. Yet, this did not prevent Mauroy from interpreting the 14 June victory that resulted from these policies as both a vote of confidence in François Mitterrand and a mandate for the socialist form of "changement" over the right's concept of it. Not until the establishment of the second Mauroy government would a more forthright leftist program for change emerge, divorced from the exigencies of electoral politics and the Gaullist imperative to mystify the state.[22] Whether that program was understood and endorsed by the electorate in 1981 remains debatable, although the party leadership intended to implement that program as much as it could. To understand that part of the Socialist victory of 1981, we must examine the ideology of the party and the context in which that ideology emerged.

The Socialist party's rise to power occurred at an inopportune time. Not only did France face a serious economic crisis with no end or remedy in sight,[23] but also the hostile ideological and intellectual environment that the party confronted in 1981 offered no compensation. As an English observer of the post-1968 French intellectual scene pointed out, in the 1970s all socialist models were discredited in the eyes of the intelligentsia, from the Soviet model to the Cambodian and Chinese. Most French intellectuals became increasingly skeptical of all forms of socialism, while Socialist intellectuals and French Socialists in general remained out of touch with the new mood that swept the nation.[24] Although numerous indications existed that the post-1971 Socialist party had reached out to include the new leftist forces that had emerged in the 1960s, the party remained tied to archaic attitudes in the eyes of the intelligentsia. The poststructuralist, postmodernist, and antihumanist attitudes of the 1968 generation seemed to condemn all political action, but especially leftist political action, as the nihilism and passivism that were explicit or implicit in these attitudes tended to support the status quo for lack of anything better. As Luc Ferry and Alain Renaut have argued in their important work on *La pensée 68*, all of the major thinkers of the 1968 generation (Lacan, Foucault, Althusser, and Derrida) declared "the death of man." "La pensée 68" constantly reiterated the idea that humanism, rather than liberating man as it claimed to do, had been one of the key forces in oppressing him. Thus, the generation of 1968 posed, Ferry and Renaut argued, "la question de l'humanisme," which became *"la* question centrale de la philosophie contemporaine." And in posing this question, "la pensée 68" equated humanism with Stalinism or Nazism, flying totally in the face of common sense.[25]

Be that as it may, the French Socialists increasingly confronted a hostile intellectual environment during the course of the 1970s, which became more threatening with the rise of each "new" movement, beginning with the new left and continuing through the new philosophers, the new right, and the new economists. As diverse as these movements were, they all embraced the common ground of condemning the state and calling for a liberal/libertarian direction in politics. All were products of the 1968 generation and all posed clear challenges to the Socialist party, challenges that were all the greater when they came from leftist circles that the party had failed to integrate into its grand coalition. The new left and the new philosophers, in particular, posed the most serious challenges to Socialist ideological hegemony on the left.[26] Rightly or wrongly, both movements gained considerable publicity during the course of the 1970s, both in the right-wing press and in such leftist journals as *Le Nouvel Observateur* and *Libération.*[27] A brief analysis of these two movements will help in understanding the Socialist predicament in the 1980s.

The new left antedated the 1968 uprising, finding its roots in the events of 1956 and the Algerian war, if not earlier, but its real impact on French political life did not occur until after the events of May.[28] This new left was not homogeneous in its ideas or political positions, but a certain core of values characterized most of its participants. These included serious reservations about the French Communist party, to the point of embracing an anti-Communist position. The Soviet government's brutal suppression of the Hungarian uprising of 1956 began this process of disenchantment. The discovery of Gramsci and the young Marx during the 1950s and early 1960s, the failure of the French political system to resolve the Algerian conflict successfully, and the rise of the authoritarian procapitalist Gaullist regime combined to create a fledgling movement that challenged the Marxist-Leninist tradition, the authority of the state, and the legitimacy of traditional political parties, including the precursor of the French Socialist party of the 1970s, the SFIO.

The participation of such divergent thinkers as Henri Lefebvre and Cornelius Castoriadis in this movement was an indication of its diversity. Lefebvre, a disillusioned Communist who broke from the party in 1958 after concluding that it would never change its Stalinist ways, criticized scientific Marxism, proclaiming that alienation was the key to Marx's thought; he claimed Marxism was not a system but rather a flexible way of comprehending and criticizing social reality, which was in constant flux. In *The Critique of Everyday Life*, Lefebvre concluded that the alienation found in capitalist consumer society would be overcome through a cultural revolution that would transform politics and the economy as well as society and consciousness. Like many new-left thinkers, Lefebvre rejected deterministic solutions to human alienation for voluntaristic ones, solutions that emerged from the base rather than from the party, from cultural and social revolution rather than from economic and political forces. In contrast, Castoriadis never flirted with French Communism, gravitating toward "new-left" ideas in the 1940s. In his journal, *Socialisme ou Barbarie*, which survived from 1949 to 1965 and influenced numerous young intellectuals, he engaged in a massive critique of bureaucracy, both Soviet and western, explaining Soviet bureaucracy as the logical outcome of the Russian revolution, which entrenched a new class of people in power, while viewing western bureaucracy as the means of coopting and integrating various movements for revolution or radical reform into the system. The only solution to the problem of bureaucracy, Castoriadis claimed, was the implementation of *autogestion*, which would eliminate hierarchical forms of organization and create real democracy—genuine socialism—with the workers in control at the base. *Autogestion* would overcome alienation and eliminate the false solution of "expertism." Castoriadis totally rejected both capitalism and Marxism, claiming that they were both based on the idea of "economic man," that both were total systems of thought, and that neither one was capable of understanding reality. As he put the matter in a 1972 statement: "The absurdity of all inherited political thought consists precisely in wanting to resolve men's problems for them, whereas the only political problem in fact is this: how can people become capable of resolving their problems for themselves."[29]

After 1968, thinkers such as Lefebvre and Castoriadis became commonplace; the new left flourished in the poststructuralist, postmodernist age. In particular, new-left thought concentrated its energies on the issue of *autogestion*, which became the catchword for radical change in the 1970s. As we shall see in more detail later, the Socialist party would be open to this new-left thrust, adopting *autogestion* as part of its program in 1971 and welcoming the *deuxième gauche* of Michel Rocard and Edmond Maire into its ranks in 1974, but not all aspects of *autogestion* were acceptable to the Socialists and even the ideas of the *deuxième gauche* were viewed, at times, with suspicion, as a sort of Trojan horse in the ranks of the faithful. In fact, the links between the new left outside of the party and the *deuxième gauche* inside were so close that it was often impossible to distinguish between them, making the Socialist job of demarcating their ideology from that of the second left a very difficult one indeed.

Still, there were clear differences. Second-left thinkers placed major emphasis on civil society, playing down the role of parties to the point of denouncing them. Anticommunism and anti-Marxism often played significant roles in new-left circles. Libertarian and liberal values were clearly placed in the forefront of their agenda, at the expense of such dearly held Socialist objectives as equality and fraternity. Less state, to the point of anarchy, was advocated by many second-left thinkers, which meant that they often opposed Socialist objectives to nationalize industry or to increase central state power for purposes of achieving equality. Of course, some second leftists were more adamant on these points than others, posing clear and present dangers to Socialist ideology. Jacques Julliard, for example, posed a very real threat as one of the leading second-left journalists with the prestigous *Nouvel Observateur*, a journal that tended to support second-left ideas, although not exclusively. Julliard's ties with Michel Rocard and the "Catho" gauche also made him an important figure on the fringes of the party. Therefore, the 1977 publication of Julliard's book *Contre la politique professionnelle* caused a good deal of consternation in party circles, for in it he attaked much of what the party stood for in the name of the spirit of 1968, proclaiming that 1968 had destroyed the notion of *politique politicienne* and had erected social groups as the center of political action. As Julliard pointedly claimed: "of all the new ideas which are in the process of transforming French society none have emanated from the political world in the past ten years; all, without exception, have been launched by small groups."[30] Although Julliard conceded that the Socialists had at least been receptive to some of these ideas, he despaired that the party was dominated by "organic intellectuals" who favored a primitive statist policy and promoted a reactionary ideology that opposed *autogestion*. To Julliard, the answer to alienation resided in the abolition of the "classe politique," which had usurped power from the people, and the establishment of a Rousseauian type of democracy where civil society dominated politics. Still, Julliard was willing to support the Socialists, with the proviso that if they took power and established "a new techno-bureaucratic power that is cynical and arrogant" he would then be justified in calling out "Vive l'anarchie!" to rally the workers and citizens against leftist tyranny.[31] In short, Julliard envisaged the Socialist party playing a very minor role in a future government. He hoped that it would finally accept his analysis that French society was moving more and more toward an American type of society, one in which "the political party is losing its influence to the benefit of a vast diversity of associations."[32] If it did, the final result would be a Copernican revolution in the party, "which would make it the champion of liberty in a society of risk and initiative," a society in which the autonomy of the individual would be the key to all relationships.[33]

In contrast to Julliard's popular journalistic approach to *autogestion*, Pierre Rosanvallon provided the penultimate philosophical arguments for the *deuxième gauche's* position. Closely tied to Edmond Maire and the CFDT trade union, in fact serving as editor of the union's key journal during the 1970s, Rosanvallon also had connections within the Socialist party's ranks and was even used by "organic intellectuals" in the party to bolster certain Socialist concepts of *autogestion*. But, for the most part, he remained suspect, along with Julliard, for his quasi-liberal ideas on the subject. In his most popular and important work of the 1970s, *L'âge de l'autogestion*, Rosanvallon made these differences clear. To Rosanvallon, *autogestion* was the dream of the anti-Soviet, anti–Social Democratic left in France, which hoped to use it in order to make the French socialist experience different from either Eastern or Western European experiences. *Autogestion*, Rosanvallon argued, would overcome Marx's reductionist concepts of class struggle and economic determinism by restoring political theory to its proper place. Because Marx and the Marxists never developed a political theory of their own, but instead attacked Lassalle's concept of the absolute state on the one hand and Proudhon's anarchism on the other, they found themselves erecting Lassallian regimes, by default, wherever they won control of the state. To correct this, a workable theory of politics in the context of *autogestion* had to be created. Rosanvallon found the makings of such a theory in the political liberalism of John Locke and Adam Smith, as refracted through Gramscian thought on the state: "the guarantee of individual and public liberties, the supremacy of the law over the power of the governed, and the principle of the state of law." These thinkers had developed a radical critique of the state and a defense of civil society that found expression in their "theory of the separation of powers and the limitation of the power of the state, ... in the context of an egalitarian society."[34] Yet, *autogestion* was not just liberalism revived; it united the liberal critique of the state with the socialist critique of capitalism to overcome alienation. Under *autogestion*, there would be no experts, no science of politics or society, no appeal to the authority of an "other." *Autogestion* was not utopian, however, for its objectives were practical, pragmatic, and open-ended. There was no conclusion to *autogestion*, no unfolding of reality, no liberating myth of the end of history. Yet, *autogestion* was not reformism, it was revolutionary, for through it the base would control the hierarchy, all planning would begin from below, and a new concept of society would prevail, one in which the productivist values of the past—the old liberal/Marxist dialogue of *bonheur*, *besoin*, and *utilité*—would be surpassed by a new model of development "based on a vigorous policy of the reduction of inequalities of income and inheritance."[35] Equally important, however, *autogestion* also celebrated social and cultural differentiation—*le droit à la différence*—in contrast to capitalism, which encouraged social and cultural uniformity to complement economic inequality. Most significant, Rosanvallon concluded, under *autogestion* society would not be reduced to and defined by economics. If it were, some form of totalitarianism would be the result: "The socialist society implies a theory of the limitation of the economic and thus a renunciation of an economic theory based on needs, which always contains the totalitarian danger of the organization of *bonheur* imposed in the name of a nature of man and society with the sole guidance of either marketing technicians or enlightened interpreters of the meaning of history."[36]

Rosanvallon's "third way" to Socialism emerged in the context of the Catho-CFDT environment, which was highly receptive to anti-Marxist and especially to anti-communist arguments. But some new-left advocates, such as André Gorz, came from backgrounds in which Marxism had been a major force. Gorz, along with Serge Mallet and many of the young Gramscian intellectuals who wrote for Jean-Paul Sartre's journal *Les temps modernes*, had been among the first to argue the new-left position in a neo-Marxist sense during the 1960s.[37] In the 1970s, Gorz became one of the leading thinkers of the ecological movement, writing regular articles on ecology for *Nouvel Observateur* and publishing extensively on the subject. Increasingly, he viewed ecology and *autogestion* as complementary parts of a critical evaluation of capitalism and authoritarian socialism. With the publication of *Adieux au prolétariat* in 1980, Gorz synthesized the work of more than a decade into what was one of the most important new-left treatises of the post-1968 period.[38]

As the title of his work indicated, Gorz broke completely with his previous belief that the skilled proletariat would lead the way toward socialism.[39] In so doing, he criticized the metaphysical foundations of Marxism: "For the young Marx, it was not the existence of a revolutionary proletariat that justified his theory: on the country, it was his theory which allowed him to predict the rise of the revolutionary proletariat and which established the necessity of it."[40] Marxist thought created the illusion of the inevitable victory of the proletariat over capitalism, but no such teleological historical message could be proved. The same was true of capitalism: both capitalism and Marxism suffered from similar metaphysical problems; each one was the mirror image of the other. Thus, Gorz was not reluctant to point out the bad news that wherever the proletariat had been victorious, a new managerial party elite had emerged to destroy working-class autonomy and perpetuate the statist, hierarchical, elitist institutions and values of capitalist society: "The seizure of state power by the working class becomes in reality the takeover of the working class by the power of the state."[41] There was no simple solution to the problem of exploitation. In modern society, neither the workers nor the bourgeoisie controlled their own destiny. Modern capitalism had created a monolith, a one-dimensional world of corporate bureaucracy that no one dominated, not even the capitalists. To Gorz, this bureaucratic power could not be reformed, for reform only led to the reinforcement of the structure, not to its transformation. He concluded: "The only chance to abolish the relations of domination is to recognize that functional power is inevitable *and to create a circumscribed place for it*, determined in advance, in a manner that disassociates power and domination, and that protects the respective autonomous spheres of civil society and the political society of the State."[42]

Here Gorz hit upon a problem that neither Rosanvallon nor Julliard had addressed effectively. But how did he resolve it? Not through traditional channels. Instead, Gorz argued, a new nonclass would lead the way, a class that vaguely resembled the old Marxian lumpen proletariat, for it included all of the outcasts of the capitalist system. In philosophical terms, this nonclass was post Nietzschean: those who knew that all gods were dead, that history did not have a transcendent meaning, and that society could be changed only in light of that knowledge. This nonclass would aim at implementing liberty, establishing a society in which the individual was supreme and where work was reduced to a minimum. Although the division of labor was a fact of life that could not be overcome, it had to be minimized to the point where individual identity was no longer determined by it. Gorz maintained that this was Marx's objective in book III of *Capital*, where he differentiated between liberty and necessity—what Gorz called *autonomie* and *héteronomie*. In light of this distinction, Gorz examined the parameters of *autogestion*, rejecting the pure *autogestionnaire* school that relegated everything to the realm of autonomy. To Gorz, the state will always be necessary, just as the division of labor will be. Only monastic communities were able to achieve pure *autogestion*, but at the expense of liberty, on the basis of complete asceticism, which was a sublimated form of necessity that justified an authoritarian order. In short, any community that repudiated the role of the state inevitably transformed itself into a type of state or perished. "The problem that 'post-industrial socialism' must resolve is consequently not the abolition of the state but the abolition of domination."[43] The state must be modified, limited in its power, by new social relations and new forms of association, but it must never be dominated by civil society just as civil society must never be dominated by the state. The careful equilibrium among civil society, the state, and politics must be maintained, with no element in the equation gaining control. Thus, politics forms an essential part of any *société autogestionnaire*. Politics in such a society must always be a process, a tension between alternatives, and never an end in itself. Politics must not confuse itself with the state and its functions, but instead must aim at limiting, orienting, and codifying power. As the space that reflected the conflict of forces within civil society, politics was the transparent connection between civil society and the state and never the locus of power.[44]

Gorz's recasting of the Marxist tradition in an *autogestionnaire* direction had profound appeal in the post-1968 intellectual and political environment that I have just outlined. Who, in the post-1968 generation, could disagree with Gorz when he maintained that the postindustrial society must be one in which human freedom realized its complete potential through the subtle interplay of civil society, politics, and the state, with each one checking the power of the other, recognizing the necessity for the existence of the other in the process of creating the greatest possible degree of liberty? But, unfortunately, Gorz's appeal to the myths of this generation was not bolstered by a convinicing theory of change, either revolutionary or reformist. The nonclass that he posited as the force for change—à la Herbert Marcuse—is unconvincing. How does that nonclass relate to a political movement? Or is it capable of creating change without politics or on the margin of politics? Because of his caveat about the political class usurping power for its own purposes, Gorz is reluctant to identify his nonclass with a political party or with such concepts as Gramscian cultural hegemony. Nor does he establish clear connections between economic forces and this nonclass, although he vaguely ties monopoly capitalism to its development. The nonclass thus serves primarily as a metaphor for the new social movements of the 1970s, from ecology to feminism to *autogestion*. It is an attempt to unite these movements behind one sprawling concept. Furthermore, like other advocates of *autogestion*, Gorz shifted the primary emphasis of his theory from equality to liberty and in so doing transformed socialist praxis, giving it a much more liberal/libertarian slant. In sum, Gorz' work presented a direct challenge to traditional Marxian socialism, a challenge that was based on earlier new-left thinkers but went beyond them, raising as many questions as it answered, but providing a framework in which to discuss civil society, the state, political parties, and, above all, the autonomy of the individual. Like all new-left thinkers in the 1970s, Gorz probably created more problems for the Socialist party than he provided solutions. No party could fulfill the agenda that Gorz outlined. His utopian program of *autogestion* could only lead to disillusionment in the real world where day-to-day political problems had to be resolved. As we shall see, however, the Socialists themselves offered nothing better.

In contrast to the *deuxième gauche*, the *nouveaux philosophes* comprised a media event and often little more than that in the course of the 1970s. Almost overnight, in 1976, they became household names as the result of appearances on such popular television programs as *Apostrophes*. In no other country in the western world did a group of so-called intellectuals command such an audience. And since they basically rejected the Socialist party's vision of society while maintaining, for the most part, that they were "on the left," their ideas loom large in our attempt to understand the atmosphere that the Socialist party inherited in 1981.

Although the *nouveaux philosophes* never organized as a coherent group of intellectuals, they shared a number of ideas and values. Almost all of them were disillusioned participants in the events of 1968. They had been philosophy students in the 1960s, studying with the great masters, Foucault, Althusser, and Lacan. Many had originally been Marxists of one shade or another, a number had converted to Maoism as an alternative to Leninism or Stalinism, and most of them ended up totally disillusioned with Marx and the "master thinkers" of their youth—Descartes, Rousseau, et al. As a result, they rejected all political movements, all masters, for all movements and masters corrupted the ideal. Reason, capitalism, and bolshevism were so many totalitarian traps, different aspects of the same will to power.[45]

The vehemence with which the *nouveaux philosophes* attacked Marxism and the Soviet Union, combined with their penchant for metaphysical concepts, led many observers to conclude that they supported Giscard and the right. Some did. Jean-Marie Benoist, for example, openly backed the liberal political camp, running for office against Georges Marchais in the 1978 legislative elections. But Benoist was an exception. For the most part, the *nouveaux philosophes* were either apolitical or antipolitical. They saw themselves engaged primarily in reinterpreting the past, reinventing the idea of France, its politics, its intellectual heritage, its present, its future. In doing so, they did not adhere to the traditional division into left and right, as they combined the ideas of Herbert Marcuse and the Catholic Georges Bernanos in a critique of consumer society or found links between Jacobinism and

Stalinism in arguing for the end of the state and a return to provincial cultures that predated the rise of Parisian supremacy over the nation. In making these juxtapositions, the *nouveaux philosophes* often came very close to the intellectual positions of the new left, but the optimism of that perspective was totally lacking in the nihilistic pessimism of their ideas.[46]

If the *nouveaux philosophes* had a leader, a spokesman, it was probably Bernard-Henri Lévy. His constant presence in the French media, from his articles in *Le Nouvel Observateur* to numerous appearances on television, made him into a minor cult figure in the mid-1970s. Yet, no one really led this disparate group of thinkers and Lévy's ideas were too idiosyncratic to form a school of thought. Although Lévy claimed to be a socialist, he rejected revolutionary change totally, turned against the hopes of 1968, embraced the idea of transcendence, rebelled against his Marxist-Leninist teacher Althusser, and ended up following the ideas of the arch-Catholic thinker Maurice Clavel. Not surprisingly, Lévy's most important work in the 1970s, *Barbarism with a Human Face*—an obvious ironic reference to the slogan of the Czech renaissance of 1968, "Socialism with a Human Face"—included a radical critique of socialism and the state. In that book Lévy argued that power was the great enemy. He found it everywhere, as the basis of language, the key to society, and, most important, the origin of the state. There is no "reality," or "history" or "progress." These are all inventions of power, used by the state to control its subjects. History is nothing but the manipulation of time by the prince, the master, whether that master were a dynastic monarch, a Jacobin revolutionary, a bourgeois capitalist, or a Bolshevik. Therefore, in order to eliminate the state, one must eliminate or transcend history. But this cannot be accomplished by revolution or individual effort: revolution and the individual are created and defined by the state and have no separate ontological existence. Socialism, therefore, is not the answer to the state but rather a mindless utopia that avoids the problems of evil and suffering that exist in this world. And Marxism is even worse: it invents a proletariat that does not exist, which is nothing but the obverse of the bourgeoisie, whose nonexistence must be represented by a party that supposedly speaks for it and in the process oppresses those who are not the "proletariat." Lévy thus reaches a total Derridaian impasse: capitalism is the final, decadent stage of western civilization which Marxism is totally incapable of transcending because it can only mimic the capitalist order of things, yet Marxism is the only real political discourse on the left, despite the monumental and inevitably futile efforts of the generation of 1968 to transform that discourse. The conversion of the French Socialist party to Marxism since 1968 means that barbarsim will be continued and entrenched in France. The little band of dissenting prophets can only protest against the dominance of barbarism for that dominance is inevitable. But, to protest does not mean to strive for power. Power will only corrupt and continue the process of barbarism one step further. Instead, protest means to rebel, to be a *moraliste* in the sense that Camus or Kant were. "But we will continue to *think*, to think to the end, *to think without believing it*, the impossible thought of a world freed from lordship."[47]

This austere, nihilistic attack on politics and the state, which represented a vulgarization of the ideas of Foucault and Derrida for the benefit of the unwashed masses, was not necessarily shared by Lévy's "colleagues." André Glucksmann, who probably ranked second to Lévy among the *nouveaux philosophes*, remained solidly anchored in the more traditional aspects of the French anarchist tradition, hopeful that the revolution would succeed one day. Although he expressed profound distrust of political parties and all forms of organization, viewing the French Communist party and the Soviet Union in an especially negative light, Glucksmann did not reject politics totally nor did he view Marx as the progenitor of the evils of communism. Instead, Glucksmann maintained that the May revolution might find expression in a new political party, one that would represent the student-worker desire for autonomy and decentralization of power, and he distinguished carefully between Marx the advocate of the anarchist Paris Commune and the perversion of Marxism in the Soviet Union. Admittedly, these views were most clearly expressed in Glucksmann's 1968 analysis of the May movement, but he did not abandon them later when Solzhenitsyn's revelations about the Gulag forced him to reevaluate earlier attitudes. In his 1975 work, *La cuisinière et le mangeur d'hommes*, Glucksmann retracted his earlier exoneration of Lenin and argued that the Soviet state was totalitarian from its inception. But, unlike Lévy, he emphasized clearly the dual origins of the twentieth-century gulag in the traditions of western liberalism and Soviet Marxism. The camps began in the European colonies, in places like South Africa, and spread from there to World War I, the Nazis, the Soviets, and on to the present. The camps, Glucksmann maintained, were the logical development of the European scientific revolution of the seventeenth century. Following Foucault, Glucksmann discovered their origins in the "hôpital général," the insane asylum, and the prison. Like those institutions, the camps were intended to impose reason, to stamp out *folie*. The camps force people to be free, they impose the work ethic upon humanity, they create economic man subservient to the system, to the state.

Glucksmann reminds us over and over that the camps are not a foreign invention, that they are not an Asiatic import, but rather they are us: Germany is us, the USSR is us; the camps are merely an extension of the western state system and capitalist rationality. But Glucksmann refuses to accept the impasse that Lévy offers us. He believes that the wretched of the earth can rebel against the system and overthrow oppression: "witness in France the spontaneous and carnavalesque occupation of the factories in 36, the Resistance, May 68." Recourse to the street, to the strike, to the takeover of bourgeois property help preserve the western proletarians from the Gulag: ". . . where the State ends, man begins."[48]

Glucksmann's Foucaultian anarchist perspective on the modern world did not provide any clear answers to the political problems of the day, but it struck a positive note with the 1968 generation and other members of the new philosophers movement. Michel Le Bris, a Breton contributor to the movement, reinforced and expanded upon Glucksmann's perspective, providing it with a regionalist twist. An extreme left-wing Maoist in 1968, Le Bris had been imprisoned for his role as *directeur* of the outlawed far-left Maoist newspaper, *La Cause du Peuple*. In the 1970s, he became an enthusiastic supporter of regionalist movements, publishing such works as *Occitaine: volem viure* in 1974, *Les fous du Larzac* in 1975, and *La révolte du Midi* in 1976 before his new philosophy masterpiece, *L'Homme aux semelles de vent*, appeared in 1977.[49] The first chapters of this work read like a regionalist manifesto. Brittany, where Le Bris was born in 1944, is depicted as an exploited area, where peasants worked from dawn to dusk in the service of the local lord, experiencing daily the inferiority of their culture to Paris and the outside capitalist world, subjected to that world and eager to imitate it. Over time, the local peasantry lost what little dignity and independence it once had, as capitalist agriculture destroyed small farmers, tourism disrupted traditional communities, and the Parisians took over the countryside, displacing the Bretons into the cities where they become part of the proletariat. Modernity meant disaster for Brittany: the ecological balance between peasants and the countryside was destroyed by new capitalist farming techniques and the proliferation of vacation homes; the scientific world required the peasants to give up their so-called archaic values and beliefs for the arid benefits of reason, technology, and the machine. By 1960, Brittany was dead, destroyed by capitalism and science.[50]

Le Bris's analysis did not end on this pessimistic note. He searched for the origins of this predicament in an attempt to understand how it could be transcended. Like Glucksmann, his guide to the past was

Michel Foucault's interpretation of the rise of rationality and the state. Le Bris argued that the period from 1750 to 1850 witnessed the rise and dominance of forces that led to the death of Brittany and other regions in the twentieth century: Hegelian thought, the Benthamite Panopticon, Jacobinism, scientific Marxism, the modern State, and the French language contributed to the destruction of individuality, provincial culture, regional languages, working-class freedom, and local autonomy for the purpose of centralizing power. But, Le Bris maintained, an important and powerful counterculture also emerged during this same time period. Basing its values on the Rabelaisian, carnivalesque tradition of premodern times, emphasizing peasant, working-class, and provincial languages and cultures above the centralizing culture of Paris, this counterculture found expression in some form or another in the works of such diverse intellectuals as the anarchist Proudhon, the liberal de Tocqueville, the socialist Lafargue, the romantic historian of the Girondists Lamartine, the Provençal writer Mistral, and the *romans populaires* authors Hugo, Sue, and Zola. Le Bris wanted to resurrect this lost tradition, to give life back to the joyless, barbarian world that capitalism and Marxism had created. But he had no faith in politics as the key to resurrection. As the title of his chapter 5 proclaimed: "The Art of the Fugue . . . since there is no science of revolution." In the spirit of the counterculture of the 1960s, Le Bris called for laughter, fêtes, carnivals to destroy the alienated world of science and reason.[51]

The joyous romantic utopianism of Le Bris's regionalist "politics" did not prevail in the work of the other major regionalist in the movement. On the contrary, Jean-Paul Dollé reflected the nihilistic despair that we have seen in Lévy's thought rather than the anarchistic *gai savoir* of a Le Bris or even a Glucksmann. Dollé is important, however, for giving us an idea of the deep sense of despair, of *angst*, that prevailed in certain French circles in the 1970s. Like Le Bris, he had been a Maoist revolutionary in 1968, expressing his hatred of Moscow by this choice. He thought that the revolution would transform France, remake the educational system and French culture. When it failed to do so, Dollé turned to psychoanalysis in order to overcome the void of existence and obtain some sense of identity. From this experience he learned that he belonged to the "abandoned generation." Born in 1939, about the same year that most of these philosophers first experienced life, Dollé believed that he and his generation were the children of defeat, raised in a France that had nothing left, no past, no present, no future. But despite the oppressive nihilism of existence, Dollé found meaning in the France of the *banlieue*, as he called it, of the Loire River valley where the Rabelaisian tradition still existed or of Brittany where Celtic culture still thrived. The state, Marxism, capitalism, and anything modern encounters nothing but scorn from Dollé. He is totally consumed by nostalgia for the past, a romantic nihilistic yearning for oblivion: "The peasantry is not a class like any other for it speaks with death after its death. The earth is not a place or a usufruct for it offers those who rest there a repose which does not end with the disintegration of the body. The earth remains."[52] The mystical tenor of Dolle's thought, the super *force tranquille* of his regionalism, emerged in his idea of true culture:

> The Patrie is the call of the native earth. I am because I was also my father, my grandmother, an oak under which my parents made love, the place where my uncle made some furniture. Champagne where my great uncles died in the war, the Palais-Royal where my ancestors came to find whores, the Fourmies miners' strike where I was killed, the Commune that I passed over rapidly. There is a patrie because there is a word which speaks to me and a native earth because there are songs of it. Beyond that, nothing exists: a despotic state, a chauvinistic nationalism, a one-dimensional and insignificant language, political terror, the death of architecture and the all-powerful "urbanistical."[53]

To Dollé, France is dead along with God. The politics of cultural despair is all that remains in a bleak, nihilistic world.

Dollé's despair and the extreme leftist, Maoist world of 1968 were totally foreign to Jean-Marie Benoist, the last of our new philosophers. While Glucksmann, Dollé, and Le Bris were on the barricades in 1968, Benoist remained aloof from events in London. Although he never accepted the appellation of *nouveau philosophe*, Benoist published the first of the movement's recognized masterworks, *Marx est mort*, in 1970, which began the long, repetitive process against Marxist thought in all of its forms. Furthermore, even though Benoist ran for public office on a rightist UDF ticket in 1978 and possessed little of the anarchism and nihilism that comprised the movement's sound and fury, his works were solidly grounded in the counterculture of the 1960s from which the new philosophers gained sustenance.[54] His 1978 work, *Les Nouveaux Primaires*, was based on the concept that a new type of man (or primate) had emerged in the twentieth century, defined in the West by the leveling mediocrity of consumer society and in the East by the brutal police states created by Marxism.[55] The commonplace themes of the gulag emerge here, with strong emphasis on the eastern form of that monster and vehement condemnations of French intellectuals who apologized for Soviet excesses despite evidence from Solzhenitsyn's pen and the concrete examples of Cambodia, Cuba, Vietnam, and China. In the tradition of Foucault, Benoist traced the origins of the

French "gulag" back to Descartes, arguing that Cartesianism had created, in the modern age, "une société organisée, informaticienne, matérialiste."[56] To counter this, Benoist hoped that a new politics would emerge in France, a politics that would do away with technocracy and centralization of power. He thought that such a politics was emerging with the union of political liberals and disillusioned Marxists of the extreme left. Although he rejected completely the Common Program of the left, which he thought was inspired by the authoritarian Marxism of the Communist party and its fifth-column CERES supporters in the Socialist party, he embraced the Fourierist tradition of decentralized socialism and its modern interpreters in the CFDT under Edmond Maire's leadership.[57] Yet, Benoist was ultimately no more realistic about the problems of the modern age than his fellow new philosophers. He sought liberation in the emergence of a new Baroque, a new Fronde, in which liberty would combine with transcendence, which he defined in the traditional Catholic sense found in Bernanos or the writings of Monsignor Lefebvre, the arch-reactionary priest of the 1970s and 1980s. Like Le Bris, Benoist discovered a French historical tradition that could overcome the evils of modernity. It embodied liberty defined in terms of a "Grand Autre," a transcendence that would replace the Marxist God of the modern clerics. He fled the modern age, much as Dollé had done, to find solace in a supposedly less complicated past.[58]

No political party could ever create a coherent policy based on the ideas of these thinkers, but still their importance in popularizing the concepts of the master thinkers of the 1970s, in a political context, cannot be dismissed lightly. For those who could not grasp the intricate concepts of a Foucault or a Derrida or a Lacan—not to mention their German predecessors—the new philosophers provided a simple formula that placed primary emphasis on anticommunism but did not neglect the themes of decadence and the destruction of all values, including those held most dear by western civilization. In pursuing their attacks on the state and European humanism, the new philosophers offered their alternative vision, a nostalgic utopia of regionalist cultures, traditional values, and a totally decentralized if not anarchical political system in which the individual prevailed over the tyrannies of political parties and bureaucratic organizations. Difficult though it may be to take this vision seriously, it resonated powerfully with deeply entrenched mythologies in French culture, which the 1968 revolution had brought to the forefront. Combining tradition and liberty, Catholicism and Rousseauian moralism, provincial autonomy and modern narcissism, a revolt against modernity and the impossibility of revolution, the new philosophers grounded their ideas in the crisis mentality of the age, popularizing virtually every aspect of that mentality in a world view that denigrated all traditional political solutions and left the individual totally isolated in a heartless world of totalitarian destruction. Since they called themselves leftists—for the most part—and gained the support of such leftist journals as *Le Nouvel Observateur*, it is not surprising that the Socialist party in particular viewed the new philosophers with suspicion. The antisocialist and antistatist ideas of this group posed a major threat to the party's ideological positions, which both mimicked the ideas of 1968 and remained aloof from the nihilistic despair contained within them. The great fear among Socialists was that the new philosophers would turn their supporters into right-wing anti-communists, emphasizing the narcissistic nostalgia of 1968 over the "progressive" values of the party. As we shall see, Socialists would pay careful attention to this threat, attempting to counter it frontally on such issues as anticommunism and political choice and to offer a better, more realistic position on regionalism and decentralization.

In this intellectual environment of *gauchisme* and new philosophy, the Socialist party attempted to outline its ideological perspective during the 1970s. From the start, however, the Socialists faced serious obstacles to the achievement of a coherent ideological position that could challenge these threats effectively. To begin with, the party emerged in 1971–72 as a coalition of numerous groups, ranging from the far-left CERES, whose concerns were to unite the Communist and non-Communist left into a grand alliance for victory, to the old-guard hangovers from Guy Mollet's SFIO, which aimed primarily at maintaining the powers of the traditional Socialist bastions and the notables that led them in such places as the Bouches-du-Rhône and the Nord. At the center of this new party, uniting its centrifugal forces, was François Mitterrand and the Mitterrandists. Elected to head the party as its secretary in 1971, Mitterrand emerged as the guiding force in determining party ideology, despite the fact that he was not very interested in ideology. At the Epinay congress, he outlined the path that the new Parti socialiste had to take in developing an ideology. First, Mitterrand maintained, the party had to be capable of conquering power, which meant that it had to take over the terrain that the Communists, the *gauchistes* and the liberals had been able to appropriate from it. Second, the Socialists had to aim at achieving the union of the left, which meant acceptance of the idea of the *rupture* with capitalism and the recognition that they could not obtain power and carry out their objectives without the support of the Communists.[59] To achieve these two aims of differentiation and common ground, the party proceeded in 1971–72 to draw up a three-point strategy composed of the *front de classe*, *union de la gauche*, and *autogestion*. That strategy would remain the basis of all Socialist ideological discussion through the elections of 1981, although the interpretation of it would vary greatly, depending on the circumstances and which current within the party happened to be dominant at any given time.[60]

Of these three, only *autogestion* could effectively fill the gap of an ideology for the party.[61] Neither the *front de classe* nor the *union de la gauche* carried such importance. The *front de classe*, for example, referred merely to a very minor part of the Marxian corpus regarding the proletarianization of the middle class. The Socialists argued that large sections of the French middle class, from artisans to the professions, had become potential allies of the French proletariat as the result of their increasing dependency upon employers for wages during the post-1958 period. This wage dependency contrasted sharply with the previous independent status of this middle class, making it ripe for ideological union with the proletariat in a front that would be able to capture power and carry out the rupture with capitalism. Despite certain problems concerning the potentially reactionary response of this middle class to proletarianization—a problem to which the new philosophers contributed—and the seemingly opportunistic nature of an alliance between workers and middle-class employees, in 1977 a leading Socialist party theorist would write, in *La nouvelle revue socialiste*, that the concept of the *front de classe* was the least controversial and least examined of the three strategies of the party.[62] And it remained that way throughout the 1970s, in part because the new Socialist party was, much more than the old SFIO, a party of the middle class, with only 15 percent of its members from the ranks of the working class (versus 35 percent in the SFIO).[63]

By contrast, the *union de la gauche* was a controversial strategy from the Epinay congress until the withdrawal of the Communists from the government in July 1984. In 1971 neither the Molletistes nor the followers of the former *gauchiste* PSU leader Jean Poperen was pleased with this new strategy. They went along reluctantly with the Common Program that the party drew up with the Communists in 1972, distrusting such an alliance as much as the new-left elements outside of the party did. In 1974, with the entrance of Michel Rocard, Edmond Maire, and the *deuxième gauche* followers of these two men into the party, the anti–*union de la gauche* elements were reinforced. Whether or not François Mitterrand encouraged these forces at the expense of the Common Program, by 1977 the Communist party had become suspicious of both Socialist electoral advances at its expense and internal changes in the Socialist party that the *deuxième gauche* had initiated. The ensuing breakdown of the *union de la gauche*—or at least the Common Program—and the defeat of the left in the 1978 legislative elections, gave the *deuxième gauche* the upper hand in the party. As a result, under Michel Rocard's leadership, the *deuxième gauche* attempted to scrap this part of the Epinay strategy in an effort to "modernize" the party. But Mitterrand, CERES, and some of the party notables—Gaston Defferre in particular—rallied behind the *union de la gauche* and saved it from new leftist attacks, despite the fact that the Common Program remained null and void.[64]

Most academic observers of the "long march" of the Socialist party have argued that the *union de la gauche* was essential if the left were to gain victory under the Fifth Republic and therefore they have viewed the triumph of François Mitterrand over Michel Rocard and the *deuxième gauche* as a sine qua non for the electoral success of the French Socialists. But, few observers have noticed the degree to which the Mitterrandists took seriously the issues involved in this debate.[65] In particular, François Mitterrand was very concerned about the new-left, *nouveaux philosophes* accusation that socialism equaled the gulag, and he proceeded to attack that simplistic observation, either directly or through proxies, on numerous occasions. In his speech at the Metz congress of 1979, where the party chose between Rocard and Mitterrand; in articles that appeared in *La nouvelle revue socialiste*, which was under the *direction* of the secretary of the party; and in a special colloquium on Stalinism, Mitterrand and his supporters in the party addressed this vexing issue.

Much has been made of the fact that the Metz congress of 1979 represented a showdown between the "two cultures" in the Socialist party, the "modern" culture that emphasized decentralization of the state, market forces, and anticommunism and the "archaic" one that represented centralization of power, nationalization of the key economic sectors, and the *union de la gauche*. But such a simplistic dichotomy is not an accurate picture of either side in the debate and it is especially inaccurate as a depiction of François Mitterrand's position. In speeches leading up to the Metz congress, before the Comité directeur of the party on 8 July 1978, and before the National Convention on 26 November 1978, Mitterrand reaffirmed the principles of Epinay, which he claimed included the *union de la gauche*, the *front de classe*, *autogestion*, and the acceptance of the Common Market. Although he made appeals to the Marxist, pronationalization elements in the party, reaffirming the ideas of the rupture with capitalism and nationalization of key industries as outlined in the Common Program, he carefully straddled the two cultures, embracing both rather than excluding anyone. As he put the matter very succinctly to the National Convention in discussing the importance of Epinay: "It was necessary to choose: either to construct a great party in which we united our forces, ideas and abilities together, or to maintain numerous small fractions, without doubt pure in their own eyes, but impotent in the course of History."[66] Always consistent, Mitterrand reiterated this theme at Metz, rejecting totally the idea that the gulag emerged out of Marxism and embracing fervently the idea that the objective of the Socialist party was to unite the left, the two cultures of Socialism, in order to win victory: "But we are together comrades, and we are together because we have conquered the two cultures and their two histories in order to make them into one! That is the task of the Socialist party. I can tell you that it is the only one that I recognize as historic, for you as well as for me!"[67] Nevertheless, the party secretary made clear that he did not accept those parts of the Marxist culture that endangered liberty: "But if one tells me at the same time that it is advisable to eliminate a type of culture, because it identifies itself with state oppression, with the elimination of the citizen, with a dominant bureaucracy, and finally with the negation of autogestion and individual values, then I sense in myself that it is necessary to eliminate this contradiction, because it is mortal."[68]

Victory at Metz did not end this careful process of definition. Increasingly, in 1979 and 1980, *La nouvelle revue socialiste* attacked those new-left, new-philosopher, and new-right elements to which previously, the review had paid scant attention. Under the pen of its editor, Alain Meyer, the journal carefully identified these movements as products of a period of intellectual crisis, which emerged with the collapse of structuralism in the mid-1970s. Clearly, Meyer saw these new intellectual developments as a threat to the Socialist party, for they appealed to middle-class groups that the *front de classe* attempted to incorporate, emphasizing irrationalism, utopianism, neoromantic *enracinement*, anti-Marxism, and Nietzschean individualism over socialist values.[69] To Meyer, the new philosophers and the new-left thinkers were unwitting allies of the extremist new right of Alain de Benoist and Louis Pauwels: their attacks on Marxism and political parties helped to create the environment in which new-right thinkers gained respectability in French political circles.[70]

The greatest danger for the party resided, therefore, in the possibility that the outcome of the two-cultures debate might affect its image among the floating middle-class electorate whose support was essential for victory. The party could not be seen as being tied to a French form of Stalinism or Leninism. It had to counterattack the new-left, new-philosopher claim that socialism equaled the gulag. In 1980, therefore, the party's research bureau, the Institut Socialiste d'Etudes et de Recherches, held a colloquium on Stalinism to which leading former Communists and Eastern European émigré dissidents were invited to speak on the subject in order to help distinguish the French Socialist party and Marxism from any form of Stalinism or Leninism. None of the invited guests disappointed the party. But more important, Lionel Jospin and François Mitterrand gave major speeches at the colloquium, revealing the seriousness of the issue to the Mitterrandist current in the party. Jospin began the assault with a slashing critique of the French Communist party (PCF) for adhering to a Stalinist position after making cosmetic modifications to appeal to the French electorate. But Jospin did not equate his vehement anti-Stalinism with an attack on the *union de la gauche*. He maintained that the *union de la gauche* was not the union of two parties into one, but the union of the people of the left: "One must understand that it is the necessity of uniting the popular forces, the social categories which need reforms that is the basis of the strategy of *union de la gauche*."[71] To Jospin, the union of the left would lead to changes in the Parti communiste that would reveal the contradictions that existed in that party and force it increasingly to accept Socialist positions or else risk the loss of its electoral support.[72]

Speaking at the conclusion of the colloquium, François Mitterrand reiterated Jospin's position on the PCF and added to it: "Our position [on Stalinism] must be recalled incessantly, for the means of communication in our country tends to assimilate French Socialism, in an insidious or fixed manner, with the totality of experiences—including the worst—of world Communism."[73] Mitterrand rejected the notion that the Common Program had compromised the Socialists, pointing out that the Communists had made major concessions in signing that program. He also pointed to the absurdity of the new philosophers' equation of Marxism with the gulag: "If Stalin is Lenin and Lenin is Marx, then from the start all advances toward the socialist world are struck with impotence; from the start this project leads to the Gulag, to repression, to the destruction of millions and millions of men and women."[74] On the contrary, Mitterrand maintained, French socialism was not tainted by totalitarianism, even though the French Communists remained infected with Stalinism:

Our party shall be the bearer of a society which shall have broken with any possibility of Stalinism, which shall have renounced without any doubt the illusions of a Leninism that extends itself to planetary dimensions, a society which will be constructed on the basis of Marx and a number of other theoreticians, on the basis of all those who have been the torchbearers of liberty, whether socialists or not, who, in their respective nations, have preferred prison, the psychiatric ward, exile or death to capitulation, and on the basis of those who accept death or the loss of their own liberty because they love, above all, the liberty of others.[75]

This cannot be accomplished, however, through the vapid schemes of the new philosophers: "We can only get rid of the master if we break the economic chains." When that is done, Mitterrand added, the Socialists had to destroy "all the forms and temptations of power" in their ranks, for all "power carries in itself its own Stalinism." Each individual will become master of his or her own destiny under a French form of socialism that will have nothing in common with Stalinism, but rather will be identified "by the defense of minorities, by the decentralization of power, by the transformation of industrial relations and economic structures, by social adaptation, and by the rejection of all exhorbitant power. . . ."[76] "Thus, the socialism of tommorow, the socialism of *autogestion*, shall be a socialism which discovers its own Montesquieu."[77]

The struggle to define and defend the *union de la gauche* from misrepresentation spilled over into every aspect of party affairs in the run-up to the 1981 elections, including the *Projet socialiste* that outlined party policy for the 1980s. But, neither the *union de la gauche* nor the *front de classe* strategy equaled, either separately or together, an ideological position that could differentiate the Socialists from the Communists and provide the party with a project for change that could appeal broadly to the French electorate. That burden was placed on *autogestion*, which became the only ideological position that the Socialists came close to adopting in the 1970s.

Beginning as a product of the 1971 alliance between the Mitterrandist and CERES currents in the party, *autogestion* was accepted reluctantly by the Mitterrandists, but soon became the vehicle for uniting the non-Communist left behind the Socialist party. In 1974, with the *Assises du socialisme* which brought together the Socialist party and the key leaders of the *deuxième gauche*, most notably Michel Rocard and Edmond Maire, the concept of *autogestion* became central to the party's ideological position, leading to the proclamation, in 1975, of the fifteen theses on *autogestion*.[78] Yet, despite the centrality of this concept to Socialist identity, leading some academic observers to claim that *autogestion* was *the* ideology of the Socialist party,[79] the concept remained very vague, defined in different ways by different currents within the party, sometimes bordering on impossible utopianism or obscurity or eclecticism. Nevertheless, *autogestion* proved to be a perfect metaphor or unifying idea, around which the Socialist party could create an identity separate from the Communist left or the Giscardian-Gaullist right, an identity that could reach out to attract the generation of 1968, especially those who might be swayed by the new left or the new philosophers.

Basically, the Socialist party included in its ranks three varieties of *autogestion*: the Marxist-CERES variety, the deuxième gauche-CFDT-Rocardian variety, and the regionalist/decentralizing variety. The three overlapped—especially the second and the third—and appealed often to the same constituencies, despite the differences that existed between them on what was meant by *autogestion*. Together, they helped comprise a Socialist identity whose vagueness and contradictory positions were often an asset, at least when it came to gaining broad-based support among the voters. To understand what *autogestion* represented in the party, we will discuss these three varieties and the differences that emerged between them, concluding with an analysis of the Socialist position on *autogestion* on the eve of the presidential election of 1981.

The CERES current in the party was the first to advocate *autogestion*. As early as 1968, CERES had developed at least some rudimentary ideas on the subject, but they did not gain currency until after the victory of the CERES and Mitterrandist forces at the Epinay congress of the party when Jean-Pierre Chevènement, the young leader of CERES, was given the task of drawing up a new party program. Although Chevènement's program proved to be too *autogestionnaire* in tone and had to be modified to appease the traditional members of the party, *autogestion* remained in the party's program from that point on.

CERES's views on *autogestion* were probably best expressed in a collective work that it published in 1975, *Les Ceres: Un combat pour le socialisme*. In that work, CERES made clear that its program was based solidly on the union of the left and the rupture with capitalism, in contrast to what it called the Rocardian program of compromise between the working class and capitalism. CERES sought to achieve a revolutionary middle way between the two monolithic systems of American capitalism and Soviet statism by implementing *autogestion,* which it viewed as the "contemporary expression of the 'revolutionary utopia.' "[80] *Autogestion* would occur first of all through the struggle for control over the workplace, but would not be "limited to the sphere of production." *Autogestion* would eventually affect "all domains of social reality" from control over urban affairs to control over public services such as education and health, and it would encompass the "droit à la différence" of cultural and linguistic minorities in their struggle against centralization and uniformity.[81] But how, precisely, would this process be initiated? To CERES, the transition from statism to *autogestion* would occur through nationalization of industry, which would allow workers to take over at the base and initiate democratic planning to replace the market. Society would be transformed by a dual process from above and below. The union of the left would be the vehicle through which change would occur, as the Common Program offered the means to accomplish a revolutionary break with capitalism. Thus CERES thought that the party was essential for bringing about *autogestion* as it would provide ideological leadership and organization for the rank and file, without subjecting the populace to either a social democratic model of oligarchical organization or an Eastern European model of bureaucracy. CERES also opposed all *gauchiste* proposals to destroy the state, for it maintained that the state was needed to arbitrate between different levels of government under *autogestion*. Better to democratize and decentralize the state in an effort to transform it gradually along the lines of *autogestion* than to dismantle it precipitously.[82]

Clearly, CERES's position was much more Marxist and statist in direction than new-left ideas on *autogestion*. As Jean-Pierre Chevène-ment argued in his major work on the subject, *Le Vieux, la Crise, le Neuf*, *autogestion* required a "strategy of rupture with the great multinational firms and with American domination over the world economy."[83] Citing the 1972 Socialist program, *Changer la vie*, which he had played a major role in writing, Chevènement defined *auto-gestion* as "the end of exploitation, the disappearance of antagonistic classes, the abolition of the salaried class, and the achievement of democracy."[84] None of this, however, could be accomplished without profound struggle by the party and the working class to take over the state and transform it. In Marxist terms, Chevènement saw *autogestion* emerging through the actions of the proletariat and the party in the factory or enterprise at the stage in which monopoly capitalism reached its final end, creating a massive movement toward decentralization of power, leading to the breakup of monopoly capitalism and the establishment of direct democracy in industry. From that base, he argued, *autogestion* would spread to replace the market with democratic planning from the bottom up, transform the patriarchal family, and redirect education from its role of transmitting the dominant ideology and class hierarchy under capitalism to creating responsible citizens able to participate in society under *autogestion*. In the process, the capitalist state would slowly wither away to be replaced by an *autogestionnaire* society.[85]

In contrast, the *deuxième gauche* of Michel Rocard and Edmond Maire adopted positions that were much closer to the new left that remained on the fringes or outside of the party. Anti-communism and anti-Marxism pervaded the ranks of this second left, which often seemed to be using *autogestion* as a means of attacking the *union de la gauche* and the Common Program—or so the CERES faction would maintain. Yet, in many respects the divisions between CERES and the second left were not as profound as they seemed. For example, when CERES stated where most of its ideas came from, it pointed directly to the new left: "Closer to us, the contribution of the 'new left' is incontestable. The colloquium of Grenoble, the theses of the P.S.U., the positions outlined by the 'opposition' elements in the P.C.F. have contributed, in the course of the last ten years, to create a community of opinion which we have borrowed from."[86] Not surprisingly, therefore, these two groups could agree on a common set of principles about what *autogestion* meant, as they did at the *Assises du socialisme* in 1974. Differences on strategy, more than on prinicples, divided the two factions.

Yet, these differences were important. Edmond Maire, the head of the nation's second largest union, the CFDT, did not choose to join the Parti socialiste until after he had been convinced that it could be transformed into a great anti-communist movement on the left. The Epinay congress and the Common Program had turned Maire away from the Socialists, but François Mitterrand's 1974 Presidential election campaign convinced him that the party under Mitterrand was moving toward a pragmatic, autogestionnaire position that was basically anti-communist in outlook.[87] Beyond this visceral anti-communism, which contrasted with the CERES-Mitterrandist policy of embracing the PCF to death, Maire's form of *autogestion* differed from CERES's by its extraordinary emphasis on the withering away of the state, the party, and any form of authoritarian expertise. Maire envisaged complete democratization and decentralization as the objective of *autogestion*, to the point where every worker and every citizen had control over his or her own destiny without any intermediaries. He rejected totally the Communist (and CERES) thesis that the state and society could be changed from the top down through nationalization of industry and centralized planning. Change, if and when it came, would occur through *social* forces primarily, rather than through political parties and the state. *Autogestion*, therefore, was "the maximum decentralization of these forms of social organization and their democratic functioning."[88] The centralized state would only be needed to provide justice, liberty, and security. Like CERES, but with more emphasis on the autonomous nature of social groups, Maire viewed *autogestion* as a process that would affect not only the workplace but all aspects of society, from urbanism to regionalism. Maire made clear that regionalism was in fact a form of *autogestion* that had emerged independently with a bias toward emphasizing traditional values rather than the more balanced approach that *autogestion* took of combining those values—"Vivre au pays" for example—with the need for creativity and progress. Thus, the *projet autogestionnaire*, as Maire defined it, was for "*une autre croissance*, for different types of social relations, that is to say, for providing development with another orientation."[89] Growth had to occur in the context of *autogestion*, in which profits and production were subjected to the culture of democratic decisions. Or, as Maire put it: "Initiatives in regard to social services, urban affairs, and working conditions can only be proper if they are the product of the choices and decisions of those involved."[90]

Within the party proper, the CFDT themes of less party, less state, more decentralization, and more civil society were the property of Michel Rocard and the Rocardians, whose ideas led CERES to complain often and loudly about the "gauche américaine" that was undermining Marxist values for a vague, catch-all American-style Democratic party.[91] Over and over again, Rocard spoke out for new-left values that he identified as the culture of *autogestion* in combat with the culture of Jacobin centralization. To him, the fifteen theses on *autogestion* were the heart of the Socialist party and not the Common Program, which he labeled as merely a "bon compromis" between the two cultures.[92] In an article written to commemorate the tenth anniversary of May 1968, he pointed to the CFDT and the PSU as the forces that carried on the spirit of May, developing *autogestion* as their driving principle, helping the French left avoid the pitfalls of authoritarianism and terrorism, which afflicted Italian and German politics after 1968. But unfortunately, Rocard observed, from 1972 to 1978 the spirit of May was reversed in France as the left placed primary emphasis on electoral politics rather than on social change at the base through *autogestion*.[93] Far more than Maire did, Rocard concentrated on the archaic nature of the party, condemning those Socialists who were still fighting the battles of the Fourth Republic and criticizing the exclusive focus on electoral politics and highly centralized Leninist organization, which made the party more interested in winning elections and taking over power at the center than in transforming civil society. Rocard wanted a different kind of party, one that engaged in the "combats du quotidien," a party of millions of militants who wanted to transform society and the state from the bottom up rather than submit to change from above, who would carry out the rupture with capitalism rather than having it done for them. "No new praxis is possible, no real responsibility or initiative, in an organization where the impetus comes solely from the top, where the Party is a mirror image of the society that it is struggling against."[94] To Rocard, the new socialism must make liberty the supreme value, the final goal of the movement—not the liberty of small, self-enclosed entities, for that often degenerated into local tyranny, nor the liberty to exploit, but "the liberty to create in every area, beginning with that of production."[95] Thus, *autogestion* restored the value of free initiative, of civil society, and it solved the problem of reform versus revolution by placing primary emphasis on social change rather than political change. In the process, the party would become an instrument for civil society to use in carrying out change rather than the force that imposed change from above. Rocard and the Rocardians consequently ended up as revisionists who viewed the rupture with capitalism as an evolutionary process rather than a smashing victory of the forces of good over the forces of evil. And they called this *autogestion*.[96]

The final component in the *autogestionnaire* mixture was regionalism, a movement that had traditionally been identified with the right, with local notables and folkloric appeals to tradition. Since the publication of Jean Gravier's *Paris et le désert français* in 1947, however, a small but important regionalist movement had emerged on the left and gained ground under the Fifth Republic as the right became increasingly identified with centralization of power in Paris.[97] In the mid-1960s, the regionalist thinker Robert Lafont was one of the first to link socialism with local autonomy and to accuse the Gaullist state and capitalism of undermining the regions of France through the process of internal colonialism. Lafont argued that exploitation of the regions by Paris had undermined local control over banking, commerce, industry, and natural resources for the benefit of the state and capitalism, leaving regions such as Languedoc and Brittany in a state of pauperization: "We are indeed faced with classical colonialism, which eliminates the local bourgeoisie as a class by undermining regional capitalist structures, by altering and absorbing them. It is proper to speak of *proletarian regions* in France." Speaking of his *patrie*, the Mediterranean, Lafont observed that the process of modernization had been blocked by capitalism and the state: "We understand the results of this situation: raw materials are exported and come back to the region, after being processed, where the users pay for this processing, which could have been done by them." Gaullism, Lafont concluded, represented the final victory of "grand capitalisme dans l'Etat."[98]

Despite his scathing condemnation of internal colonialism, Lafont offered no convincing solution to the problem in this early work. In this respect, he reflected the frustration of many new-left thinkers in the 1960s, who spoke vaguely about a socialist revolution but had no idea where the leadership for such a revolution would come from. Neither the Communist party nor the SFIO appeared capable of implementing regional autonomy. Yet, by the late 1960s parts of the socialist movement had embraced regionalism: the writings of the Breton professor of geography, Michel Philipponeau, who was a close associate of both Gaston Defferre and François Mitterrand, combined with the analyses of Michel Rocard and the PSU, were helping to prepare the ideological ground for the Socialist party's adoption of regionalist ideas in the 1970s.[99]

The changes that occurred in the Socialist party during the early 1970s made it into a more hospitable environment for regionalism to thrive. By 1976, therefore, Robert Lafont had discovered the solution to the problem of internal colonialism in the Socialist party, especially in the form of socialist *autogestion* in the region. In Lafont's version, this entailed the creation of democratic representation for each *pays* in each region. For instance, the Languedoc-Roussillon region would be broken down into fifty *pays*, each one a natural subunit of the region, composed of about thirty thousand voters apiece. Each *pays* would choose representatives for a regional council that would become the central ruling body for the people of the region as the department and the state were eliminated or reduced to a minimum. An Assembly of the Regions, with limited powers, would replace the Senate and allow the regions to coordinate policy through "the harmonization of regional plans among the regions and the discussion of intranational and international contracts . . ." that the regions would engage in.[100] All planning would begin at the local level, rather than at the top, and proceed democratically from there to the Assembly. Ultimately, the regions would control everything, from the kind of educational system they wanted to the bulk of the budgetary process. Regional taxes could be imposed on tourists, capitalists, and goods leaving or entering the region. Each region would also be allowed to control its own banking system, totally independent of central state supervision. Energy resources, mineral rights, forests, agriculture, and industry would all be carefully monitored by the region to keep control in local hands. The end result of regionalist *autogestion* would be the establishment of a new socialist kind of citizenship that would replace the bourgeois, democratic concept of citizenship, as Parisian centralization and capitalist control of the provinces were broken down under a socialist government. A France composed of autonomous regions would in turn inspire the creation of a Europe based on the principle of socialist *autogestion* and a new postcapitalist, poststatist age would be inagurated as a consequence.[101]

Exactly how the Socialist party would achieve such sweeping changes, other than by simply winning the next election, was not explained by Lafont, leaving his optimistic analysis ripe for eventual disillusionment. But that did not deter the Socialists from adopting Lafont's arguments on internal colonialism in drawing up their 1981 regionalist manifesto, *La France au pluriel*.[102] That important document, which received the enthusiastic support of François Mitterrand, who wrote the preface to it, pointed to *déracinement* as the great problem the nation faced.

Echoing Lafont and Gravier, it argued that regional cultures were being destroyed due to the predominance of Paris and capitalism over the regions. The Socialists pledged to reverse the course of rural exodus and underdevelopment, which the Gaullists and the Giscardians had promoted, by encouraging productive work—industry above all—in the regions. The slogan "Vivre au pays" would become reality, the document claimed, as the Socialists gave the regions control over their own economic, cultural, and political destinies under "a state which, while remaining united, would be decentralized and *autogestionnaire*: a state that France has never seen before and of which few examples exist in the world."[103] Under this new state, the cultural uniformity that capitalism had created would be reversed by the restoration of the teaching of local languages and cultures, while the dual economy of "dynamic" and "traditional" regions would be eliminated. The region would emerge under socialism as an autonomous entity in control of its own cultural and economic destiny, capable of carrying out the objective of "Vivre au pays."[104]

Yet, in spite of this massive outpouring of *autogestionnaire* ideas, the party never totally agreed on whether *autogestion* should be the ideological underpinning of socialism. The closest that the party ever came to such an idea was in the mid-1970s with the *Assises du socialisme* and the fifteen theses on *autogestion*.[105] But these developments were countered by skepticism over what the adoption of any set ideological position would do to the party's structure and political appeal, not to mention the fact that the concept of *autogestion* was not clearly defined and meant quite different things to different currents within the party. In 1977, therefore, the party's research arm held a colloquium on the matter of whether the Socialists should adopt *autogestion* as an ideology. Strong, convincing arguments were made in favor of such a move. Alain Meyer, the editor of *La nouvelle revue socialiste*, pointed to the inroads that nihilism, populism, new leftism, and the new philosophers had made in the *front de classe* that the Socialists hoped to create. To counter this, he argued, the party could adopt an ideology that reflected the *front de classe*, in other words an ideology that included flexiblity, liberty, and openness in the spirit of *autogestion*. But Meyer did not come out solidly in favor of such a course, nor did most of those attending the colloquium. Their views were probably best expressed by the Mitterrandist participant, Lionel Jospin, who believed that the party was too diverse to adopt one ideological position. To do so, Jospin maintained, would lead to the suppression of the rights of some elements in the party. But more important, Jospin claimed that he was "très méfiant sur le terme idéologie autogestionnaire," because he did not understand what *autogestion* meant. Although he could accept *autogestion* as a social experiment, he could not accept it as an ideology that defined what the party was. François Mitterrand, in making the closing speech to the gathering, reaffirmed Jospin's position that a dominant ideology in the party would breed intolerance rather than openness.[106] The colloquium concluded that the party should avoid committing itself to any ideology.

Jospin and Mitterrand were right: to choose between the new-left *autogestion* of Rocard and Maire and the Marxist form of *autogestion* supported by CERES presented too many problems for the party. One last example will suffice. In January 1979, the *Nouvelle revue socialiste* held a debate on social experimentation that pitted Jean-Pierre Chevènement against Michel Rocard, with others participating as well. The debate centered exclusively on the issue of whether significant social change could occur in a political environment that was hostile to such change. The Rocardians, whose belief in the powers of civil society to bring change was paramount, maintained that significant change could occur in a hostile environment and that parties were secondary to the process of change. To Chevènement and his supporters, however, the central issue was who controlled the state: "to conquer the state, to transform it fundamentally, to achieve in the real structures of society the transformations which shall give the workers, that is to say the majority, the means to allow a new politics to prevail." Chevènement believed that social experimentation could only achieve limited reform, that it was not *autogestion*, and that those who maintained that they could "changer la vie sans changer l'Etat" were engaging in "a sort of historic compromise with the grande bourgeoisie."[107] Rocard could only respond with doubts about the efficacy of state power in bringing real reform, but they were doubts that smacked of the new philosophers and the new left: "What kind of power is one going to create? How will one provide against the absolute powers that Marxist societies have all created? All ... there is not any countermodel, which is dreadful!"[108] But Chevènement gained the upper hand over his rival when he pointed to the United States as the prime example of social experimentation, with women's liberation, gay power, ecological movements, and other movements, which had made absolutely no impact on the powers that be: "Ten years after [1968] conservatism triumphs! The little desire machines can function as much as they want in the shadow of the great bureaucratic machines of the Pentagon, the State Department or the multinational societies." No party in the United States contested these forces, in contrast to France, where a powerful left existed. Even so, Chevènement continued, the French bourgeoisie has erected "a fantastic ideological offensive" that aims to "substitute for the political conception that it calls traditional, *politicienne*, dirty, in short the Epinay line, a conception that it presents as new, romantic, proper, joyful, *fêtarde*, which is called social experimentation."[109] Although the CERES leader did not label Rocard as one of the enemies, he strongly implied tht Rocard might be sympathetic with their cause. With divisions of this kind, *autogestion* became impossible to implement as the ideology of the party.

Yet, the party returned over and over to the values of *autogestion* in defining itself vis-à-vis the left and the right. The *Projet socialiste pour la France des années 80*, which Jean-Pierre Chevènement played a major role in writing, imposed CERES' view of *autogestion* on the entire party on the eve of the 1981 presidential election campaign. Beginning with an analysis of the international economic order by tracing the origins of the second "crisis" in the twentieth-century capitalist system to 1974, when the post-1945 capitalist order, under the hegemony of the United States, reached the limits of exploitation of the working class, the *Projet* attacked Giscard d'Estaing for addressing the crisis by favoring the marketplace over planning, promoting the antidemocratic ideas of thc new right, and accepting American economic and cultural hegemony over the French nation. Although the *Projet* engaged in a Marxist analysis of this situation, the heart of the document was concerned with the theme of "values," which Chevènement had come to believe was the most important issue that the Socialists had to address. The 1980s faced a major "Crisis of Values" the authors argued. This crisis had already found expression in numerous ways: in the ideas of the new philosophers, in the new right, in the rise of irrationalism. All of these responses were false. The new philosophers and their compatriots, the new economists, were bastard children of 1968, who apologized for capitalism and the cult of the individual, while attacking the left maliciously by falsely equating Marx and the Gulag. All of these movements, the *Projet* maintained à la Chevènement, were part of capitalist hegemonic culture, part of a totalitarian social order that "was in the process of installing itself in the name of the struggle against 'totalitarianism.'"[110]

The *Projet's* response to the crisis combined both new and conventional elements. In the conventional vein, the authors maintained that France faced "un monde incertain" in which the values of socialism confronted the powerful capitalist enemy. To overcome this, France must place itself "in the avant-garde of a new internationalism" that will prevent the capitalist solution to the crisis from prevailing.[111] But in addition to forming alliances with the Third World and promoting international socialist solutions to the crisis, the *Projet* advocated an *autogestionnaire* system of values to replace the old. Thus, it called for worker control over "daily affairs" through the "conquest of information, the transparency of salaries, the mastery of production and the organization of labor," and it promoted the extension of socialist democracy to as many citizens as possible: "Diffusion of power, control by the workers and the users, decentralization, vigorous regionalization, free circulation of information, abolition of administrative secrecy, respect for pluralism, separation of powers, no confusion between the State and parties...."[112] In tune with the regionalist advocates of *autogestion*, the program aimed at uniting the individual with the community: "the concrete individual can live and thrive only when connected with an actual community which ties him with both the past and the future." The sense of alienation and isolation that capitalism created will be transcended: "Our aim is to give back to the individual the sense of enrootedness, of history, of his neighborhood and all that he owes to the work of others and more generally what Blum called 'la grande vie humaine' which expresses itself through art, knowledge or the work of the generations."[113]

The *Projet*'s concept of *autogestion* placed key emphasis on the need for state control of the economy through nationalization of leading industries and state-directed research and investment projects. But it did include at least a passing reference to the Rocardian-CFDT position. In discussing "Les droits nouveaux dans la cité," for example, the authors referred to thesis ten of the 1975 program on *autogestion*, which stated that socialism could not be implemented in the French state "unless the function and the nature of the state were transformed and new forms of power appeared."[114] In that light, the *Projet* advocated sweeping changes such as the decentralization of power to the regions, departments, and municipalities and the protection of local culture and languages. But the authors also spoke of the state encouraging *autogestion* at the local level, promoting proper associations and discouraging "false" ones. And they made much of the role of state-controlled education, advocating a system that would shape young minds in the ways of *autogestion* at a very early age—"La lutte pour l'égalité commence à la maternelle"—and continue through adult life.[115] However, the *Projet*'s emphasis on the national mission of a Socialist France and the central role of the party in mobilizing workers to act, guiding the *front de classe* and promoting the *union de la gauche*, distinguished it most clearly from the Rocardian position. To the CERES authors of the *Projet*, *autogestion* may have been the objective, but *autogestion* with a strong state, a strong Socialist party organization and leadership role, a united left with the Communists, and a major presence for a socialist France in the world.[116]

The Marxist, *autogestionnaire Projet socialiste* divided the party as much as it united it. No wonder that every current within the party, except CERES, refrained from referring to the *Projet*, despite the fact that it was accepted as the official party position. Simply put, the divisions within the party made it impossible to adopt any coherent ideology, such as *autogestion*, for no one could agree totally on what the contours of such an ideology should be or on how to implement it once the party gained power. In lieu of an ideology, the Socialist party accepted a catchall, grab-bag approach. Jean-Pierre Chevènement and his CERES supporters were absolutely correct when they accused Rocard and his followers of wanting to establish a *gauche américaine*. But Rocard and the CFDT were not alone in this enterprise. François Mitterrand himself rejected the *Projet socialiste* in the 1981 election campaign and chose to run, instead, on his own pragmatic program, the *110 propositions pour la France*, which played down the more extreme positions of the *Projet* and attempted to unite the currents in the party behind a minimalist program that eschewed ideology for concrete propositions that a Socialist government would implement.[117] To Mitterrand, ideology was irrelevant compared to the task of gaining power. This political opportunist, whose political roots were in the intrigues of the Fourth Republic, sympathized with *autogestion* and Marxism, but took no clear position on ideological matters. He had not become a Socialist until late in his career, after the 1968 uprising. And when he did, he vascillated between the two cultures that Rocard referred to in the late 1970s, refusing to accept either one. This was clear as early as 1970, when Mitterrand stated his position on decentralization and *autogestion*: "I am a supporter of everything that leads to decentralization: the plan, municipal control, *autogestion*. I am not a Girondin in politics, but a Jacobin. But on the other hand, I am a staunch supporter of decentralization."[118] In the debate on the two cultures, as we have seen, he reiterated this position and added his profound distaste for petty ideological quibbling. Yet, in the end, Mitterrand came down most clearly for the second left's form of *autogestion*, despite his ties with CERES. In 1980 and 1981, he embraced totally the idea of "Vivre autrement," identifying his program with decentralization, the *droit à la différence* for cultural minorities, ecology, spirituality, freedom for associations vis-à-vis the state, and the greatest possible extension of liberty.[119] In his 1980 conversations with Guy Claisse, the chief editorial writer for *Le Matin de Paris*, whose views were known to be close to Michel Rocard's, Mitterrand played down the Marxist aspects of the Socialist program and emphasized the second left's agenda. In ranking the key ingredients in a Socialist program of government, Mitterrand did not mention the *union de la gauche*, but emphasized instead "our theory of the *front de classe*, our theses on *autogestion*, our projects for decentralization, our method of planning, our approach to the relations between the plan and the marketplace, and above all our will to found socialist society on the intransigent respect for the rights of man"[120] Michel Rocard and his followers would have found nothing to quibble with in such a program.

By 1981, therefore, the Socialist party was in a state of total ideological confusion. Although one could argue that the party ran on a program of *autogestion*, such a statement means virtually nothing, since so many definitions of *autogestion* existed and no clear-cut definition could be established, either within the party or outside of it. On the broadest— and vaguest—level *autogestion* meant freedom: freedom from the state, freedom of assoiacation, freedom to control one's own destiny. At that level, almost everyone could agree with it and the Socialists stood to benefit politically by appealing to anti-Communist, anti-statist elements on both the left and the right. But once *autogestion* became concrete, advocating, for example, the rupture with capitalism as part of the process, the party stood to lose votes. Clearly the best course the Socialists could take, in terms of their electoral chances in 1981, was "to promise and claim little."[121] And that was precisely, as we have seen, what François Mitterrand did.

Victory *pour quoi faire*? The result in 1981 was not clear. *Autogestion* and the Common Program were weak guides in light of an electoral victory based primarily on a vague appeal to change, coupled with economic policies to save jobs. Although the *Projet socialiste* was the official party position on the issues, only CERES accepted it as a guide. To a great degree, the Socialist party had fallen victim to the "presidentialist" bias of the Fifth Republic. François Mitterrand determined party policy, not the party itself, in 1981. He would choose a government loyal to his conception of ideology, not one that came out of the party's conception, whatever that might be. Because victory in the presidential election of 1981 had been based on Mitterrand's ability to appeal to disaffected Gaullists, the party in power would most likely move to the right, away from the more extreme proposals of the CERES current. Precisely what would emerge from this ideological muddle, however, was not clear in May 1981. In looking back on this situation in 1985, with the hindsight of four difficult years of Socialist rule, Jean-Pierre Chevènement would claim that the French Socialists lost the battle with the right before 1981: "the French left, in more or less accepting the 'Satanization' of Marxism, which was identified with the 'Evil Empire,' ended up throwing out the baby with the bath water." The Socialists lost their intellectual autonomy in this debate, Chevènement claimed, leading directly to the difficulties of the 1980s: "For one cannot transform the world when one does not understand it, not to speak of when one has given up trying to understand it!"[122]

2

"The Rupture with Capitalism," 1981–1983: Utopia and Reality

The overwhelming Socialist victories in May and June 1981 caught everyone by surprise. Suddenly, the outcasts of the Fifth Republic had taken over the Palace, as though a countercoup had occurred some twenty-three years after the events of May 1958. Oddly, neither the left nor the right had been prepared psychologically for this contingency. Although the Socialist party had drawn up numerous statements and programs from 1971 on, no one was quite sure what the party would do now that it had conquered Paris. Whether the party could reconcile the potential contradictions between its economic objectives and its desire to transform the state and civil society remained to be seen in light of an election campaign that had been fought almost solely on economic issues. Still, the ideological imperative was strong within the party and the new government. The years in the wilderness had encouraged the rank and file to pursue utopian goals. Power merely reinforced the penchant to put such goals into effect, despite the economic consequences. The "rupture with capitalism" and various other socialist revolutionary slogans rose to the surface during the summer of 1981, without much thought given to what they meant or how they would be implemented. No matter. The desire to change the system, to engage in radical reforms prevailed over caution among the party faithful and their representatives in Paris. The old order would be swept away and the new ushered in within six months or a year at most. The 110 propositions would become law before the right would have the opportunity to reverse them. The Socialists looked over their shoulders and saw 1936 without realizing that they were living in 1981.

The men and women who came to Paris in July 1981 to sit in the newly elected National Assembly and form the new government differed profoundly from the former Giscardian group of Enarques and technocrats. They were less formal, more political, less well dressed, more meridional and provincial, and younger and bearded—at least the men.[1] While almost half of the Socialist deputies were teachers only 1 percent came from the working class. Yet, the new party did not merely replicate the old SFIO mix of instituteurs and the petit bourgeois class for it had shifted its center toward the lower professorial ranks and the mainstream of the bourgeoisie.[2] The Mitterrandist and Mauroyist currents in the party, in particular, reflected the new political elite: they tended to come from modest backgrounds rather than from the bureaucratic elite, their highest educational degrees tended to be in letters rather than in the Grandes Ecoles, and their political training began on the local level rather than in Paris.[3] In short, they were provincial outsiders.

The ministerial elite that emerged out of the party generally reflected this outsider element. The administrative republic that had dominated since 1958 gave way to a republic of the professors. In comparison with the Fifth Republic cabinets from 1958 to 1981, the ministers in the Socialist governments of 1981–84, did not come from the ranks of the self-employed to any great degree (17.9 percent of them were self-employed compared with 44.2 percent of ministers prior to 1981) nor from the bureaucratic elite (23.8 percent versus 40 percent) but rather from the teaching profession (30 percent against 5 percent prior to 1981). Furthermore, the majority of Socialist ministers received their training in local politics: 56.5 percent of them began their political careers in local office, as opposed to only 22.5 percent of all ministers from 1958 to 1981. And, thirteen of the twenty-nine Socialists in the second Mauroy government were mayors, including the prime minister and two of the five ministers of state.[4]

The same pattern of promoting outsiders to positions prevailed in appointments to the Elysée staff and to the ministerial staff. Mitterrand chose his staff primarily from those outside of the senior civil serivce. Only one-third of the new Elysée staff came from the bureaucratic elite, as compared with 89 percent under Giscard. Political appointees, best represented by the head of the Elysée secretariat, Pierre Bérégovoy, predominated. The new ministerial staff, in comparison with the Barre government, was recruited more from teachers (50 in Mauroy's staff to 13 in Barre's), lower-level civil servants (37 to 11), union members (15 to 2), and women (71 to 20). Yet, the number of Enarques in the Mauroy ministry remained roughly the same (about 100), and the new government did very little to purge the old guard from key posts in government, with the one notable exception of the educational elite, the rectors in particular, which was changed substantially in composition. The pro-opposition journal L'Express commented in January 1982 that the Socialists had done little to transform the state into a partisan political vehicle, much to the consternation of the party faithful. The outsiders took over, but in the fragile form of a political elite intent on compromising and working with the Fifth Republic's bureaucratic system of government. The need to find a common ground between the party's economic agenda and its provincial, outsider desire to dismantle the state ended up with the old bureaucratic elite maintaining much of its power, for as Michel Crozier argued, the Socialists had to rely upon the Grandes Ecoles graduates to carry out their ambitious program of nationalization.[5]

Still, the new political elite was very conscious of its provincial, outsider status and acted in the context of that cultural mentality. When Roger Quillot arrived in Paris from Clermont-Ferrand, where he was mayor, he was turned off by the ostentatious trappings of ministerial office. As minister of urban affairs and housing, he was entitled to his own Renault 30, with a driver, but he preferred something simpler. On his first day on the job he arrived in his office far earlier than any of his staff did, yet it was the hour that the workers of Clermont-Ferrand and the provinces would have begun the working day, he claimed. At his first ministerial meeting, he identified his colleagues by their provincial ties: Jean Auroux was his neighbor from Roanne, whereas Louis Mexandeau was a fellow citizen of Normandy, where Quillot had been born. But Quillot was also sensitive about his provincial roots. He expressed amazement that his colleagues were so inexperienced at national politics, pointing out that most of them were local politicians, unaccustomed to national affairs.[6]

The same outsider theme ran through the writings and musings of other ministers. Yvette Roudy, the minister of women's rights, wrote of her provincial upbringing in a poor lower-middle-class family as one of fear, paternalism, and male chauvinism, which she only overcame by enormous effort and ability. Her outsider status was of course compounded by her gender. In turn, the abrupt sayings and writings of Gaston Defferre, the minister of state for the interior and decentralization, revealed a similar attitude. In the preface to Michel Philipponneau's work on decentralization, Defferre talked of the need for decentralization in terms of finding one's roots, restoring the rights of minorities, overcoming the Parisian distaste for and mistrust of provincials, and restoring economic vitality to the nation from the base up. But, the most important provincial in the government was Pierre Mauroy, the prime minister. Mauroy was a true man of the North and the working class, who took pride in his peasant, working-class family origins, which he could trace back to the sixteenth century. Until the twentieth century, the family remained solely engaged in day labor and woodcutting. Pierre's father was the first to break from the family tradition, becoming an instituteur and eventually a school principal in the steel community of Haussy, outside of Trith-Saint-Léger. Although Pierre followed his father's career, becoming a technical-school teacher, his strong socialist convictions were soon translated into a second career in the local party, where he rose to secretary of the powerful SFIO federation in the Nord by the time he was thirty-three and to mayor of Lille and deputy from the area by 1973, at age forty-five. As a provincial with deep roots in Lille, the Nord, and Flanders, Pierre Mauroy soon found himself caricatured by the Parisian press as a Flemish beer drinker, a trencherman of unlimited capacity, and a bon enfant lacking intelligence or initiative, despite evidence to the contrary. Rather than attempting to dispel these Parisian prejudices and run the risk of being corrupted by the city's cosmopolitan decadence, Pierre Mauroy chose to remain the provincial. As he put it, not without a strong dose of sarcasm, "I have never tried to fit into 'Parisian society.' I have never pursued the 'dîners en ville' circuit. Since I was twenty years old, I have tended to live with my neighbors, with my friends, with all those who share my commitments."[7]

This strong provincial sense, although a dominant mentality in the new government, did not pervade every corner of the new Socialist elite. Michel Rocard, for example, might be superficially included among the provincials, as one of the Socialist mayors who rose from the periphery to the center, but in reality Rocard's ties were much closer to the Grandes Ecoles elite administrative class that he came from. The same was true of Rocard's bête noire in the government, Jean-Pierre Chevènement, whose Enarque background was also well known. Yet, despite these and other notable exceptions, the central political powers in the new government, from the president through the prime minister and the first minister of state, Gaston Defferre, were controlled by provincials, that is by outsiders with strong regional ties and generally anti-Parisian attitudes. This new, inexperienced Socialist elite would attempt to translate its attitudes and values into a set of policies that would reverse the statist, capitalist course that the Fifth Republic had followed. *Autogestion* and decentralization should have been central to such a set of policies, given the ideological debate that preceded the Socialist victory of 1981 and the mentality of this elite, but the parameters of Socialist action would be established instead by economic imperatives. Economic policy, to a great degree, shaped all other policies that the Socialists undertook after May 1981, as the realities of unemployment and economic crisis impinged increasingly on the party's ideological program. Any attempt to understand the success or failure of the Mitterrand government must therefore begin and end with an analysis of its economic policy.

Socialist Economic Policy: The First Phase, May–December 1981

The Byzantine complexity of French Socialist economic policy virtually defies description, even though many have attempted to plumb the depths of it. Possibly a few sketchy preliminary remarks will help to put this policy into some sort of perspective. First, there was and there was not a French Socialist economic policy. On the one hand, the entire Socialist program, as contained in virtually every document from *Changer la vie* to the 1981 *110 propositions*, could be interpreted as a statement of economic policy. To the Socialists, such issues as *autogestion*, culture, Third World policy, and defense came under economic policy. Not that they would be determined by economic factors. On the contrary: Socialism would change relations to the degree that attitudes and institutions would be transformed totally, most particularly and profoundly in an economic sense. Cultural and economic revolutions, therefore, were viewed as two sides of the same phenomenon, not diametrically opposed developments or separate paths to reality. Which leads to the second, seemingly paradoxical part of this first point, that the Socialists had no economic policy, for the definition of economic policy in such broad terms made policy extremely difficult to define in a strictly economic sense. If everything is policy, nothing is, at least not precisely, as every actor can claim that he or she is implementing policy by, for example, setting up a countercultural group or carrying out some aspect of decentralization of government. The dominance of ideology and political action over economic factors emerges clearly from these Socialist documents. In short, they offered little guidance for what the realities of Socialist economic policy might be.

Second, the implementation of Socialist economic policy, once that policy had been determined, faced serious obstacles. In any bureaucratic system the distance between policy and reality is vast, but in the French system the complexity of economic mechanisms, combined with the aim of decentralizing the state apparatus to allow economic policy to be carried out at the local level, made this problem even greater. Two English observers of the French scene counted some three hundred different mechanisms for carrying out industrial policy. Only very tight ministerial control of this situation could have created a coherent economic policy.[8]

Third, ministerial control over policy was not coherent, as numerous different voices emerged in competition over what economic policy should be, with no one minister possessing final jurisdiction. In that environment, the minister of planning, Michel Rocard, fought for dominance over economic policy with such powerful figures as the minister of research and technology, Jean-Pierre Chevènement, the minister of economics and finance, Jacques Delors, the minister of industry, Pierre Dreyfus, and the minister of the budget, Laurent Fabius. No one ministry was given final authority by the president or the prime minister. Only time would tell who would become dominant. Not surprisingly, in the end, the old pattern that had prevailed under the Fifth Republic would emerge supreme: monetary and fiscal policy as defined by the minister of economics and finance would dominate planning and economic policy decisions.[9] But before we reach that stage, we much go beyond these preliminary remarks to investigate in some detail the evolution of policy making during the period 1981–83.

By the fall of 1981, something that we can identify as an attempt at a Socialist economic policy had emerged in France, but it existed in a very precarious state.[10] This policy emerged in ad hoc fashion, with ideology playing a major role in some cases, most notably in the nationalization of leading industries. The ad hoc aspect of this policy was due to the internal squabbles that plagued the government and to the vagueness of what policy should be. Foremost and least controversial, the government implemented a *relance* of the economy. During the spring presidential election campaign, every political party advocated a massive *relance* of the economy, except the Socialists. François Mitterrand had called for a relatively moderate expansion, which his finance minister, Jacques Delors, began implementing shortly after the formation of the first Mauroy government. No one, on either the right or the left, opposed this policy, which included measures of solidarity with the poor such as increases in the minimum wage and old-age pensions, as well as programs for paring down unemployment such as aid to the building industry and the hiring of additional teachers and administrators. Jacques Delors pointed out that the entire *relance* program equaled only a stimulus of 0.5 percent of the nation's gross national product, which was hardly inflationary.[11]

Still, differences did emerge about the impact of this minor *relance* of the economy. Both Delors and Mauroy defended the government's position by making constant public references to the need for rigor. Discussing the *relance* in early June, Delors defined the government's policy in the following terms: "La rigueur dans la solidarité et la vigilance dans la relance économique." He argued that this position was necessary because of the weak economic condition of France and the bleak international economic situation.[12] Mauroy backed up Delors shortly later when he cautioned that the *relance* would not be carried to the point of undermining the "grands équilibres économique du pays."[13] The advocates of rigor proved to be so strong that their views were even included in the declaration of government signed by the Socialists and the Communist party after the second round of the parliamentary elections. That declaration stated that solidarity could be implemented only within the parameters "of the status of the *crise*, the fact that the French economy was open to foreign imports, and the essential economic and financial equilibrium." The Common Program, by contrast, took a secondary position in this declaration.[14] By late July, François Mitterrand was therefore openly calling for a "budget de rigueur," one in which a "relance des investissements" would be the primary objective.[15]

There is little doubt that the policy of *relance* that Delors pursued marked a victory for the social democratic camp within the Socialist government. Pierre Mauroy, who believed that his final objective was to implement socialism in France, argued in his memoir of the first year of Socialist rule that the *relance* was nothing more than a conjunctural policy, within the limits of the free enterprise system, whose purpose was to clear the path for structural reform in the future.[16] In turn, a close political colleague of Michel Rocard maintained, at the time, that the "effect of these measures on employment, prices and economic growth will be negligible."[17] Delors himself later discussed the opposition to his moderate policies, referring vaguely to the unrealistic Marxist theorists in the government, who believed in socialism in one country, which they constantly tried to implement until they were ultimately defeated in March 1983, and mentioning specifically the constant, although diametrically opposed, criticisms that Michel Rocard and Jean-Pierre Chevènement levied against his cautious policies in the name of pursuing a more imaginative economic course during 1981. Delors countered their points by arguing incessantly and successfully that the restraints of the capitalist world made it necessary to follow a policy of rigor.[18]

But the Socialist militants did not accept this social democratic vision of reality. They interpreted the victories of May and June as a mandate for fundamental change, such as the "rupture with capitalism" and the implementation of *autogestion* and decentralization, and the *relance* represented only a minor step in that direction, one that was too statist and too "capitalist" for the vast majority of the militants to accept as the government's key objective. By September 1981, therefore, Delors found himself on the defensive, despite the increasing evidence that even the limited *relance* had been too much for the relatively weak French economy to absorb. In face of a strengthened German mark and a rapidly weakening French franc, the Socialist government finally decided to devalue the franc in early October 1981. On the surface, this seemed to mark another victory for Delors and the social democratic camp, but in reality the exact opposite was the case. To be successful, devaluation required the implementation of rigorous deflationary economic controls, such as wage and price restrictions, and cuts in the 1982 budget. Delors obtained neither of these. No controls were placed on wages or prices, and the 1982 budget was one of the most inflationary state budgets in the postwar period. Delors had fought hard, during September, to limit the budget increases, and he argued again in October for rigorous measures to accompany devaluation, but the constituencies involved were too powerful for him and he lost decisively in the Council of Ministers on 7 October 1981. This time, rather than obtaining the support of Mauroy and Mitterrand, as had been the case with the relatively mild *relance* of 1981, he was left out in the cold. Laurent Fabius undercut Delors at every point, drawing up a budget that included a 27.6 percent total increase in spending and a large projected deficit of 95.4 billion francs.[19] Jacques Fournier, a CERES militant, best summed up the prevailing sentiment of the time when he stated later:

> We were preoccupied more with growth, with protecting jobs, with structural reforms. We believed that it was necessary to move faster in sensitive areas such as decentralization and nationalization. The defense of the currency emerged only on the second plane of our preoccupations.[20]

Fournier and militants like him were not satisfied with the slow progress that the government made in 1981. They believed that the moderates in the party had taken over at the top, eschewing the "rupture with capitalism" for compromise. In spite of Delors's defeat in September and October, or possibly because of it, they stepped up their attacks upon their opponents, both within and outside of the party, when they met with their fellow socialists in the congress of Valence at the end of October 1981.

The Socialist congress of 1981 took place in the context of increasing political frustration among the rank and file, whether in the National Assembly or in the nation at large. Many had already concluded that the program of *autogestion* and decentralization would not be implemented, at least not to the degree that they had expected. Notably, the small but important "seond-left" party, the PSU, met in late September to condemn its leader's position of compromising with the Socialist government, claiming that there was no sign that the Socialists supported the PSU policies of *autogestion* and decentralization. In addition, Edmond Maire, the head of the CFDT, denounced the government's policies as "statist" and Michel Rocard threatened to resign from the cabinet over its failure to support the policies of the "second left." More immediately, however, the congress unfolded amid the highly partisan debates in the National Assembly over the Socialist bill on nationalization of industry. In such an environment as this, the center and the right in the party had no chance to express their social democratic views at Valence. Instead, the left lashed out against the "mur d'argent" and the failure of the government to undertake significant changes in personnel and institutions. Paul Quilès, who was nicknamed Robespaul by the right, stated at Valence: "It is not sufficient to say that heads will fall. It is necessary to say which ones."[21] Quilès was convinced that a conspiracy of some sort had been hatched within the administration against the Socialist program, while Louis Mermaz pointed to an "economic counterrevolution" that had to be stopped: "It is necessary to strike quickly and powerfully against the sabotage of our economy. It is essential to put an end to the dictatorship of the banks."[22]

Originally, the Mitterrandists had expected only minor rumblings at Valence and had prepared in advance with a statement on the "rupture with capitalism," a typically Olympian gesture to the toiling masses. Posing the question, would the struggle between capitalism and socialism end in "choc" or compromise, the statement claimed that the party would work hard for compromise, based on the "contract that we have signed with the French people" in the elections of 1981. But by the time of the congress, this looked mild indeed. At Valence, even Gaston Defferre was swept up by the spirit of life and death struggle between capitalism and socialism, proclaiming, in a fit of passion, "c'est eux ou nous!" And Pierre Mauroy, although more moderate than some, felt it necessary to remind the opposition that popular suffrage had expressed its will and it had no right to oppose that will. The congress decided to vent its anger by issuing a statement entitled "The Appeal to the People of France." It claimed that the opposition's virulent objections to nationalization of industries and banks were based solely on greed, the desire for private profits above the public benefits of Socialist policy, and added that the party would "work to unite the profound forces of the people" against this onslaught from the right. The statement presented the Socialist program for jobs and economic revival in almost apocalyptic terms. "The grand humane enterprise that we are engaged in stimulates hope among the people of Europe and the entire world," it claimed. If the Socialists succeeded they would pave the way for a "world redistribution of wealth, the condition for the real emancipation of all people. . . . " "With the people of France we shall change life and assure peace!"[23]

For all the rhetorical excess that came out of Valence, the reaction of the government was cautious. Although Pierre Mauroy promised to make some significant changes in administrative personnel, he qualified this move by pointing out that only political appointees would be considered for replacement, not career bureaucrats.[24] The prime minister also refused to accept the confrontational economic policy that Valence thought necessary between socialists and capitalists. Mauory made this clear in a speech that he delivered to the Senate on 20 November 1981, in which he outlined what he called the new rules of the game in the wake of government nationalization of the banks and key industries. The rules resembled a social democratic model rather than the apocalyptic one of Valence. First of all, Mauroy established, the "économie mixte" was the foundation stone of the French economic system: the government recognized that entrepreneurs had a major role to play in this system. Furthermore, he claimed, the government would not change the accepted rules of the marketplace, whether in domestic credit matters or in international trade. And it would do as much as it possibly could to stimulate the economic environment for private enterprise by reducing fiscal and social security taxes on businesses so that their profit margins, investment portfolios, and employment policies could be improved. Finally, Mauroy added two other rules, one aimed at controlling inflation and the other intended to establish "concertation et négociation" among the social partners. In short, Mauroy's speech represented a major acceptance of the social democratic agenda of compromise and reform against the Valence congress's notion of "rupture with capitalism."[25]

The culmination of this tortuous struggle to define a centrist policy in the midst of Socialist ideological imperatives came, appropriately, from Jacques Delors at the end of November 1981. In what became a famous, if not notorious, interview, on 29 November Delors called for "a pause in the declaration of reforms," adding that it was dangerous to think that "the left possessed miracle solutions," and cautioning "that those who think that France is inevitably moving toward radicalization are fooling themselves." In remarks that stunned the Socialists, Delors called on the government to concentrate on implementing the reforms it had already undertaken rather than continuing the process to the end. He stated openly that the government needed to convince the patrons, whether they were in charge of large, medium, or small establishments, that it favored improving their profits and creating "a climate which is more stimulating for business." He made clear that the key economic priority must be investment, which had been stagnant since 1974 as the result of bad economic policies and not because of any "conspiracy" of business against the Socialists.

And he bluntly expressed his views about social security, pointing out that it was impossible to maintain intact a social security system based on low economic growth rates, unless some rather spectacular efforts at solidarity were made. He summed up the situation by stating that France could not invest heavily, innovate in new areas, and maintain its standard of living as long as economic growth rates remained low. Unlike the far left, Delors believed in the limitations that the capitalist order placed on the French economy. Those limitation had to be taken into consideration in formulating economic policy, unless the nation was willing to pay the price of economic stupidity.[26]

The reaction to Delors's *coup de brumaire* was surprisingly muted. Pierre Mauroy was evidently furious with him for speaking so bluntly, but he essentially accepted what Delors said, interjecting one qualification on the reform program of the government: "These reforms are the condition for the transformation of French society and thus for the success of the government's policies."[27] The basic difference between Mauroy and Delors arose over the definition and implementation of "rigor." To Delors, "rigor" meant both an economic policy and a "pause" in reforms; to Mauroy, "rigor" did not apply to reforms, for the rank and file of the Socialist party would never accept a policy that stopped the ideological agenda of the government from being fully implemented.[28] To make the distinction clear in the minds of the party faithful, Mauroy proceeded to outline three major areas of reform for 1982, highlighting social security, worker democracy, and fiscal reforms.[29] Nevertheless, Delors's point had been made. Economic rigor, at least, was now accepted, reluctantly, as a part of Socialist policy.

The argument that the Socialists had no coherent economic policy, but rather a series of pragmatic responses to developing situations, is supported by Pierre Mauroy's writings on his government. Mauroy himself was a practical, urban politician and not an intellectual concerned about economic theory or socialist ideology. He preferred to point to specific accomplishments, such as the five-week annual holiday for workers or the reduction of working hours from forty to thirty-nine per week, rather than outlining a logical, coherent policy. To Mauroy, the reforms that his government implemented were socialist because it was a socialist government. No need to quibble about the fine points or to worry about things like *autogestion*.[30]

One specific example of Mauroy's economic policies that illustrates the point of pragmatism above ideology was his handling of the important issue of unemployment. The Socialists had come to power, as we have seen, on the basis that they could deal with unemployment better than any other political party. To their dismay, however, unemployment did not decline after the June *relance* but continued to climb throughout the summer of 1981 into the fall, reaching the point where the electorate would soon begin to blame the Socialists for this state of affairs. In September, Mauroy launched his plan to combat this deteriorating situation. Speaking before the National Assembly, he called the battle against unemployment the "priority of all priorities" for his government. The resources of the state were to be fully mobilized to engage in it. This meant the passage of a budget that would achieve a minimum of 3 percent growth in 1982, even though this would lead to a deficit of approximately the same percentage of gross national product. The budget would include further increases in social security outlays to achieve solidarity with the disadvantaged, more money for public housing projects to spur on a weak sector of the economy, aid to industry—especially small and medium-sized industry—through state loans and subsidies, a program of solidarity contracts to allow young workers to replace early retirees, early-retirement plans, training programs, and work-sharing arrangements to create jobs.[31] Although this budget included specific socialist objectives, especially from the "second left," it was not specifically socialist. Early-retirement schemes, solidarity contracts, aids to industry, and similar programs had all been part of various rightist programs in the 1970s. In fact, as one observer noted, the Mauroy plan was quite timid, aimed at creating only about a hundred thousand jobs through solidarity contracts, in contrast to the Giscardian scheme, hatched during the election campaign, to create a million.[32]

Yet, despite the timidity and pragmatism of the Mauroy plan, it was opposed by virtually every interest group from the patrons to the unions. Only the CFDT welcomed it, most likely because its leaders helped formulate parts of the plan. The prime minister's plea for unity—"We must overcome the challenge of unemployment by working together"— went unheeded. Why? The answer lies clearly in ideological and corporatist attitudes. The olive branch held out to the patronat did not tempt many businessmen, for they felt betrayed by the actions of the Socialists. Even though Delors and Mitterrand had close ties to the business community, the party was clearly hostile to it. No amnesty had been offered to businessmen in the summer of 1981, although other groups such as workers had been pardoned of previously committed crimes. The tax on "grandes fortunes," which Laurent Fabius introduced in August, was deeply resented by the patrons, as were the plans to implement legislation that promised workers extensive rights in the management of factories. Furthermore, for ideological reasons, the Socialists decided to work with the small and medium-sized businesses and not with the main union of patrons, the CNPF. This decision proved to be disastrous, as the Syndicat national de la petite et moyenne industrie (SNPMI), under the leadership of a former Vichyite, totally rejected all Socialist attempts at rapprochement, while the CNPF used the occasion to oppose not only Socialist initiatives but also social policies that it had supported reluctantly in the 1970s for the purpose of maintaining social peace with the unions.[33] Mauroy's pragmatism was sorely tested under these circumstances. Caught between ideology and economic necessity, the prime minister found himself encouraging employers to "engage in the battle for employment" and arousing the party faithful against "those who teach us lessons and put their capital in Switzerland" on the same day![34] In November, the deterioration of business confidence in the government's economic policies was confirmed in a poll of *chefs d'entreprise*: 83 percent said that they were not planning to hire any workers in the next six months and 53 percent claimed that they would not be making any investments. The president of the General Confederation of Patrons of Middle-Sized Enterprises stated that "we no longer believe in dialogue" with the government and the outgoing president of the CNPF compared 1981 with 1936, claiming "that the present situation is a great deal worse."[35]

To the unions, the Mauroy plan had different pitfalls. The dominance of the CFDT in the government, with CFDT officials ensconced in the Elysée, the Ministry of Solidarity, the Commissariat au Plan, and the Ministry of Labor, convinced the other unions that policy was being made by the "second left" at their expense. The Communist-dominated CGT's proposals for massive reform in the workplace went unheeded by the government, while particular CFDT reform measures were put forward as Socialist priorities.[36] In turn, the third major union, Force Ouvrière, maintained its total opposition to any political involvement of unions in governmental affairs. On numerous occasions, FO's leader, André Bergeron, expressed openly his opposition to CFDT involvement in the government. For instance, in the 10 June 1981 edition of the union's weekly paper, Bergeron wrote: "We are not in favor of what is a kind of interpenetration between political power and the syndicalist movement."[37] Furthermore, Bergeron scoffed at the Socialist claim that such reforms as five-week vacations, early retirement, and shorter working weeks had been initiated by the new government. In every case, he claimed, the unions had carried out such reforms before the Socialists arrived in power. The new government had merely jumped on a successful bandwagon, extending these measures to the few who did not yet benefit from them and taking credit for a struggle that the unions had fought and won, and not the politicians.[38] In short, long-standing corporatist struggles and ideological positions in union affairs assured the Mauroy government of a lukewarm reception, at best, for its proposals, especially since they were seen as part of a grand CFDT package of reforms that could lead to a CFDT-Socialist state, at the expense of the other unions.

Possibly Jean-Marie Colombani analyzed the Socialist dilemma best in his *Le Monde* article on six months of Socialist rule. He noted that the Socialists had acted with alacrity to implement changes, but without any mass mobilization behind what they were doing. No union movement (with the possible exception of the CFDT), no patronal organizations, no institutions supported these changes. As a consequence, Colombani argued, Socialist reforms may be undermined by a number of forces, ranging from the Communists to the bourgeoisie, from the CGT to the conjuncture in economic affairs. To succeed, Colombani maintained, the Socialist party must go beyond electoralism to become entrenched in the ranks of the working classes; otherwise it will have only the state to rely on to implement its program.[39]

Colombani may have missed the real problem, however, which can be stated simply as the pursuit of diametrically opposed short-term economic policies to achieve the goal of full employment. Possibly the simplest way of illustrating this more fully is to look at the problem of the Social Security budget in 1981. As we have already indicated, Mitterrand appointed the CERES militant, Nicole Questiaux, to the post of minister of national solidarity. Questiaux made clear from the beginning that she would not be a "ministre des comptes." In other words, she would not preside over a social security system that engaged in cutting benefits in order to balance the books. But the Socialists placed very heavy demands on the system at the same time that they were sympathizing with the patrons about the abnormally heavy financial burden that social security placed on them. Businesses payed about half of all social security taxes, one of the highest percentages among advanced industrial nations. How could the government justify increasing this burden at the same time that it was encouraging business to increase investments, which had reached unacceptably low levels by 1981?[40] Yet, under the new government, massive increases in social security outlays occurred in 1981 on top of the deficit of about 7 billion francs that the Giscard-Barre administration had left for the Socialists to make up. The Mauroy budget of September 1981, which included hefty increases for old-age pensions, housing allowances, health benefits, and family allowances, added another 8 billion francs to the system, on top of a future projected deficit of around 24 billion francs for 1982. In this grim financial environment, Nicole Questiaux was given the task of bailing out the system. Her solution, which was announced in November after tortuous negotiations, merely copied what had been done before rather than engaging in significant reform. No attempt was made to place social security financing on the general tax roles, no income tax increases or other new types of revenue support were introduced, nor were significant cuts made in social security. The Questiaux plan required the patrons to pay an additional 16 billion francs in taxes and reintroduced the 1 percent surcharge on salaries (to bring in 14 billion francs) that the Socialists had opposed so strongly when the previous administration had used it. Not only were the patrons disaffected by this seeming reversal of Socialist promises to keep taxes down and improve the business environment, but also the unions and the workers viewed the Questiaux plan as a reversal of Socialist electoral commitments. The government found itself divided and in disarray over the Social Security problem.[41] Those divisions and that disarray revealed the limitations of both pragmatism and ideology as instruments for forging economic policies in 1981, in an environment of mistrust and competing objectives that pitted patrons against workers and both against the government.

If budgetary matters and the conjunctural area of economic policy fell victim to compromises between pragmatism and ideology, they did not comprise the heart of Socialist policy. The Socialists had come to power to nationalize leading industries and banks, implement new planning procedures for the economy, and carry out decentralization and *autogestion* in an effort to transform capitalism. The issue of nationalization, in particular, was at the center of the party's ideological agenda. It was the key to the Common Program with the Communists and the main cause of ideological contention between the two parties in 1977-78, when the Common Program broke down. For the left, no other piece of economic policy had a higher priority in 1981 than nationalization. The fate of the Socialist-Communist alliance for government hinged more on the success of this policy than on any other.

Oddly enough, nationalization had not been a major factor in leftist ideology before the 1970s. The right, rather than the left, had been the main advocate of state control of leading economic institutions. Charles De Gaulle, and not Léon Blum or Guy Mollet, had been in charge of the greatest wave of nationalizations in the postwar period. Not until the Epinay revolution and the signing of the Common Program did the Socialists make nationalization a major part of their economic policy. Colbertism or Republicanism, rather than Socialism or Communism, had been the main ideological basis for nationalization until the 1970s.[42]

This massive shift to nationalization as one of the Socialist party's major ideological positions occurred at the same time that *autogestion* was making a substantial mark on the party and the left in general.

Seeming opposites, they were supposedly reconciled through the theory that the state would have to guide civil society toward *autogestion* by permitting and encouraging social experimentation in the nationalized sector of the economy, which would culminate in the creation of *autogestion* in state enterprises and lead the private sector to imitate the public. The early justifications for nationalization were couched in terms of the "rupture with capitalism," which included the concept of *autogestion*. Nationalization, in short, was conceived of as a revolutionary act. But it also proved to be a divisive point in the Common Program. In the 1978 legislative election campaign, the unity of the left broke down on the issue of the degree to which a leftist government should carry out nationalization, with the Socialists opting for a minimalist program against the maximalist one put forward by the Communists. The Communists wanted more emphasis on workers' control in the future state enterprises, mainly because the PCF believed that "its union," the CGT, would be able to dominate in any situation involving *autogestion* in the workplace, whereas the Socialists moved away from *autogestion* to the idea that nationalization should be limited and carried out primarily for the purpose of restructuring French industry.[43] After the election, François Mitterrand analyzed his party's defeat in terms of what its future program should be regarding this crucial issue: "If we want to put into effect the Socialist project, we will not cut back on nationalizations. Where property exists there is power."[44]

In the 1981 elections, however, the Common Program was not a factor and the Socialists succeeded in ignoring Communist maximalist demands on nationalization. The victorious Socialists could more or less define nationalization on their own terms, with only minimal concern for the Communist agenda. To François Mitterrand and a large part of the Socialist elite, this meant scrapping the more ideologial aspects of the left's program for a more pragmatic approach to the subject. The appointment of Pierre Dreyfus, the former head of Régie Renault, as the minister of industry in the first two Mauroy governments, indicated clearly that the maximalist and *autogestionnaire* positions regarding nationalization would not be dominant in the new government. Dreyfus staunchly believed in the Renault model of running state industries, which entailed granting almost total freedom to the heads of these firms to run their own operations with only minimal interference from the government in the form of *lettres de mission* or planning contracts. No one in the second Mauroy government was able to challenge Dreyfus on this matter, in part because he had the full support of Mitterrand, but also because of his reputation as the great director of the state's most successful nationalized industry, Renault.[45]

Consciously or unconsciously, the new government spoke less and less of nationalization in terms of the "rupture with capitalism." Instead, the rationale for nationalization shifted from that ideological position to more pragmatic arguments such as the need to save jobs, to recapture the internal market, to restructure industry in the face of massive international competition and the uncompetitive nature of French industry, and to control credit in order to direct investments toward productive enterprises. There was nothing particularly Socialist about these objectives; they seemed much closer to Gaullism than to *autogestion*. But this did not seem to bother the party leaders, as they combined their "Gaullism" rather easily with parts of the old ideological agenda, without noting any discrepancy. Pierre Mauroy, in particular, deftly mixed the new realism with the old ideological justification for nationalization. For example, in July 1981, Mauroy explained the government's reasons for carrying out massive nationalization by claiming that if the left did not move in this direction it would be confronted with "un pouvoir d'argent" that would undermine democracy. But he quickly added that the nationalized firms would have total "liberté de gestion."[46] In the fall of 1981, Mauroy told an Austrian television audience that the main goal behind nationalization was to create "a sector of reference" in the French economy, "where some very advanced experiments would be undertaken on the division of responsibilities between the managers and the managed, a field of experimentation where we shall be able to apply what we call 'autogestion.' "[47] Yet, a few weeks later, speaking before the National Assembly in the debate on nationalization, Mauroy played down *autogestion* for the pragmatic argument that state run industries would provide France with "growth, jobs technological development and a world position."[48] Much later, in 1985, one of the key actors in the Ministry of Industry when Laurent Fabius headed it, Lionel Zinzou, would write the Socialist history of these nationalizations, entitled *Le fer de lance*. In that work, Zinzou would justify nationalization on the basis of one major point: it saved French industry from destruction in the world recession of 1981–82. Without nationalization and the restructuring of industry that it allowed the state to engage in, he argued, France's industrial establishment would have either been bought out by foreigners or allowed to go bankrupt.[49] Later on we will consider the validity of this argument, but for now it is sufficient to note that Zinzou's rationale for Socialist nationalization was already prominent in 1981. Time and events would make it the dominant explanation four years later.

Still, in 1981, a good part of how the Socialists undertook nationalization was determined by the ideology of the Common Program.

Mitterrand and Mauroy both insisted on taking over 100 percent
of all firms nationalized, as the Communists had argued, rather
than gaining only majority control, even though Jacques Delors and
other prominent cabinet ministers opposed such a policy on the
pragmatic grounds that it was both unnecessary and too expensive.
The president and the prime minister feared a Communist reaction
similar to 1977–78 when the Common Program broke down over
nationalization.[50] Using the same logic, only the industries and banks
mentioned in the 1972 Common Program were nationalized in
1981–82, despite changes in the economic environment since then or
reservations regarding the necessity of nationalizing some of them.

The concessions made to maintain the Common Program and appease
the Communists assured that France would become the most statist
of western industrial democracies, with 40 percent of industry and 90
percent of banking placed under state control at a cost of 45 billion
francs.[51] Unlike earlier nationalizations, which were undertaken
primarily in infrastructure sectors, the Common Program called for
the nationalization of major competitive sectors of the economy, giving
the state control of heavy industry such as chemicals, aluminum, and
steel; high technology such as communications and computers; the
armaments industry; and parts of the consumer and health industries
such as glass, paper, and drugs. Many of these competitive industries
were in serious economic trouble by 1981. Heavy industry, especially
steel, was in danger of total collapse, while high tech, the computer
industry in particular, was losing out rapidly to foreign competition.
Massive amounts of money were needed to help these industries regain
their economic health. Thus, despite the Common Program's belief that
nationalization would bring an end to capitalist profit and surplus value,
resulting in untold benefits for the workers, the situation in 1981–82
dictated that the primary objective, once the state took over, would
be to return industry to profitability through restructuring and increased
funding for investment and research. Given that perspective, the
Socialists opted for continuity rather than rupture, fearing that an
extended period of social chaos in these newly nationalized firms would
exacerbate the economic crisis, decrease the competitiveness of French
products, and lead to increased unemployment. In February 1982, when
the new heads of nationalized banks and industries were chosen, no
purge of the old order occurred: the criterion for selection was clearly
competence and not political ideology, as only one Socialist became
a PDG of a newly nationalized state industry. François Mitterrand
claimed on the occasion that "the nationalized enterprises would have
total autonomy to make decisions and act."[52] Although the superficial
imperatives of the Common Program had been adhered to, the need

to regain industrial competitiveness dominated the government's actions. The pragmatic and the conjunctural triumphed once again over the ideological agenda of the left.

As a general rule, the closer Socialist economic policy came to implementation, the more pragmatic and conjunctural it became. We could use many other examples to prove this point, but possibly energy policy offers the simplest and most direct insight into how the government operated. During the 1981 election campaign, the Socialists accepted the general principles of the ecological movement. Nuclear energy, in particular, would be curtailed under a Socialist government, the party proclaimed, and the Giscardian government's high-handed imposition of nuclear plants on local communities would be ended by allowing communes to reject nuclear projects. But the reality, once the Socialists had obtained power, proved to be quite different. Without nuclear power, they now argued, France would be held captive to foreign sources of energy, prices for energy would rise, industry would become less competitive, and unemployment would increase. Not surprisingly, therefore, in the fall of 1981 the Socialists reneged on their earlier promises to the ecologists, proceeded to endorse most of the previous administration's program for nuclear energy, and placed such tight restrictions on the rights of municipal councils to veto nuclear projects that the promise of local democracy on the subject became meaningless.[53]

Only in areas that were sufficiently divorced from day-to-day economic reality could Socialist economic policy avoid the pragmatic compromises that constantly corrupted it. In the realm of foreign relations, for example, the government could advocate improved European cooperation as the means to solve common economic problems without fear of having to back down. Soon after the 1981 elections, a flurry of activity occurred on this front, as François Mitterrand addressed the European Community on the need for its members to follow a concerted economic policy of *relance* and improvements in social welfare. In July, at the first Franco-German summit under Mitterrand, Jacques Delors announced a package of reforms that the French government would submit to the European Community on such issues as employment policy, energy, and regional and social development funds.[54] Although none of these measures received much support from other countries, Socialist advocacy of them served domestic ideological needs, providing evidence of the government's sincere support of the Common Program in spite of the skepticism of a hostile world. As François Mitterrand observed in the introduction to his collection of speeches on foreign affairs, domestic and foreign policy were inextricably interconnected.[55]

Within the field of foreign affairs, however, Socialist Third World policy played the most important role in shaping overall economic policy. The ideological agenda of French Socialism emphasized greatly a third way of economic development, one in which France would be the model and not the Soviet Union or the United States. François Mitterrand spent a good part of his first year in office advocating various ways to support development in the Third World, from international monetary reform to guaranteed minimum prices for Third World primary materials. He traveled to Africa, Mexico, the Middle East, and eventually India spreading the same message. He hosted a Franco-African conference in Paris on the problem of underdevelopment. He committed his government toward increasing the percentage of gross national product devoted to Third World aid. And most significantly, he took action to implement part of this policy by signing the Algerian gas agreement. The president believed that Franco-Algerian relations could serve as a model for North-South relations and in that context his government agreed to purchase Algerian natural gas at prices that were considerably above the going market price, with Algeria using the profits for the purpose of economic development.[56]

But there was a darker side to this magnanimous Third World policy. At the same time that the Algerian gas accord was being signed, Claude Cheysson and Charles Hernu were busy selling Egypt twenty Mirage-2000s at a cost of 1 billion dollars. They justified this deal on the basis that France offered an alternative to superpower control over Middle East foreign policy and military affairs.[57] Despite the Socialist party's expressed opposition to the sale of arms to Third World countries, the government continued pursuing such sales on the basis that the arms industry needed a larger market than France in order to be profitable. Very early in the history of the new government, both the minister of defense and the minister of commerce presented similar arguments to justify sales abroad.[58] Here too the pragmatism of saving jobs and French industry modified Socialist ideology, along with the additional factor of defending the nation.

Finally, economic policy was determined by the Plan. The party had persistently criticized the Giscard-Barre administration for neglecting the planning mechanism, insisting that a Socialist government would correct this state of affairs. Despite these sentiments, François Mitterrand chose his main opponent, the man he despised the most in the Socialist party, Michel Rocard, to head the Ministry of the Plan, dooming it to almost certain oblivion. And oblivion is what the plan obtained under Socialist rule. Rocard's *Plan intérimaire* for the years 1982–83, existed in the realm of pure ideology, untainted by the pragmatism we have observed elsewhere. The Plan was all things to

all people, advocating contradictory policies of statism and decentralization, solidarity and modernization, technocracy and new
citizenship, the *relance* of the French economy and Third Worldism,
and ad infinitum. The contradictions contained in the temporary plan
were so great that no real economic policy could be derived from it;
rather, the Plan became a politicized document, for the purpose of
spurring on the party faithful by now including their hopes in a
government document and not just as part of a political manifesto.
Under those circumstances, the Plan became nothing more than an
article of faith, filled with pious hopes, incapable of providing effective
leadership or direction for economic policy.[59]

Although it would be incorrect to conclude that Socialist economic
policy had become nothing more than a series of pragmatic responses
to perceived economic realities by the end of 1981, the evidence certainly
indicates that the party in power had come a long way from the
ideological positions found in the Common Program and the *Projet
socialiste*. The social democrats in the party had not won out by 1982,
but they had made considerable progress toward weaning the rank and
file away from the simplistic idea of the "rupture with capitalism."
The unexpected advantages of extended political power—the so-called
durée—would allow this generation of socialists to undertake an
experiment in day-to-day government that no other generation had been
allowed to make. Ironically, Charles de Gaulle's constitution had created
the conditions for Socialist pragmatism to shape the party into a social
democratic alternative to the right, a party of government rather than
a party of perpetual opposition.

Decentralization and *Vivre au pays*

Leading up to the elections of 1981, the manifestos of the second
left and its regionalist compatriots played a key role in shaping the
Socialist agenda. *Autogestion*, decentralization, and related themes were
at the center of Socialist rhetoric, at least equal to nationalization and
economic policy. In fact, decentralization and *autogestion* were
conceived of as central parts of Socialist economic policy; through them,
the state and capitalist society would be transformed, the rupture with
capitalism would be carried out. After the elections, however, these
powerful ideological concepts often underwent quiet transformations,
or were even forgotten in the case of *autogestion*. Part of the reason
for this was the new pragmatism that the party in power began to pursue.
Still, by 1983 the Socialists had set in motion a number of reforms in
government, in cultural affairs, and in worker-employee relations that
often resembled the ambitious agenda established by the party in

opposition. Let us examine each of these areas to establish the interrelationships between ideology and action, pure socialism and pragmatism, in the evolution of Socialism in power.

Decentralization stood at the center of the government's program in 1981, theoretically superior to nationalization in importance. A conjunction of political and ideological factors made this the case. The Socialists had been in opposition for twenty-three years, during which time they had exercised political power almost exclusively at the municipal and regional levels of government. We have already noted the outsider mentality that pervaded the Socialist government and the large number of city mayors who sat in the Council of Ministers. Two of the most important members of the government, Prime Minister Pierre Mauroy and Minister of State of the Interior and Decentralization Gaston Defferre, had made their mark politically as mayors of two of the nation's most important cities, Lille and Marseille, and as heads of the regional councils' of the Nord-Pas-de-Calais and Provence-Cote d'Azur. They, and others like them, had personally experienced the frustrations of running local governments under the restraints of Parisian control and wanted to do away with that domination. In addition, during the course of the 1970s, the Socialists gained a number of regionalist converts, in Brittany in particular, who developed a successful regionalist ideology for the party, in stark contrast to the Jacobin position of the right. These new party members, who had contributed greatly to the Mitterrand victory, now looked to Paris for their reward.[60]

As political constituencies developed for policies of decentralization and regionalism, they became major parts of Socialist ideology. As we have already noted in the previous chapter, this ideology was often expressed in rather extreme, revolutionary ways while the party was in opposition. In 1980, for example, the Socialists introduced a bill for decentralization of government that they claimed would create "one of the most powerful levers for the rupture with the capitalist system." The bill would end the centralized state, which the Socialists identified as "the instrument through which capitalism maintains its grip on society as a whole."[61] Even after the conquest of power, such rhetoric persisted. Pierre Mauroy called the law on decentralization the "most important reform undertaken by the left" because it was the key to creating a "démocratie quotidienne," while Gaston Defferre claimed that decentralization would "abolish the causes of conflict" in France by "giving to the regions the potential to be themselves."[62] Yet, some were skeptical about this "*grande affaire du septennat*." Bernard Stasi, the president of the Centre des démocrates sociaux and a major supporter of decentralization, thought that the Socialists undertook decentralization as a substitute for economic change and a diversion from the overwhelming economic problems facing the nation.[63]

The grand hopes that decentralization raised proved difficult to realize in concrete terms. The gap between rhetoric and reality was impossible to bridge. For one thing, serious constitutional restraints prevented the establishment of any sort of federalist system, which many regionalists had advocated. Decentralized power could only be administrative, not legislative, unless the government was willing and able to undertake a major, contentious reform of the Gaullist constitution. In addition, the Socialist concept of direct democracy or new citizenship, could only be realized through a major shift in power away from elected officials toward a Rousseauist ideal of popular sovereignty, but the hard-headed, realistic Socialist mayors and officials who sat in the Assembly did not believe that such a system could work and proceeded instead to pass a law that increased the powers of the representatives of the people, maintaining that this equaled a form of direct democracy. The problems of bureaucratic jurisdiction and control of the various levels of government also prevented the realization of the ideal of citizens control of local government. The reforms that the Socialists carried out tended to increase the need for bureaucracy rather than devolving power to the people. From the beginning, decentralization had little chance of achieving any sort of rupture with capitalism or break from the old state system. Minor reform, some devolution of power, was all that could be expected.[64]

Despite the limitations of reform, the Socialists spent a considerable amount of time decentralizing the powers of government. A total of about thirty laws were passed, concerned with seven distinct areas of decentralization. Once decentralization was set into motion, almost every aspect of the state had to be reconsidered, including the areas of competence of various levels of government, finances, planning mechanisms, and the interface between levels of government and the law in general.[65] The new relationship between Paris and the provinces began with the simple elimination of the prefect's *tutelle*—that is, the right of the central government to prevent actions taken by local governments from being implemented. A priori control of government, whether regional,departmental, or municipal, was eliminated. In place of the *tutelle*, the commissaire de la République, as the prefect would henceforth be called, could only refer local actions to an administrative tribunal for consideration of their legality. A similar procedure applied to budgetary matters, which were to be reviewed by a new body called the Chambre régionale des comptes, an auditing board set up in each region under the control of the Cour des comptes. In both cases, judicial authority, after the fact, replaced political and administrative authority, before the fact, over local decisions.[66]

With the elimination of the prefect's arbitrary executive powers went the democratization of every level of local government. The first article of the law of 2 March 1982 proclaimed that "the communes, departments and regions shall be administered freely by elected councils." The executive branch of the government at these levels now came under the control of elected officials, rather than under the centralized state.[67] Governmental responsibility was clearly established, as each level of government obtained competence over distinct matters. Municipal government gained control over urban planning and development, the departments became responsible for solidarity, social aid, and financial equalization among rural communes, and the regions gained certain counterpowers over planning, economic action, and management of the territory.[68] A clear, hierarchical pattern of responsibility was created by the law, although some doubts still remained about conflicting jurisdictions.

Yet, the law did not undermine the power of the state, as Socialist rhetoric had indicated it would. One of the most positive assessments of this situation was provided by André Laignel in the *Nouvelle revue socialiste:* "Decentralization is not synonymous with weakening the state. Quite the contrary. By intervening only in those sectors that are key for the nation's future, and relying on powerful and democratic local governments, the efficacy of state intervention cannot fail to grow."[69] Possibly true, but hardly an evaluation that the second left would endorse. More common were the criticisms of the severe limitations that still existed on local initiative. Had the *tutelle* really been abolished or had it merely been transferred to another level? The evidence increasingly supported the latter interpretation. For example, one of the main Socialist ideological objectives in carrying out decentralization was to allow provincials to live and work in their *pays*. To assure that this would be possible, local governments were to gain the right to intervene in the economy, to support failing businesses, and offer incentives of various sorts. But the reality, after the laws had been passed, was quite different. A circular issued by Defferre on 24 June 1982 established very strict criteria for offering local aid to failing industries. Local governments had to carry out studies, in each case, to determine the state of the local economy, the social climate, the condition of local finances, and whether aid to a failing business would save jobs. The use of any state funds for aid was strictly controlled by Paris, leaving the financially limited local governments in the position of having to rely on the central government for approval in most cases.[70]

In fact, wherever the interests of the state were involved, some element of the *tutelle* remained in effect. The system of a posteriori control over finances, through the Chambres régionales des comptes, seemed to end the *tutelle* in financial matters, but the law provided the Chambres with extensive powers to control local budgets, in some cases similar to the old *tutelle*: the Chambres had the right to take over local budgets if they were in deficit and they could intervene when no budget was agreed on or when a budget did not balance.[71] In planning at the local level, the law also maintained strict limits on autonomy. Although in theory the new planning mechanism allowed for give and take between the central government and the local level, the state imposed national norms for such things as construction permits and housing projects on the basis that local governments were highly susceptible to the corrupt practices of unscrupulous developers and that housing was a national priority. The state also required all local planning to take place within the confines of a *Schéma directeur*, which was a document that reconciled the interests of the various partners in local urban development, including the state, state agencies such as EDF (the state electrical company) and the SNCF (the state railroad company), the region, and the local government. All local Plans d'occupation des sols had to be drawn up in accordance with the Schémas directeurs, with all the complications of reconciling various government and corporate interests that had existed under the old Prefectorial system.[72] And, of course, the national government reserved certain areas such as the seacoast, the forests, the police, and the national patrimony for its jurisdiction, outside of any local control.

The second left's simple demand for *autogestion* and decentralization looked quite different by the time the new laws had been implemented. To achieve either required massive legislative changes, a careful balancing of rights and responsibilities among levels of government. And in the end the question remained whether the changes had made any real difference. Was decentralization so complex that, inevitably, the experts had to take over in order to make the system work? Two of the leading commentators on the process, Gontcharoff and Milano, concluded that in some cases the laws were so involved that they defeated the purpose of decentralization. In discussing the law of 29 December, 1983, they commented, in obvious frustration: "*La complexité byzantine qui atteint la législation financière locale* va à l'encontre de l'objet même de la décentralisation qui était de rapprocher le citoyen du pouvoir et fait de son élaboration (et son application) un dialogue entre initiés."[73]

In the words of another key observer of decentralization: "The reforms . . . have served neither to change the management of local authorities nor to enhance the participation of the population. Nor do they constitute a simplification of procedures or decision making. . . . They merely confirm processes which had been under way for the previous ten to fifteen years."[74]

Oddly, however, the opposition viewed decentralization as a revolutionary upheaval that threatened the very existence of France. Olivier Guichard, who had been the head of a commission on decentralization under the Giscard administration, claimed that Defferre's law would "destroy everything. It is based on mistrust of the state and its agents." Guichard believed that it would "disadministrate" France rather than decentralize it.[75] Michel Debré, the author of the Fifth Republic's constitution, claimed that he could support decentralization if it were carried out in the spirit of "rejuvenating the State and revitalizing the provinces," but not if it dismantled the nation, which he believed the Socialist bill would do. "To weaken the nation is to return again to very dangerous notions of ethnicity and race," he asserted.[76] Jean-Emile Vié, a former prefect who wrote a carefully argued work against Socialist decentralization, came to a similar final conclusion about the negative effects of the Defferre law. Vié believed that centralization was crucial for the grandeur of France; without a strong state, France would become weak, unable to maintain its freedom. Decentralization equaled balkanization, to Vié; the next step in the process would be the rise of independence movements in the regions, leading to the weakness and decay of France.[77]

There was a grain of truth in the fears expressed by the right. The implications of decentralization, especially if one believed Socialist rhetoric, pointed clearly toward something like balkanization. Michel Philipponneau, a Breton regionalist and Socialist, who was close to Gaston Defferre, dreamed of the day when Europe would no longer be based on the principle of the nation state but rather on regions that cut across national boundaries. He thought that a socialist France would lead the way in dismantling the nation state by setting up strong regional authorities that would have control over regional banks, resources, industries, energy supplies, culture, and other entities.[78]

Although Pilipponneau's dream did not come true under Socialist rule, the opposition perceived a domino effect at work, beginning with decentralization, moving on to autonomy for Corsica and the overseas departments and territories, and ending with independence for those autonomous areas. The Socialists, however, rejected totally these fears, claiming that autonomy for minority cultures would strengthen France by offering those cultures real powers over their own affairs and by defusing demands for total independence as home rule proved to be effective. The reality proved to be somewhere in between the two positions. The Socialist victories in 1981 aroused great expectations in the overseas departments and territories (DOM-TOM) and among Corsican advocates of autonomy and independence. Aware of this, the new government proceeded rapidly to introduce a regional government for Corsica, one that would even include legislative powers. In the summer of 1982, under the new law, Corsica held elections to a regional assembly that had received limited autonomy over administrative affairs but not the right to legislate, as originally planned. Although the elections revealed clearly that the Corsican independence movement had little support—a fact that had been known previously—the new assembly did not convince Corsicans that autonomy was the answer to their problems. Bitter political divisions in the assembly made it almost impossible to set up a government and the failure of Paris to decentralize necessary technical and bureaucratic support made it difficult to administer the island without relying heavily on the French government. Meanwhile, the independence movement stepped up its terrorist activities and most Corsicans concluded that Socialist autonomy was not much better than the old system of Parisian administration. However, the effect of autonomy for Corsica upon French attitudes was quite different: in a 1980 poll, 43 percent of the French thought that Corsica would eventually become independent, as opposed to 44 percent who believed it would remain a part of France; by early January 1983, only 28 percent thought independence was a possibility versus 66 percent who thought the opposite.[79]

The Corsican model, which allowed a considerable degree of control over the local economy and culture, did not become the rule for other cultural groups. For example, the Socialists had promised to create a separate Basque department and support financially the teaching of the Basque language, but neither of these promises was carried out.[80] Other groups experienced similar disappointments over the failure of the Socialists to fulfill regionalist promises. It seems that the rightist critique of Socialist decentralization played a role here. The Socialists may have concluded that the domino theory could work or at least that regional autonomy was not important enough to waste limited government energies on, especially in light of the economic situation that the nation faced.[81] No matter what the reason, the Socialists began to have second thoughts about regional autonomy when they faced the rising expectations of the Kanak population of New Caledonia. Originally, the Socialist party had called for the "libération du peuple canaque" under a Socialist government. Although this was an ambiguous phrase that could be interpreted in terms of either independence or autonomy, the Kanak population and the French living in New Caledonia viewed it as a call for independence. As a consequence, the Kanaks voted overwhelmingly for the Socialists in the 1981 elections, while the French settlers backed Giscard and the right. After May 1981, New Caledonia turned into a battleground between the two groups, with the Socialists attempting to work out a compromise between them that would offer the natives some rights without endangering French sovereignty and without alienating the French nationals in the territory. The situation soon became impossible. In August 1981, Henri Emmanuelli, the secretary of state for the DOM-TOM, visited the South Pacific islands to sort out the competing claims. Emmanuelli referred to what he called a "colonial situation" in New Caledonia, raising the hopes of the Kanaks, but he proposed to end this through social and economic reforms that would respect the democratic rights of everyone in the territory, not through granting increased political power to the natives. Despite this relatively moderate program, the response of the French settlers was total opposition to any reform and the recourse to violence if necessary. In September 1981, a leading moderate Kanak nationalist was assassinated by a French vigilante group. By the end of the year Paris had to resort increasingly to ruling by decree in New Caledonia. Attempts to create some sort of "third way" between independence and French domination was not working.[82]

Although the Socialists set up elected assemblies in the *départements d'outre-mer* in 1983, the Corsican and New Caledonian experiments had dampened their enthusiasm by then. Regionalism was not working the way the party had hoped it would. In Corsica, regionalist autonomy changed little if anything; in New Caledonia, Socialist rhetoric had raised hopes that could not be realized. Yet, the party's vision of *Vivre au pays* and *Droit à la différence* remained a powerful element of both its ideology and its political base. That vision had to be expressed in some concrete form. In the relatively safe, highly visible actions of the Ministry of Culture under Jack Lang's ebullient leadership that vision finally obtained its due.

Of all the Socialist ministers, none represented the spirit of 1968 better than Jack Lang. Lang had been a student at the Sorbonne at the time of the May uprising, which he remembered as a revolution based on hope, aimed at establishing "a new world." As minister of culture, Lang believed that his task was to implement the ideals of 1968, uniting the student movement with a Socialist government. To him, 1968 "prefigured the changes that we in the government are currently entrusted with inscribing in everyday life."[83] Lang's vision of 1968 was closer to Régis Debray than to the anarchists. Strong doses of Third

Worldism and anti-Americanism shaped his idea of culture as he carried the outsiders mentality that infused the Socialist cabinet to the level of a world view. That world view was expressed most forcefully in the Minister's speech to the 1982 UNESCO meeting in Mexico on the cultures of the world. Although Lang never mentioned the United States by name in his speech, he clearly had it in mind when he called upon the peoples of the world to stand up against those who would make culture into a money-making proposition of vulgar standardization. He condemned the "system of multinational financial domination" of culture, especially in regard to the cinema and television, and the "uniform way of life that they would like to impose on the entire planet" through "standardized, stereotypical productions." He asked those present, "Is it our destiny to become the vassals of the immense empire of profit?" And he answered by calling on the world to carry out "a veritable crusade against this financial and intellectual imperialism." Lang wanted "to oppose the international of financial groups with the international of the peoples of culture." To help achieve these goals, Lang announced that in 1984 Paris would be the site of an "états-généraux of the creators and researchers of the five continents."[84]

This vision of a culture independent of great power domination, and in this case especially American domination, resonated with the main themes of the *Projet socialiste*, especially the theme of the French Socialist way between Soviet communism and American capitalism, the way of *autogestion* and the Common Program. Probably more than any other member of the government, Lang believed that he was successfully creating the conditions for this Third Way, at least in the realm of culture. Everything conspired to make him believe this. Lang's impatient desire to create a new world coincided with François Mitterrand's vision of an active, expansionist Socialist cultural policy. As a result, Mitterrand gave Lang virtually everything he wanted, even when Pierre Mauroy objected. Lang was one of two or three ministers who appealed regularly and successfully to the Elysée to override the authority of the prime minister.[85] During the Lang years, the Ministry of Culture received the largest increases in funding of any government office, as the ministry's budget tripled between 1981 and 1985. Only the research budget obtained anything close to such favorable treatment.[86]

With such largesse, Jack Lang could pursue his 1968 agenda with relative ease. Numerous studies on the cinema, popular songs, books and reading, the plastic arts, cultural democracy, and the culture of work were undertaken by the ministry to determine where action was needed. Gabriel Garcia Marquez was appointed to head a committee to determine the viability of uniting Latin and Third World cultures into a sort of Third Cultural Way under French leadership, a project that was dear to Lang.[87] The minister convened a meeting of about one hundred world-class intellectuals, which included such Americans as John Kenneth Galbraith and William Styron, to consider the relationship between creation and development. They concluded that the two could be united most effectively under a French model in which the state provided "harmony between creation and development," rather than under an American model, which would be totally commercial, or a Soviet one, which would be directed from the center.[88]

But the most tangible and significant developments of the Lang years were related to the decentralization of culture to the provinces, to coincide with the decentralization of government and the establishment of citizen's democracy. Creativity, Lang believed, could only flourish in an atmosphere free from state control and Parisian domination. In the tradition of the physiocrats, Lang used the state for the purpose of dismantling it; cultural largesse to the "exclus de la culture" was the first step toward freedom and autonomy from central government. In every area, from the provision of aid to provincial art museums to the establishment of local archives for working-class affairs, the ministry decentralized the cultural patrimony. Probably no other action undertaken by Jack Lang was as important as the massive increase in funding to provincial libraries. As the result of improving the national library budget from 163 million to 677 million francs, seventeen departments without a *bibliothèque centrale de prêt* in 1981 obtained one by 1986. Ten million more people obtained access to major lending library resources as a result of the Socialist library program.[89]

As Paris' share of the cultural budget declined from 60 percent to 45 percent between 1981 and 1985, the provinces gained new ballet companies, music halls, artistic centers, theaters, and popular culture facilities. Lang did not neglect any aspect of either high or low culture. He respected both the theories of his director of music and dance, Maurice Fleuret, who believed that one should make culture available to as many people as possible and forget the attempt to achieve great works of art, and those of the director of the Théâtre National de Chaillot, Antoine Vitey, who believed in lifting up the population to higher levels of artistic appreciation and consciousness, in a Brechtian sense.[90] But possibly the clearest expression of how Lang's cultural philosophy related to decentralization came from Pierre Mauroy, in June 1982, when he and Lang dedicated the Musée Matisse du Cateau in the department of the Nord. Defending the vast increases in the Ministry of Culture's budget, Mauroy referred to the need to reach the "exclus de la culture" and to see centers of culture emerge and prosper outside of Paris. "It is essential that the future Matisses and the future Debussys can flourish in their own natural family setting without being forced to go into exile. The political and administrative decentralization engaged in by the government must also extend to cultural decentralization." But Mauroy did not confine his remarks to high culture and decentralization. He concluded that "artistic creation is both the sign and the driving force of the dynamism of a society." Culture and work must be interconnected in this process; culture must be made an integral part of the daily lives of working people.[91]

Mauroy and Lang believed that the forces of decentralization, cultural progress, the new citizenship, and the Third Way were part of the same process, the so-called rupture with capitalism. The battle for culture was a battle against Paris, the Americanization of France, and capitalism, and for the Third World, Latin civilization, and French socialist democracy. Jack Lang fought the battle long and hard, never compromising his ideals. Although not everything he did was successful, in general Lang's high popularity ratings among the French electorate—the highest for any member of the government—reflected the outstanding job he did in decentralizing French culture. He deserves to rank among the leading Socialist ministers even though the challenges he faced were not on the same scale as the ones confronted by other ministries.

In conjunction with decentralization and the democratization of culture, the second left's agenda also aimed at establishing some form of *autogestion*. Pierre Mauroy justified the nationalization of leading industries in terms of the need to carry out social experiments along the lines of *autogestion*. His minister of labor, Jean Auroux, began drawing up laws for the democratization of the workplace in1981 and the government passed a series of four major laws on the subject in 1982–83. The patronat universally opposed these changes on the basis that industry in France could not afford the social problems that democratization would create, but the reality of the Auroux laws proved to be far less revolutionary than either the left or the right had anticipated. By the end of 1983,the patronat had become reconciled to the reforms while the working class and the unions concluded that they did not translate into major changes in the workplace.[92]

The Auroux laws did not implement anything remotely close to *autogestion*. From the publication of the government report on democratization of the workplace in the fall of 1981, it was clear that any reform would be relatively minor. While Jean Auroux justified democratization on the basis of the rights of workers to control their own destiny, he also argued that improvements in working-class conditions in industry would increase productivity and produce better-qualified workers, both of which were necessary for French industry to compete in the international marketplace.[93] The realism of competition therefore qualified the imperative of democratizaton and *autogestion*. The result was a series of laws that were much closer to the moderate recommendations contained in the 1975 Sudreau report than to the thesis of autogestion. Not that these reforms were inconsequential. For example, the Auroux laws implemented mandatory collective bargaining at the firm level of industry, something that had never existed before in France, although branch-level collective bargaining had existed since 1950. The laws also strengthened the rules on health and safety in the workplace, giving the Comités d'hygiène et sécurité more powers, although not the right to stop production in case of extreme danger, a right the patrons opposed vehemently and the far left believed absolutely necessary. They also granted working-class representatives release time, recourse to expert consultants, and training for involvement in the comité d'entreprise and other representative bodies in the firm. Worker representation on the comité d'entreprise, which had been instituted by law in 1945 to bring workers and management together to discuss common concerns, was increased and the comité itself received additional powers, including the right to obtain confidential economic information from the firm to use in advising it on policy. Unions obtained rights to organize, to hold meetings in firms, and to call in outside speakers to address the workers. A degree of free speech was inaugurated through the unions, but no freedom to proselytize indiscriminately was allowed in the workplace.[94]

Still, the Auroux laws granted very little real power to the workers. The comité d'entreprise remained a consultative body, with little influence on economic policy. The laws reinforced the power of the unions as intermediaries for the working class rather than devolving freedom and power to the individual worker. Only large firms were required to provide their comités d'entreprises with economic information, which meant that almost two-thirds of the workers were excluded from exercising this limited oversight function. As a result, the central objective of the Auroux laws shifted perceptibly from *autogestion* to the implementation of collective bargaining, as a first tentative step toward social dialogue. The increasing gap between Socialist ideology and practice was reflected in the bizarre reception of the laws: by 1984 the patronat had accepted them as beneficial to business, whereas the workers viewed them as insignificant changes and only one major union, the CFDT, expressed positive sentiments about them.[95]

In all of these areas of concern to the second left and the ideology of *autogestion*, the "Jacobinism" of the main stream of the Socialist party prevailed over "Girondist" solutions. But this was not the old authoritarian Jacobinism; rather, a sort of "Democratic Jacobinism," as one writer called it, emerged in the process of adjusting the ideal to reality. Regionalism, federalism, and *autogestion* were either greatly modified or scrapped in that process. Only a very visible cultural Girondism survived totally intact of the second left's agenda. Beyond that, the changes that the Socialists made in local government and in employee-worker relations represented the culmination of ten to fifteen years of reform rather than the beginning of a new era.[96]

Socialist Policy under Fire: From the Pause of 1981 to the Austerity of 1983

When Jacques Delors called for a pause in reform at the end of November 1981, the Socialist government faced the prospect of the end of the state of grace and the beginning of a long period of increasing disenchantment with its policies. In March 1983, after a second devaluation of the franc in June 1982 and the imposition of strict wage and price controls, the electorate sanctioned the left by voting for the opposition in municipal elections, uprooting the urban power base that had been the heart of the Socialist and Communist parties in opposition during the 1970s. Increasingly, the left was judged on the basis of its economic policies, which became more and more "realistic" and "pragmatic" as time passed. Yet despite this conversion to realism— or possibly because of it—almost every organized group, from business to the unions, opposed the government's policies. March 1983 marked the final benchmark in this slow conversion experience; after the third devaluation of the franc and the imposition of further austerity measures in March, utopianism was dead and social democracy was alive and well, in fact if not in name.

The "pause" of 1981 marked the first step in the process of the struggle for the total victory of Socialist "realism." Although both Mauroy and Mitterrand opposed a pause in reform, they were concerned about the disaffection of business from government policy. While they forged ahead with such reforms as the decentralization and democratization laws, they also tried to appease the patrons. Polls of businessmen had indicated in November that 83 percent of the *chefs d'entreprise* would not hire any workers in the next six months and that 56 percent would not invest in industry. In early January, a poll taken by the journal *l'Expansion* revealed that 91 percent of the patrons believed the economy would deteriorate in 1982 and that 80 percent of them had a high opinion of Delors. Because such pessimism could be disastrous for the success of the *relance*, the government launched a campaign to win back the patrons. François Mitterrand inaugurated it in a speech given to the Haute Ecole de Commerce on 8 December 1981, where he called for a partnership between the patrons and the government instead of the adversarial relationship that prevailed. He repeated this theme in the second press conference of his *septennat* on the following day. In early January, Mitterrand sent Jacques Delors to speak before the CNPF and to lunch with the newly elected head of the patron's union, Yvon Gattaz, all in the spirit of cooperation.[97]

These verbal overtures were backed up with action. Delors and Anicet le Pors, the Communist minister of the civil service, began negotiating with service industries and civil service unions to restrict price and wage increases to somewhere between 10 and 11 percent for 1982, in an effort to ease inflation and improve profit margins for industry. When the heads of newly nationalized industries were appointed in February 1982, the government chose qualified businessmen over party ideologues in an effort to convince the patrons that pragmatic policies would be followed by the state. On the occasion of the installation of the new state PDGs, François Mitterrand proclaimed that "the nationalized enterprises would have total autonomy to make decisions and act," while Pierre Dreyfus made clear that the government intended, as its first priority, to modernize and improve the competitive position of these firms. The patrons in the private sector were also relieved to hear that the government would maintain the membership of these newly nationalized industries in the CNPF, bringing millions of francs a year in dues to the organization's treasury.[98]

The culmination of this opening to the patronat occurred in April 1982, when the Mauroy government and the CNPF reached an agreement on a number of outstanding issues. According to that agreement, the government promised to freeze increases in social security taxes until July 1983, reversing the trend of higher and higher taxes on business to support the system. It also pledged to reduce the much despised professional tax by 11 billion francs during 1982–83, to assume the cost of aid to handicapped adults, and to drop support of any further mandatory reductions in the work week, leaving such reductions up to negotiations between employers and employees. To make up for lost revenues, the Socialists aimed to cut the budget, to restructure the value added tax (TVA) to tax nonindustrial items more heavily, and to place levies on banks and credit institutions. Finally, to aid small and medium-sized industries, the government provided a billion francs in loans at subsidized interest rates of 6 percent for 1982 and 8 percent for 1983. In return for these major concessions, the patronat promised to invest in industry, increase employment, train people for jobs, inagurate solidarity contracts to replace early retirees with young workers, and engage in such experiments as work-sharing plans. Although many patrons scoffed at the compromise publicly, they were privately pleased with the realism of the government. In contrast, *l'Humanité* castigated the agreement as "Les cadeaux au patronat."[99]

The "cadeaux" to the patrons were granted for a good reason: by the spring of 1982, the Socialists knew that the *relance* had failed and that a second devaluation of the franc would be necessary within a few months, at most.[100] The left had not suddenly gone soft, accepting the "pause" totally. The April compromise was a calculated risk to gain time and possibly revive industry. It has to be understood in the context of the chaotic results of the February negotiations on the work week and the electoral defeat of the left in the cantonal elections of March.

When the Socialists implemented the thirty-nine-hour week, the law stipulated that only minimum wage earners (SMICARDS) would be guaranteed a salary equivalent to forty hours of work. Everyone else would have to negotiate the issue. The CFDT had favored this approach as a means of achieving solidarity between the better-off workers and the unemployed. Edmond Maire's union hoped that creative agreements could be reached between employers and employees to cut working hours and pay in order to hire more of the unemployed. The metallurgical federation of the CFDT, for example, proposed to maintain intact the salary pool for metallurgical workers, but under provisions that preserved the lowest salaries at 100 percent and reduced those above the minimum wage by a progressive amount that would be used to create new jobs in the industry. Although Jean Auroux came out solidly in favor of the CFDT solution to the problem, arguing that solidarity would help solve unemployment better than any other device available, the CGT and the Force Ouvrière (FO) totally opposed this "second-left" approach as a plot hatched between the government and the patrons to undermine the social and economic gains that the workers had achieved. André Bergeron, for one, refused to accept the "idées fumeuses de l'autogestion."[101]

The impasse in industrial relations that emerged from union opposition to the second left's agenda turned February into a month of massive strike activity, as the deadline approached for completing negotiations on the terms of the thirty-nine-hour week. In this troubled situation, François Mitterrand decided to intervene over the heads of his prime minister and his minister of labor, proclaiming that "not one worker must fear a decline in his standard of living as the result of the reduction of the working week." The CGT and the FO won out over the CFDT, as every worker was guaranteed an income equal to what he had earned previously for forty hours of work. Maire's and Mauroy's attempts to achieve a "partage du travail" and an increase in employment were scrapped for social peace and at a cost that the patrons found exhorbitant. The patronat estimated that the combination of another week of paid vacation and one hour less work per week would cost them 2.5 and 2.8 percent more, respectively, in wages, greatly undermining their competetive position in the world marketplace.[102] The government's attempt to gain social peace helped undermine whatever support it had gained from the patrons in early 1982.

The turmoil of February occurred amid preparations for the first national referendum, so to speak, on Socialist policies, the cantonal elections of March. Already, in January, the Socialists had received a warning of impending trouble, as the party lost three National Assembly seats in by-elections. In the March elections, disaster was averted as the left slipped only 3 percentage points from its comparable 1976 showing on the first round, while the right barely won the election with 0.33 percent more of the votes than the combined left. The Socialists and their Radical party allies did better in 1982 than they had done in 1976, increasing their share of the vote from 29.02 to 31.63 percent, but the Communists slipped percipitously from 22.8 to 15.87 percent, bringing the combined left's share of both the vote and total seats down considerably. Although the Socialists ended up winning the largest number of seats in the two rounds of voting, losing only 5 seats in going from 514 to 509, this occurred in a field that included 167 more seats than in 1976 and in the context of heavy losses for both the Communists, who went from 242 to 198, and the Radicals, who declined from 88 to 61. The right gained 266 seats in the elections, while the left lost 99.[103]

The meaning of the cantonal elections was not clear, although they did represent the first national defeat for the left since the smashing victories of 1981. Nevertheless, after the results were known, opposition groups became increasingly critical of government policies. In late March, about a hundred thousand peasants protested in Paris against government agricultural policies, one of the largest rural demonstrations to occur in the capital under the Fifth Republic. A month later, probably a hundred thousand showed up to protest the government's policy on private schools, with numerous opposition political figures present, including the president of the UDF and the general secretary of the RPR. Opposition leaders began questioning the legitimacy of leftist rule, as Michel Debré did in an article in *Le Figaro Magazine* on 9 April 1982. By May the right had labeled Mitterrand as "a sort of usurper," identifying the republic as belonging to them exclusively. Clubs such as Avenir et Liberté announced that they would stand up against "la mainmise de l'Etat sur l'enseignement, l'entreprise, l'administration, les médias, la justice." Some political figures, such as the former minister Philippe Malaud, adopted extreme rightist attitudes, accusing the Socialists of opening up the frontiers to the "pègre étrangère," of releasing gangsters frpm prisons, of using agit-prop in the factories to attack the patrons, and of putting Marxists in charge of education. Even the *patronat* engaged in the act: the vice president of the CNPF, M. Guy Brana, claimed that the April agreement with the Socialists was totally inadequate, as it provided only 11 to 12 billion francs in aid after the government had imposed 90 billion francs of new taxes on business.[104]

At the same time, the left began sqabbling openly about its policies. Michel Rocard criticized the government for not pursuing the agenda of the second left on "partage du travail" and solidarity. The minister of justice, Robert Badinter, and the minister of the interior, Gaston Defferre, debated publicly over police tactics regarding immigrants. When Pierre Mauroy justified such open debates in an article in *Le Monde* on 20 April, entitled "Gouverner autrement," in which he claimed that issues of public importance must be discussed broadly before reaching a final decision, Pierre Joxe, the president of the Socialist group in the National Assembly, countered that Mauroy had committed serious mistakes in communicating the government's program to the public as incoherence seemed to be the main outcome of these interminable squabbles. But Joxe's warning did not squelch expressions of disenchantment. The number-two man in the party, Jean Poperen, gave the patrons and the government notice about the tax concessions granted to business: if the patrons did not translate these concessions into jobs by September, "un question, très sérieuse, se posera." And Claude Evin, a leading Rocardian and the president of the National Assembly's Committee on Social Affairs, blasted Pierre Joxe for criticizing Mauroy, seeing in Joxe's attack more of "a personal animosity than concern for the general interest."[105]

Disarray also emerged in other leftist circles. The unions, especially the CFDT and the CGT, found themselves losing support in 1982, as their close identification with the government began to turn the public and workers against them. The CFDT, the union most closely associated with the Socialists, had gained little from that relationship, as its membership increased by only 1 percent in 1981 and very few of its second-left proposals received support. By May 1982, divisions appeared in the union over what sort of strategy to follow. On the one hand, Edmond Maire preached moderation at the CFDT congress, while on the other the former general secretary of the union, Eugène Deschamps, attacked the patronat and the bureaucracy for blocking change, raising the prospect of massive strikes of the 1936 or 1968 variety. Similarly, dissidents emerged in the CGT, as working-class support for the union declined in its traditional automobile industry strongholds. They blamed this decline on the union's moderate position, which passively accepted Socialist attempts to reach a consensus with the *patronat*, and the government's failure to do enough to reduce unemployment.[106]

Signs of leftist disillusionment with government policies also emerged in the provinces: in the coal and steel communities of northeastern France workers and union organizers concluded that Socialist plans to revitalize these declining industries were not working, while environmentalists in the Midi and Brittany came to the conclusion that they were better off under Giscard. Even the Communists took up the refrain, despite their status as partners in the government. At the end of May a party notable criticized the government's inaction on implementing social reforms in nationalized industries: "We have not nationalized in order to perpetuate the old principles of management."[107]

In the midst of this critical, postcantonal election atmosphere, the Socialists were suddenly faced with a major economic crisis. Evidence mounted that the *relance* and devaluation of 1981 had not worked. Inflation jumped 1.2 percent in April, translating into a 14 percent annual rate for the first months of the year, in comparison with West Germany's 3.6 percent annual rate. Wages, which the government hoped to contain at 10.5 percent for 1982, increased 4.8 percent during the first quarter of the year or close to 20 percent on an annual basis, while unemployment approached the 2 million mark by May, an increase of 17.1 percent since the Socialists took over in 1981. In addition, the trade deficit reached a new high in April, as imports headed toward a record 26 percent share of the internal market for 1982 and economic growth, which the government had predicted would reach 3.3 percent in 1982 after a weak 0.2 percent advance in 1981, had to be revised to 2 percent or less for the year. A major debt and investment crisis was in the making as a result of these dismal economic facts: businesses spent more on salaries and invested less, as the cost of workers increased from 69.8 percent of a firm's added value in 1980 to 71 percent in 1981, on the way to even higher levels in 1982, while the government budget went from a surplus of 2.9 billion francs in 1980 to a deficit of 61.2 billion in 1981, with worse figures to come in 1982 in the wake of declining gross national product estimates.[108]

To Jacques Delors the most shocking aspect of all this news was the comparison between France and its leading trade partner, West Germany. Delors pointed out that labor costs in France had risen by massive amounts since 1979: in 1980, French labor costs went up 14.5

percent compared with 8.2 percent in Germany; in 1981 the figures were 14 and 4 percent; and in 1982 they could possibly be 12 and 2.5 percent. The consequence of this continuing discrepancy, which could also be seen in the inflation rates for the two economies, was a rapidly mounting French trade deficit with the Federal Republic: in 1981 the French deficit in trade with Germany totalled 22.6 billion francs, a 34.8 percent increase over the 1980 figure of 16.8 billion francs, whereas in the first quarter of 1982 the deficit rose 80 percent over the comparable 1981 period, translating into a projected 30 billion franc imbalance for the year.[109] To Delors and other realists in the government, these facts pointed to the need for more rigor, even austerity.

To add to the government's woes, the spring of 1982 also produced a startling array of statistics on the status of nationalized industries and some leading private ones. In May the final audit on the newly nationalized industries revealed that they had suffered enormous losses in 1981. The steel industry, as predicted, led the pack with a 6.6 billion franc deficit for the year, but three of the other new state enterprises also lost money: the aluminum giant, Péchiney, lost 1.7 billion; Rhône-Poulenc, which was supposedly in good shape, lost 500 million; and CII-Honeywell-Bull lost 400 million. Many of these industries were on the verge of insolvency. As a result, the government allocated 9 billion francs for the sole purpose of eliminating these debts, rather than for use in productive investment. The minister of industry, Pierre Dreyfus, noted the seriousness of the situation, which he thought could end with the destruction of the nation's steel, chemical, and electronics industries if nothing were done to correct indebtedness and promote investment. In an unusual step, on 29 May Dreyfus announced the establishment of a national investment society to handle the problem of adequate financing for these industries. By the terms of the agreement, the nationalized banks and the state created a 6 billion franc fund, divided equally between them, to lend money to these industries at preferential interest rates. This amount came on top of the 9 billion franc debt clearance fund and was to be used solely for investment. In desperation, the government had finally done what the Valence congress had called for: the state banks were required to serve the nation, but only in a limited fashion and in a manner that would not undermine their international banking credibility, through a new investment device, separate from the conditions of the marketplace.[110]

The crisis was much more profound than anyone had expected. The nation's automobile industry, which had been the European leader in the 1970s, faced serious problems by the spring of 1982. In April, foreign automobile manufacturers captured one-third of the French market, the highest percentage in history. For Renault, Michelin, and the related machine tool industry, this merely reinforced their problems. In 1981, Renault lost 875 million francs, mainly because of stiff European competition, while Michelin suffered its first loss since World War II, going 661.7 million francs into the red, forcing it to borrow publicly in 1982, for only the fifth time in its history. As a consequence of the automobile crisis, the general crisis in capital investment, and the declining productivity of French businesses, the machine tool industry collapsed, capturing only 40 percent of the home market and manufacturing 40 percent fewer machine tools in the first part of 1982 than it had produced in 1981. Although the government did nothing to aid either Michelin or Renault, which was totally independent of state financing, it moved rapidly to aid and restructure the vital machine tool industry. In early June, the state committed itself to invest 4 billion francs over the next few years in such areas as robots and computerized controls, while aiding the industry to restructure itself around two main poles in order to become more competitive. Once more the Socialists accepted the realities of a capitalist economy: the restructuring of the machine-tool industry included the loss of about six hundred jobs.[111]

While the economic situation deteriorated, the government drew up plans for a second devaluation of the franc. In early May, Mauroy, Delors, and the Elysée reached a consensus on what to do.[112] The only outstanding issue was the timing of the devaluation. When should it be done and how could the government prepare the party faithful for such a drastic act? In late May, in conjunction with the bad news on the economy and the status of nationalized industries, the Socialists began debating openly the need to implement more austerity measures. It was a very odd debate, however, for most of the participants accepted the necessity of taking unpopular actions. Jacques Delors began it when he appeared on television on 20 May. He warned the nation that it would have to make sacrifices in order to get the economy back on its feet, sacrifices that might entail cuts in salaries and reductions in social services. "Patience, solidarity, effort" were the key words that Delors emphasized in his lengthy interview. They went virtually unchallenged by the left. With the exception of negative comments from the *gauchistes*, whose representatives concluded that the French Socialist party was more concerned with saving capitalism than with building socialism, every element of the left gave at least minimal support to Delors. André Lajoine, the President of the PCF group in the National Assembly, offered the least support, claiming that he could accept Delors's proposal if salaries of the lowest-paid middling workers were maintained at their current purchasing power, if the tax system were reformed along more progressive lines, if industrialists were held responsible for creating more jobs in return for receiving relief from taxes and social charges, and if enterprises were democratized to give workers more influence in them.[113]

In the ranks of the Socialist party, however, Delors's statement did not arouse any major dissent, in contrast to his November appeal for a "pause." The most circumspect support came from Lionel Jospin, who warned that there could be no deviation from the program of "struggle against unemployment, the *relance* of consumption and production, the reduction of inequalities," although within those parameters he could accept the idea of "effort." More positive was Michel Rocard's reaction. He gave Delors's realistic analysis oblique approval when he stated that "our nation can no longer support unlimited health costs," but must move quickly to contain the expenses of social security before they got out of control. But the most enthusiastic reception came from CERES militants. Jean-Pierre Chevènement rejected totally the *gauchistes* who thought the party had capitulated to capitalism. They failed to understand that "the objective in the current period is not socialism [but] to construct progressively the modern Republic." In this he was supported totally by Michel Charzat, who went even further, arguing that wage and price controls must be implemented, although not on industrial goods, in order to halt inflation and increase investment, especially in the area of new technologies. Charzat added that social security expenditures had to be contained as France could no longer afford to pay for unlimited protection. Consequently, by June 1982, large parts of the party agreed substantially with the establishment perspective on economic affairs. How far, for example, were Delors, Chevènement, and Charzat from the views of Michel Albert, a graduate of the Ecole nationale d'administration, an inspector of finances, and general commissioner of the Plan from 1978 to 1981, when he warned that unemployment could only be controlled in the next decade by increasing investment, which meant reducing salaries in order to obtain the needed capital for that purpose?[114]

With general consensus in the party and the seeming support of the French people, who responded favorably—in a poll taken in early June—to the implementation of austerity measures to control inflation and contain unemployment, Delors and Mauroy prepared to act after the Versailles economic summit meeting, where François Mitterrand attempted vainly to gain support for world economic planning to increase investment, reduce unemployment, promote new technologies, and provide economic assistance to the Third World. On 12 and 13 June, France worked out the details of a second devaluation with its partners in the European Monetary System. As a result of those talks, the franc was devalued 5.75 percent, the mark was revalued 4.25 percent, and the French government agreed to take measures to curb inflation, increase investment, reduce the trade deficit, and generally bring the French economy into line with the West German economy.[115]

Despite the careful preparation of public opinion for this second devaluation and the need for austerity measures in connection with it, the Socialists faced universal condemnation after applying this new shock to the French economy. Both the unions and the patrons reacted negatively to the government's plan to introduce wage and price controls as part of the austerity program. Originally, the government hoped that the two sides would reach an amicable understanding on the matter, but very quickly this had to be scrapped. Instead of voluntary contracts on wages, the government had to force its program on the nation, much to the disappointment of the second left, especially the CFDT. For the first time since 1950, a French government imposed controls on salary negotiations. From 1 June until 31 October, salaries were to be frozen, along with most prices, with exceptions allowed only for those who signed salary agreements that limited wage increases to 10 percent for the year.[116]

Businesses were not treated any better. Although they were allowed to pass some costs on to consumers, such as increases in the prices of imported goods, they could not increase their margins nor could they pass most cost increases through the system to the customer. From the perspective of the patrons, however, the most controversial and despised aspect of the June freeze was the decision to increase TVA taxes by about 4 billion francs without allowing businesses to pass on this added expense by raising prices. The April agreement between the government and the patrons, to limit and even reduce taxes on business firms in order to encourage investment, was modified drastically by that one provision.[117]

The government did not totally neglect solidarity with the lowest paid in carrying out Delors's austerity program. The scheduled 1 July increase in the minimum wage went into effect, even though businesses would be adversely affected because they could not pass on such salary costs to consumers, and certain groups of low-wage earners were allowed to negotiate salary increases above the 10 percent level. But these concessions were greeted with skepticism by those who knew that major cuts in the social security and unemployment systems were needed in order to make them solvent by the end of 1983. Nicole Questiaux, who had proclaimed that she would not be a "ministre des comptes" as the minister for national solidarity (social security), resigned under pressure at the end of June when she refused to go along with these austerity measures. On the eve of the second devaluation she had argued in public that France could afford to pay for its social security system and even increase the scope of that system. Such views were not supported by François Mitterrand, Pierre Mauroy, and Jacques Delors. Questiaux, an Enarque and a CERES militant, was replaced by a loyal party politician and CFDT figure, Pierre Bérégovoy, François Mitterrand's secretary general in the Elysée and one of his closest associates. To isolate Nicole Questiaux and appease the CERES left, which had generally supported the government's measures, Jean-Pierre Chevènement replaced Pierre Dreyfus as the minister of industry, while maintaining control over the Ministry of Research and Technology, making him one of the most powerful members of the government.[118]

The strong dose of realism that the government applied in June could not be absorbed easily. The Socialist party tried to explain the events away by blaming the "heritage" of the right, the "bad will" of the capitalists, and the "pressures of international capitalism." In that light, the party faithful believed that the necessary pragmatism of June had to be followed by radical reform of the tax system, more emphasis on reconquering the internal market, massive restructuring of banking and industry, and other socialist measures to assure that socialism would triumph in the end. The opposition also found this new environment disconcerting. While it continued to attack the Socialists for incompetence and a host of other sins, the opposition discovered that it possessed no alternative to the pragmatic policies that the government was pursuing. A great deal of sound and fury emerged from the right, but little in the way of substantive policies that the electorate could evaluate.[119]

Without other viable options, the government had no alternative but to follow the economic policy outlined in June. This meant careful control of welfare spending, major restrictions on the 1983 budget, increased rigor in economic planning, and the pursuit of ways to contain wages and prices once controls were repealed in November. Although solidarity with the weakest in society was to be maintained and the "pause" in reforms was not admitted, in reality the poorest would not improve their lot in the future and the "pause" had been implemented in fact if not in name. These very unpopular actions aimed at achieving two objectives, which were closely intertwined: economic revival and victory for the left in the 1983 municipal elections. In both cases, the imperatives of the system shaped Socialist policy far more than ideology did.

With the appointment of Pierre Bérégovoy to replace Nicole Questiaux at the Ministry of National Solidarity, all the key ministerial posts for shaping economic policy came under the control of economic realists, even though some of these ministers were recent and reluctant converts to that viewpoint. Bérégovoy seemed to relish the difficult task of trying to salvage the social security system through massive, unpopular cuts in programs. By the end of September he had come up with a plan that met with François Mitterrand's approval. Mitterrand had become convinced that businesses could not afford to pay any more social security taxes, especially since the deflationary environment that the government had created adversely affected those industrialists who had accumulated large debts based on the belief that inflation would continue unabated in the future. The Bérégovoy plan kept the government's promise of no rise in social security charges by increasing taxes on such items as alcohol and by making major cuts in the system. Medical expenses, which had increased by an average of 16.8 percent a year over the past ten years, were contained through salary freezes and rigid state controls of hospital costs. But the plan also blocked increases in family allowances, temporarily raised user payments for such things as glasses and dental work, increased hospital costs for patients, and cut inflation adjustments for pensions. Bérégovoy had clearly placed rigor above solidarity. Unfortunately, however, these measures did not solve the problem of future deficits; more "reforms" would be needed within a year in order to make the system solvent. And these reforms caused serious difficulties with the Communists who protested that the government had given in to the patrons at the expense of the working class. In Toulouse, François Mitterrand was greeted with Communist placards that proclaimed "Rigor for the patrons."[120]

A similar crisis occurred in the unemployment insurance system, which suffered from a massive increase in costs as the result of the economic crisis. The patrons stubbornly resisted any increase in unemployment taxes, opting instead for cuts in payments and the elimination of questionable claimants from the system. The unions, too, were reluctant to accept higher charges on workers as long as salaries were frozen by the June decrees. However, when the unions agreed in October to pay increased taxes in order to avoid major cuts in benefits, the employers refused adamantly, insisting that businesses in France paid far more toward unemployment insurance than their German competitors did. In November, the state finally intervened to force the social partners to accept a compromise which increased the tax by 1.2 percent, with 0.48 percent paid by the workers and 0.72 percent by the patrons. The patronat accepted this arrangement only because Pierre Mauroy offered them a package of incentives that included lower interest on loans that had been taken out previously at very high rates, better depreciation allowances for investment, a guarantee that social security taxes would not be increased until the end of 1983 at the earliest, and the gradual assumption, over a five-year period, of payment of family allowances by the state budget instead of through social security taxes on business.

In evaluating these measures, the head of the CNPF, Yvon Gattaz, proclaimed that the government "revealed a certain economic realism."[121]

The same could have been said about the 1983 budget proposals. In the spirit of rigor and austerity, the government proceeded to draw up a budget that aimed at reducing inflation. Although the budget projected an 11.8 percent increase in spending, this was only slightly above inflation estimates and it was divided very unevenly among ministries. The main winners in the fight for funds were the "realistic" areas of research, investment, industry, and aid to the unemployed. Research funds were increased by 17.8 percent, while aid to industry went up by 23.7 percent. As a consequence, other areas received increases that were at or below the projected inflation rate. No radical principles found their way into this budget. Despite calls by Socialist and Communist militants for major revisions in the tax system, the government introduced only minor changes, including a small increase in the wealth tax from 3 million francs to 3.2 million and the establishment of a 65 percent bracket in the unreformed income tax, which continued to collect less in revenue than any other such tax in a developed capitalist country, even though the Socialists governed France. On the other hand, this budget did not reverse the trend of increased government spending: under it the state would take 44.5 percent of the gross national product in taxes during 1983, compared with 43.9 percent in 1982.[122] Still, even with certain fudges by the government to accommodate all factions, Lionel Jospin viewed the 1983 budget as a de facto recognition of the "pause" in reform. In contrast to Delors, however, Jospin believed that there would be "some other budgets after this one in which we shall continue to advance." Increasingly, however, advances of the sort that Jospin wanted had to be postponed until after the municipal elections.[123]

While Pierre Bérégovoy and Jacques Delors defined the short-term strategy for attacking the *crise*, through social security reforms and state budget restrictions, Michel Rocard and Jean-Pierre Chevènement, through the Plan and the industry and research ministries, defined the long-term approach. Of the two, Rocard and the planning process played the lesser role, although not a totally insignificant one. From the first months of Socialist rule, Rocard had been the outsider in an outsiders' government. François Mitterrand had appointed him to a post that Socialist neglect made into one of the least important ministries, despite the party's protestations in opposition that the Plan would be the linchpin of any leftist government. Rocard had accepted his fate in a typical Rocardian fashion. He isolated himself from virtually everyone in the Council of Ministers and proceeded to offer periodical pronouncements about the errors of the government. The fall of 1982 provided him with one of his best forums, the inauguration of the planning mechanism for the next five-year period.

At the installation ceremonies for the Commission national de planification on 8 September 1982, Rocard delivered his extremely pessimistic analysis of the world economic situation, surpassing Delors in applying reality medicine to French socialism. He saw France and the world capitalist economy moving toward a situation in whch "growth shall be weak if not inexistent, quantitative social protection stagnant, international competition more and more severe, and instability, indeed insecurity, generalized." A profound structural crisis was sweeping through the western economies, a crisis that Rocard maintained went beyond economics to the core of western civilization.[124]

Rocard playing the role of Oswald Spengler did not go over very well in the Council of Ministers. Mauroy, Laurent Fabius, Charles Fiterman, and Jean-Pierre Chevènement, to name the outstanding figures, demanded that he modify his views on employment and growth in the document d'orientation for the ninth plan. Although he complied with the will of the majority, his revisions incorporated much of the same language and structure as the original. In an odd alliance of opposites, François Mitterrand expressed full approval of this slightly modified Rocardian statement, making clear that rigor and austerity were to be the rule in the ninth plan. The Council of Ministers acquiesced in this judgment and the new document d'orientation was approved in early October. By November, the authors of the ninth plan were claiming that "absolute priority" had to be given to industrial investment, in order to combat unemployment and reduce the trade deficit.[125]

While the call for industrial investment and economic realism advanced at the Planning Ministry, the Ministry of Industry and Research under the new leadership of Jean-Pierre Chevènement took an activist approach to economic problems. In contrast to his predecessor, Pierre Dreyfus, Chevènement intervened directly in the affairs of nationalized industries in order to restructure them and cut their losses. In the summer of 1982 this caused friction with the PDG of Rhône-Poulenc, Jean Gandois, who resigned in protest against the minister's tactics. When questioned about the extent of state control over nationalized industries, Chevènement claimed that he expected his PDGs to "support employment, reestablish the commercial balance, develop research and technology, ameliorate the social dialogue and working conditions in the enterprise."[126] By implication, everything else remained the prerogative of the minister of industry, who could restructure industry, direct investments to key sectors, and determine general economic policy. Under Chevènement's leadership, therefore, the government inaugurated plans for building the Airbus A320, constructing the TGV-Atlantique, and restructuring the electronics industry.[127]

Chevènement's plans for the electronics sector represented the Socialist government's most ambitious attempt to revitalize high technology and the economy in general. In the grand tradition of the Gaullist sectoral plans of the 1960s, François Mitterrand gave his minister of industry and research total support for a five-year, 140 billion franc investment program in the nation's electronics industry, with special emphasis on those areas, such as computers and component parts, in which France had lost ground to Japan and the United States. In justifying this ambitious project, Chevènement claimed that the success of the electronics industry would be instrumental in determining "the future of all of our industries." Despite severe limitations on investment funds and the fear that workers might view this plan as proof that the government's austerity program was nothing but an attempt to divert money from salaries to investments, François Mitterrand decided to forge ahead with the plan in July 1982, on the basis that the survival of the nation was at stake.[128] The Marxist Chevènement and the Gaullist Mitterrand conspired in the summer of 1982 to protect France from the evils of foreign economic domination.

Although the electronics plan probably marked the first step toward an industrial policy based on modernization, in 1982 the Socialist government still conceived of industrial policy in broad terms of saving traditional sectors and modern ones by reconquering the internal market. In that light, the minister of industry continued and inaugurated policies for saving the steel and chemical industries and for bailing out such traditional sectors as paper manufacturing, shipbuilding, the clothing industry, and furniture making. But, in his role as a modernizer, Chevènement also began the process of cutting the state's losses in the coal industry. His 1983 budget called for closing down three mines, cutting coal production, and dismissing mine workers in an effort to contain the enormous losses that the industry had accumulated in 1981–82 when the government implemented an ill-conceived, unworkable Socialist-Communist plan to revive it.[129]

Chevènement's industrial policy, at least in some cases, embraced the emerging themes of realism and modernization, although his rhetoric and ideology often obscured the fact. At the end of August, in a passion for modernization, he proclaimed to the heads of the nationalized industries that "our historical task is to organize the profound technological, social and cultural mutation of France," referring to the need "to reconcile France with its industry, to provide the nation with a competitive industry, to give priority to productive investment . . ." before announcing his four priorities: to unite science and industry better, to improve training for industrial jobs, to increase savings and investment for industry, and to inaugurate a social dialogue.[130] In November, however, when he had a chance to express his views before his own conference on industrial policy, he confused matters by mixing the new with the old, tortuous rhetoric with bizarre ideology. Embracing the spirit of entrepreneurship, he called for the modernization of the nation's industrial base, but cautioned that the Socialists rejected totally the Giscardian idea that parts of the French economy must be sacrificed to the exigencies of international competition. He called upon industry to pursue "a strategy *de sortie de crise*, to secure jobs and to reconquer national independence." The nation was involved in a struggle for survival, he maintained, which required the mobilization of the population behind industrial revival. Social dialogue would help win that struggle, for more democracy in the workplace would lead to economic growth and national revival. But dialogue and modernization were not enough for Chevènement. In concluding his remarks he called for the revival of the spirit of the resistance, using such terms as "mobilization," "defense," and "anti-Pétainism" to arouse France against the world, against the vultures who would strip it bare if France did not defend itself.[131]

Despite Chevènement's confused "struggle for survival" speech, the November conference on industrial policy resulted in a very sober assessment of France's economic position. The conferees, who were mainly Socialist economic experts or leading bureaucrats in the Ministry of Industry and related offices, presented papers that tended toward Saint-Simonist and technocratic points of view. The need for social dialogue was discussed only in terms of improving productivity and not as a step toward *autogestion* or worker control over industry. No mention was made of the "rupture with capitalism." On the contrary, the conferees argued that the main problem with French industry was the lack of entrepreneurship, the failure to develop a capitalist economy in the course of the nineteenth century. The goal of industrial policy, therefore, must be to use the state for the purpose of promoting change, modernization, innovation. The French state had historically played the role of the missing capitalist, a role that still remained important in the 1980s. But, the conferees warned the government that it would have to be a more cautious leader in the future. It could not embark on another *relance* because of the international economic situation; the weakness of the world economy made it impossible for any advanced industrial country to expand rapidly as expansion would cause imports to increase at a massive rate, similar to what happened in France in 1981–82. As a result, slow growth was the only solution. The state could not do everything, the conference pointed out; the government should finance only those projects that would lead to long-term industrial progress and energy independence. Beyond that, industrial policy should concentrate on the limited but essential goals of cutting the budget deficit and reducing the indebtedness of the nation's industries.[132]

If Chevènement provided the nation with a policy that mixed together state intervention, protection of the internal market, and economic modernization, this both reflected his own attitudes and those of the Socialist party in the fall of 1982. Although the government moved toward a form of left-wing "Barrism," its supporters—especially the party militants—found this U-turn difficult to accept. Pierre Mauroy, more than any other figure in the government, epitomized the agony of the party elite over this turn of affairs. By force of circumstance, although not by conviction, Mauroy had become a convert to the economic position of Jacques Delors. The eternal optimist and the eternal pessimist joined forces in the spring of 1982 to carry out the June devaluation and the accompanying economic measures. Furthermore, Mauroy and Delors agreed that wage and price controls of some sort would be necessary until at least the end of 1983. The problem was, how could Mauroy convince the unions and the party to accept this *dirigiste* solution to the country's economic problems when just the opposite had been expected of a Socialist administration?[133]

In the fall of 1982, Pierre Mauroy attempted to explain what the U-turn meant, in an effort to gain the support of the doubters for an extended period of rigor. He denied totally that any sort of "pause" had occurred. Only adjustments to the original program had been made. The objectives of decentralization, social progress, and the creation of an "économie mixte" with rough parity between public and private sectors had been adhered to from the beginning, although always within the context of a policy of rigor, for the Socialists had been left with a very precarious economic situation by the previous administration. The economic problems bequeathed by Giscard and Barre proved to be greater than expected and thus greater rigor was needed in 1982, but in no way did this mean the acceptance of a right-wing economic program.[134]

By October, Mauroy had placed his policy of rigor in a broader context. Taking some lines from Rocard and Chevènement, he argued that the *crise* was worldwide in scope and would endure for a long time: "This international crisis is linked to a technological mutation which challenges the system of production. We must adjust to it and modernize France. A technological challenge exists that we must overcome." But he denied that the government had adopted an austerity policy to combat the *crise*: "Rigor is not a policy. It is a method. The opposite of austerity, which is a condition, rigor is a means in the service of a policy whose objective remains, for us, economic growth." The problem for the left, Mauroy maintained, was to reconcile rigor and social progress. He reiterated that rigor had to be pursued for at least fourteen months after mandatory wage and price controls ended in November: "Rigor will be scrapped only when we shall be faced with a definite, vigorous international *reprise*."[135]

Mauroy and Delors meant what they said, partly because they knew by November that a third devaluation might be necessary in 1983. Despite mounting protests from trade unions, civil servants, and businesses, the government proceeded to maintain most wage and price controls after the expiration of the four-month freeze. Although businesses were allowed to improve their margins in November, they were not allowed to make up for supposed losses in revenue during the period of the freeze. The same condition applied to unions and workers in general. The government scrapped the indexing of salaries to inflation and controlled carefully any increases in the wages of bureaucrats. Even increases in the minimum wage were limited to inflation. Although Delors and Mauroy promised that the lowest paid would not suffer any decline in their standard of living during 1983,most wage earners would.[136] Mauroy kept his promise to link rigor and solidarity in these perilous economic conditions, but at a potentially high political cost.

Even though Pierre Mauroy struggled hard to reconcile socialism with his government's economic policies, to make the link between rigor and reform instead of between rigor and the dreaded "pause," his arguments lacked plausibility. The evidence indicated that a change in economic policy had occurred in the upper ranks of the government by the end of 1982. The rank and file in the party reflected this change, as they grew increasingly frustrated by the failure of the government to implement "socialism." In November and December, demands for radical action, such as stringent controls over capitalists who obtained state aid or the establishment of a state-controlled investment bank to promote leftist investment projects, reemerged once more from the party faithful, but those at the top continued to move inexorably toward modernization, increased rigor, priority to industrial investment, and similar economist objectives.[137] Reluctantly, the militants capitulated to the leadership, for no one in the government was willing or able to support their position. Electoralism and economism replaced the intransigent militancy of the party in opposition, as the militants and the leadership united to fight the municipal elections of March 1983.

Those elections would offer some indication of popular support for the government's policies and help determine the next stage in the struggle for control of France.

The March 1983 municipal elections were no ordinary event. The right viewed them as a referendum on two years of Socialist rule. For the left the elections placed its record of local hegemonic control on the line at a time when its decentralization program moved toward increasing the powers of provincial governments at the expense of Paris. A Socialist defeat in March would deal one more blow to the implementation of *autogestion*, for by definition the right could not carry out such a program at the local level. Defeat would also undermine the leftist contention that the government represented the true interests of the people. Long ago, François Mitterrand had learned that the true interests of the people often diverged significantly from the ideological preoccupation of the political elite. His 1981 presidential campaign made that clear. By 1983, polls indicated that the main concerns of the populace remained basically what they had been in the spring of 1981: jobs, financial problems, and inflation, in that order.[138] For better or worse, therefore, the government moved toward rapprochement and moderation in the election campaign. The president's New Year's address set the tone. He rejected totally the idea of class struggle and the rupture with capitalism, favoring in their place the harmony that the Auroux laws promised to create and the "économie mixte" that promoted cooperation between the public and private sectors for the good of the nation. His program for 1983 emphasized four objectives: adequate training of the nation's youth to reduce unemployment; increased support for the family through aid to children; solidarity with the unfortunate through the implementation of social justice; and, most important, the encouragement of enterprise. The president placed great emphasis on his fourth objective, for without enterprising industries the others meant nothing: "It is necessary to produce, to produce more and better products. But this can only be done under three conditions: by moderating social and financial charges, by having all workers recognize their responsibilities, and by inventing, investing, and learning how to sell in order to become competitive."[139]

Within a fortnight, Pierre Mauroy had seconded this move to moderation by presenting his objectives for 1983. Although they numbered six instead of four, the prime minister merely repeated the president's list in his first three proposals and added the seemingly innocuous objectives of reorganizing health care, protecting French citizens better both at home and abroad, and supporting liberty and democracy in France.[140] Almost nothing from the militant Socialist agenda remained in the president's or the prime minister's proposals for the year. Ideology clearly lost out to electoral necessity and pragmatism.

Yet, electoral necessity and pragmatism did not represent a united position. In early 1983, the two often conflicted with one another in ways that caused serious trouble for the party. When Jacques Delors attempted, in January, to reduce interest rates on the *caisse d'épargne* popular savings deposits from 8.5 to 7.5 percent, the outcry from the party faithful was so great that Mauroy and Mitterrand forced Delors to back down. Although Delors's initiative embodied the pragmatic spirit of aiding investment and jobs, through lower interest rates, electoral necessity required that such an unpopular move be reversed until after the March elections.[141] But the most difficult issue remained the contentious one of defining rigor and its duration. From a pragmatic perspective, rigor would have to remain in force for some time, but from the perspective of winning the March elections, rigor represented an albatross around the necks of Socialist candidates. Pierre Mauroy, who was placed in charge of the municipal election campaign for the party, attempted to make rigor into a left-right issue, alluding to what a Raymond Barre might do with rigor, as opposed to Socialist rigor. In an interview with the Socialist weekly, *l'Unité*, he claimed that "the debate on rigor is between the right and the left, not in the ranks of the left and still less in the ranks of the government."[142] But, on 1 February, Edmond Maire proclaimed, after meeting with François Mitterrand, that "a second *plan de rigueur* must now be envisaged" for the period following the municipal elections. He went on to demand that this plan include ironclad guarantees for the lowest paid and the unemployed and to condemn those who tried to "hide the truth," a clear allusion to Mauroy and the electoral opportunists in the party.[143]

Edmund Maire's bombshell became one of the leading election issues, seriously dividing the left. The Communist leadership attacked Maire for intervening in politics, while André Bergeron, speaking for Force Ouvrière, claimed that rigor had already gone too far, to the point where social order was threatened. On the other hand, Michel Rocard supported Maire, accusing the political leadership of misleading the public, since they knew that the French standard of living would decline in 1983, and arguing that another stage of rigor was inevitable. Lionel Jospin countered with an emphatic denial of Rocard's charges, but cautioned that the French should buy French goods and increase productivity in order to maintain their purchasing power, while Pierre Mauroy denounced the "donneurs de leçons," wondering why they had not been enthusiastic supporters of the first stage of rigor. Meanwhile, the Mitterandist controlled *l'Unité* drew the lines between the pragmatists and the electoral opportunists, accusing the second left of wanting to lose the March elections and labeling them the "gauche maso."[144]

The issue did not fade away in the course of the campaign. When Pierre Mauroy proclaimed, on 16 February on television, that "the great problems are behind us," a torrent of dissent spilled forth, leading the prime minister to explain what he meant two days later: "The most difficult is over since we have all agreed to assume the course of rigor."[145] Edmond Maire and the CFDT might have agreed, but they wanted the "course of rigor" spelled out in detail. They did so on 18 February, when the CFDT National Executive defined its support for "rigueur sélective," which would decrease inequalities of salaries, maintain the standard of living of the poorest, and aim at achieving three major positive objectives: "to stop the increase in unemployment, to expand investments, to finance social protection."[146] The second left clearly did not believe the party's optimistic position on rigor. With such statements as that of 18 February, Maire and the CFDT were laying the groundwork for the next round, after the March elections.

One the eve of the March elections, Mauroy's optimistic position on rigor received some severe blows. The government announced that inflation had picked up considerably since the end of October, increasing by 0.9 percent in January, well above the rate for the rest of the industrial world, while balance of payments figures continued in the red with a huge 9.58 billion franc deficit for January. Public opinion polls added to Socialist woes, revealing that most citizens did not believe Mauroy's rhetoric. A SOFRES poll taken in mid-February indicated that 71 percent did not think the government was succeeding in its struggle against unemployment, up from 65 percent the month before, while 54 percent believed that things "are going to become worse," versus 52 percent in January.[147]

The left tried hard to explain away the bad January figures. Mauroy pointed out that they were the "least bad" (or "the best") for the past four years of January statistics, adding that the left needed at least two years to succeed with its policy of rigor and making favorable comparisons between his economic policy and Barre's. But the *Canard enchaînée* made Mauroy's task more difficult by publishing internal government communiques that revealed that the franc would have to be devalued after the elections and perhaps again within the next eighteen months. Mauroy did not deny that the memos existed, but he argued that they did not represent policy, merely technical advice, which had no chance of being transformed into policy.[148]

The debate on rigor and economic policy in general dominated the election campaign, dividing the left and offering the right the opportunity to speak of incoherence and incompetence. But another issue, closely related to rigor, emerged on the fringes of the campaign, playing a nebulous role in March, foreshadowing what was to come in the future. That issue was immigration, or insecurity as some chose to call it. To understand its importance, we need to mention briefly the Socialist record on immigration and the related issue of law and order.

The themes of liberty and "droit à la différence" played a major role in the Socialist program in 1981. The appointment of Robert Badinter as minister of justice revealed clearly the deep commitment of François Mitterrand to implementing these objectives. Badinter was not a member of the Socialist party, but he represented all of the libertarian values that the party stood for. As minister of justice he moved rapidly to abolish the death penalty, to eliminate such exceptional penal jurisdictions as the *cour de sûreté*, and to provide liberty for oppressed groups such as immigrants, political prisoners, and homosexuals. By 1982, however, Badinter began to face serious opposition to his libertarian agenda. His attempt to repeal the Peyrefitte law, which gave the police *carte blanche* to interrogate immigrants and suspicious individuals, proved to be more difficult than either he or the Socialist party had anticipated. As the *relance* faltered, the fear of insecurity, of the unknown, increased.[149]

In tandem with Badinter's reforms, the Ministry of the Interior under Gaston Defferre moved to solve the immigrant problem once and for all by pursuing the three-pronged attack that the party had adopted. First, no new immigration was to be permitted, which reaffirmed what had been the status quo since the mid-1970s. Second, illegal immigrants who could prove that they entered the country before 1 January 1981, would be granted legal status, whereas all clandestine immigrants would be expelled and employers of such immigrants would be fined heavily. Third, the government would move to integrate legal immigrants as fully as possible into the mainstream of French society.[150]

In theory, the Socialist party's policy on immigration solved the problem totally. In practice, however, the Socialist government ran into serious obstacles. The first phase of the government's program proved to be disappointing, as only 131,000 of an anticipated 300,000 illegal immigrants applied for legal status. Partly because of this, in May 1982, the Ministry of the Interior imposed stringent restrictions on all North African visitors to France and inaugurated a tough policy on control of the frontiers, refusing entry to large numbers whose papers were not in order and expelling numerous illegal immigrants. At approximately the same time, Gaston Defferre and Robert Badinter debated openly over the rights of the police to search suspects, with Defferre arguing for the maintenance of the Peyrefitte law.[151]

Still, the government's policies contained much that was positive for immigrants. The Socialists prohibited the expulsion of certain categories of immigrants such as minors, those who had resided in France for more than fifteen years, and those who were parents of a French child. In addition, a number of restrictive laws were repealed, such as a 1932 law that had established quotas for immigrants in certain professions and economic activities and a 1939 law that restricted the right of association for immigrants. The government also appointed immigrants to the Fond d'action sociale's administrative board, set up a National Council for Immigrant Populations to consult on matters related to the immigrant condition, gave foreigners the right to vote in elections to Prudhomme councils, made naturalization easier, and provided subsidies for worthy immigrant associations. But the Socialists did not follow through on their promise to grant immigrants the right to vote in municipal elections. When Claude Cheysson raised the prospect in August 1981, during a diplomatic visit to Algeria, the government in Paris immediately countered that no such reform would be carried out during the *septennat*.[152]

Despite some vascillation on key points, the Socialists were clearly far ahead of public opinion on the immigrant issue and the related issue of civil liberties. Polls had consistently revealed overwhelming support for the death penalty, massive feelings of insecurity, backing for measures that would severely punish criminals, and major concerns about the size of the immigrant population. Yet the Socialist government implemented libertarian policies that ran counter to these sentiments. It should come as no surprise, therefore, that serious opposition to the government's supposed leniency emerged by the spring of 1982. The combination of deep-seated public fears that were often exacerbated by the right-wing press, the failure of the Socialist *relance* to redress inflation and unemployment, the revival of terrorism, and the increased visibility and assertiveness of immigrants in labor disputes led to the emergence of the "immigrant problem" in French politics by 1983.

The Socialists became aware of this reaction to their policies as early as the spring of 1982 when the so-called "letter to Mustafa" began circulating widely. The letter, supposedly written by a French Moslem to his friend in Algeria, asking him to join his coreligionists in France, claimed that "we [the Moslems] have become the masters and lords of France."[153] From that point on, whether planned or not, the Socialists tempered many of their libertarian positions. For example, they backed away from repealing the much-despised Peyrefitte law, maintaining some of the provisions for surveillance of suspects, which were expanded in 1983 to levels approximating the original legislation. In addition, the government overreacted to criticism of its law-and-order policies after the bloody rue des Rosiers terrorist attack in August 1982, by setting up a special antiterrorist police bureau with computer facilities for keeping track of sixty thousand suspected terrorists. Another similar organization was created after the Corsican independence movement stepped up its activities in January 1983. Even when François Mitterrand capitulated in December 1982 to the president of Algeria's vigorous protests against the government's visa policy for North African visitors to France, the Socialists ended up adopting a new system that continued to discriminate against the citizens of the Maghreb.[154] Increasingly, the public mood pushed the left toward positions that were often opportunistic, geared toward winning votes and appeasing the unknown forces of racism and fear.

By January 1983, at the beginning of the March election campaign, the immigrant issue had become the great unknown. The Socialists did everything they could to defuse it or, if that could not be accomplished, to be on the right side of it. When a poll revealed that 63 percent of the public thought the Métro was not a very safe place, the government responded by putting six hundred more police underground, despite statistics that showed that only four or five incidents occurred in the system per day. Late in the month, after strikes in the automobile industry had been widely publicized by French television, revealing the strong immigrant involvement in the protests, Pierre Mauroy accused the immigrant strike leaders of being motivated by religious and political interests that had "little to do with French social realities." Mauroy did not attempt to intervene when management at the Citroën factory of Aulnay-sous-bois dismissed militant Moslem union leaders in early February. Instead, he and Gaston Defferre were more concerned with creating new police posts to quell the grand fear of insecurity that the commission des maires had pointed to in their January meeting in Paris.[155]

The immigrant issue was clearly present in the March campaign, although it was used more on the right than on the left. The UDF mayor of Toulon, Maurice Arreyx, alluding to the immigrant presence in his city, protested that he would not allow Toulon to become the "poubelle" of France, while Jacques Chirac accused Defferre and Badinter of creating insecurity—shorthand for immigrant crime—through their lax policies on law and order. Numerous Socialist cities were bombarded by rumors about Algerian mistresses, favors given to Moslems, and mosques that the left had built. In Dreux, the rumor spread that the local Socialist government had hired a large number of Arabs and Turks while neglecting the needs of the "bons Français." On the other hand, the left mainly tried to avoid the issue. The most notorious example of this behavior occurred in February, when two million copies of François Autain's pamphlet on immigration, Vivre ensemble, les immigrés parmi nous, were printed by the government for distribution.

At the last moment the Socialists concluded that statements such as "Immigration does not create unemployment," were provocative in the context of the campaign and Autain's work was never released. However, in one local campaign, the bitterly fought race in Marseille, the Socialists matched the right in invective. The local party, under Gaston Defferre's leadership, appealed openly to anti-immigrant sentiments, posting signs that said "With the right, *l'immigration sauvage*; with the left, *l'arrêt d'immigration*."[156]

When the March elections were over, the issues of insecurity and immigration had meshed with the broader issue of the economy, making it impossible to disentangle the two. Clearly, however, March represented a loss for the left, although not as great a loss as many had expected. After two rounds of voting, the left ended up losing control over 31 cities of more than 30,000 population. The biggest loser was the Communist party, which dropped from control over 72 cities to 57, a net loss of 15, while the Socialists went from 81 to 67, losing 15 and gaining 1. The right had hoped to win more than 40 cities of over 30,000 from the left, but a stronger than expected vote for the left on the second round saved the government from a disastrous defeat. Still, the election witnessed a total reversal in vote percentage from 1981, as the left obtained approximately 47 percent of the vote in 1983, to the right's 53 percent. Talk of Socialist hegemony went out the window: the party's share of the centrist vote, which had been crucial to victory in 1981, dropped from 29 percent to 18 percent. About half of the voters claimed that they cast their ballots as a protest against Socialist policies, especially against the course of the government's economic policy. According to a SOFRES poll taken in April and May, the voters who were most disillusioned with the Socialists were the ecologists (63 percent) and rightists (71 percent) who had voted for Mitterrand in 1981. The RPR and Jacques Chirac were the biggest gainers from this disillusionment. Eighteen cities with populations of 30,000 or more came under RPR domination in March.[157]

To François Mitterrand, the results were disappointing but at least they did not add up to the total defeat that seemed likely after the first round. For the time being, the immigrant issue had been neutralized; it did not play a significant role in determining contests, despite its presence in many municipalities. Economics remained the key issue as the failure of the left to solve the problem of unemployment during its two years in office led voters to stay at home or switch to the right in protest. As a consequence, on Monday, 14 March, after the second round was over, everyone expected the government to announce major changes in economic policy. François Mitterrand and the Socialists had reached a turning point where they would have to choose between rigor and a peculiar Socialist solution to the nation's economic problems.

What happened during the hectic days that followed is not totally clear, despite numerous accounts of what various actors did. Of course, François Mitterrand was at the center of all of these negotiations and in the end his choice determined the direction that the government pursued. But what Mitterrand wanted to do in March is not clear. Whether he had a definite position on rigor or a Socialist solution to the nation's problems cannot be determined on the basis of the evidence, even though numerous journalistic accounts of Mitterrand's attitudes indicated that the President detested the policy of rigor. Supposedly, Mitterrand had told Mauroy in August 1982 that he had until the end of the year to solve the nation's economic problems. By October, relations between the prime minister and the Elysée had evidently become distant. During the fall of 1982, Mitterrand convened his "cabinet du soir" comprised of Laurent Fabius, Pierre Bérégovoy, the industrialist Jean Riboud, and the Radical Socialist Jean-Jacques Servan-Schreiber. They began discussing ways to promote economic growth, including the use of tariffs against foreign competitors and the withdrawal of the franc from the European monetary system. If one is to believe these accounts, Mitterrand agreed to the "cabinet du soir's" little-France policy and proceeded to implement it after the second round of the March elections, telling Pierre Mauroy that he could stay on only if he accepted this new policy and the appointment of three of the four members of the "cabinet" to key positions in his government.[158]

Yet it is highly implausible that the pro-European, antiprotectionist François Mitterrand could have converted so easily to this little-France position. Although it is speculative, a far more likely scenario is one that views Mitterrand as the Machiavellian politician who wanted the little-France solution to be expressed as openly as possible, knowing that Pierre Mauroy and Jacques Delors, in particular, would never accept it and that the rejection of it by the economic realists both inside and outside of the government would help convince the party militants and the general electorate that the government had no other alternative than to continue the policy of rigor. In addition, Mitterrand's March position, which became public knowledge shortly after the second round of the elections, could also be construed as an attempt to bluff the West Germans to agree to a revaluation of the mark, for fear that the Socialists might be serious about little France. Be that as it may, whether planned in Machiavellian fashion or arrived at through the evolution of events, in the end François Mitterrand opted for rigor, weeding out the hard-line protectionists and interventionists from his government. As Jacques Delors put it, after the events of March 1983, the Socialists became the greatest supporters of capitalism that France had ever known, aiding small and middling enterprises, encouraging the stock market, and advocating entrepreneurship.[159]

By the end of March, a third devaluation of the franc had been undertaken, an additional set of economic controls had been imposed on the nation, and a new, more Mitterrandist government had been appointed under Pierre Mauroy's continuing leadership and with Jacques Delors's increased control over the economy. If rigor had been part of Socialist government policies since May 1981, it had always been accepted grudgingly. After March, however, rigor and socialism became interchangable as social democracy prevailed over utopianism, the hard left capitulated before the economic realities of the day, and the CERES Marxists gave up their vision of rupture with the system. Although the conversion was not total, by late March 1983 the Socialists had undergone one of the greatest transformations from opposition to power that any political party had experienced. The wide gap that had divided left and right for more than a century had narrowed in a brief period of time. Still, questions remained over whether the French had moved towards consensus politics and if the party faithful would accept this bleak, pragmatic vision after years of Socialist dreams of profound change and appeals to the downtrodden.

3

"Rigueur encore une fois!":
From the Municipal Elections of March 1983
To the Fabius Government of July 1984

Although the March elections revealed clearly that the left had lost much of its support in the nation since 1981, the need for continued economic rigor remained paramount. The March crisis, if one existed, witnessed the "conversion" of François Mitterrand to the Delors camp, away from the protectionist thinking of Jean-Pierre Chevènement, Jean Riboud, and others who had advocated pulling out of the European monetary system. A new round of austerity, the so-called Delors plan, became the realist response to the protectionists that a new government implemented, under Pierre Mauroy's continued leadership. On the surface, change seemed to occur, but in reality the March crisis merely reinforced the path that the government had followed since at least June 1982. The big question remained whether the government could control the rank and file in the Socialist party, convince the nation that its program of rigor differed from a rightist course, and solve the deep-seated economic problems that France faced. After March, reform gave way totally to *gestion*, as the Socialists attempted to prove that they could run the nation effectively, solve major economic problems, and provide a positive balance sheet to the electorate by the time of the 1984 European elections or, if that proved impossible, by 1986.

The long battle to achieve economic recovery that Pierre Mauroy thought had been won in February became the center of government concern once again during March 1983. Soon after the municipal elections, Jacques Delors began negotiations in Brussels for a thrid devaluation of the franc, using the threat of a French withdrawal from the European monetary system as a lever to convince the Federal Republic of Germany to revalue the mark. In the end, after a grueling series of meetings, the members of the system agreed to devalue the franc by only 2.5 percent and revalue the mark by 5.5 percent, with the understanding that France would apply severe measures to halt inflation and reduce both internal and external debt.[1]

The Brussels agreement, which François Mitterrand accepted as the umbrella under which Socialist economic policy would have to function, necessitated changes in the government. The defeat of the protectionists, which this agreement clearly indicated, meant that Delors's position would be enhanced, with implications for virtually every other ministry involved in formulating economic policy. For a brief moment, Mitterrand seemed to consider appointing Delors prime minister, but such a choice would have concentrated too much power in the hands of one super minister, undermining the president's freedom to manoeuver. Instead, the March reshuffle of the Cabinet adhered to the doctrine of countervailing powers. Pierre Mauroy remained as prime minister, in charge of the delicate political agenda of uniting the left in the face of hard economic realities, while Jacques Delors emerged as second in command, with enlarged powers over the economy in his newly defined post of minister of the economy, finance and budget. With the resignations of Jean-Pierre Chevènement as minister of state for research, technology, and industry and Michel Jobert as minister of state for trade, coupled with the demotion of the minister of state for planning to the position of secretary of state under the prime minister's office, which forced Michel Rocard to give up that thankless position for the Ministry of Agriculture, Delors remained as the cabinet's elder statesman and most powerful figure on economic matters. But, to make sure that Delors did not overstep his domain, Mitterrrand chose two of his closest associates to watch over him in the truncated fifteen-member Council of Ministers. Pierre Bérégovoy, who was reappointed minister of social affairs and national solidarity, became the number-three figure in the council, behind Mauroy and Delors, while Laurent Fabius moved to the Ministry of Industry and Research, from which he could counter any outlandish move that Delors might make in that area. Still, when all the countervailing powers were in place, no doubts remained about who controlled economic policy in the cabinet; Jacques Delors had taken over the major part of the government's economic policy apparatus.[2]

The full implications of this shift were not immediately apparent. The Communists enthusiastically agreed to join the third Mauroy government, accepting the need to devalue the franc and the policy of rigor, as long as the earnings of the lower classes were protected. No one disagreed with François Mitterrand's 23 March charge to the new government in which he outlined six major objectives for it to meet: to train youth for the professions of the future, to reduce inflation, to eliminate the trade deficit, to support business in innovating and exporting goods, to balance the social security accounts and contain the national budget, and to direct savings toward investment in industry and housing. But, when Jacques Delors announced how some of these objectives were to be implemented in specific terms, on 25 March, everyone cried foul. The Delors plan called for cuts and tax and revenue increases equal to 65 billion francs, or 2 percent of gross national product, almost double the amount of the *relance* of 1981. Although the bulk of the tax and revenue increases fell on the top one-third of taxpayers in the form of a forced loan equal to 10 percent of their 1982 income tax payments, two-thirds of all taxpayers had to pay a 1 percent social security surcharge on their taxable income to help balance that account and almost everyone had to pay increased taxes on petroleum and an 8 percent rise in the cost of utilities and public transport. Households lost 37 billion francs as the result of these measures, almost 20 billion of which came from the forced loan on wealthier taxpayers, while social security, the state budget, and nationalized industries gained revenues that helped restore their financial health. The Delors measures would reduce consumer buying power by 1 percent in a year, which in turn would decrease demand for foreign goods, especially since most of the tax increases applied to the top third or so of wage earners who tended to spend more on such products. Severe restrictions on foreign travel, which again affected the well-to-do more than the lower classes, capped this effort to correct a serious foreign trade deficit that had contributed to the third devaluation of the franc in March.[3]

Opposition to the Delors plan came almost immediately from both the left and the right. The CFDT head, Edmund Maire, was especially critical of it, in light of his own warnings about the need for further austerity measures and the government's condemnation of his "maso" position. Maire saw no difference between the Socialist measures and those of the right; both sacrificed jobs in order to combat inflation and the deficit rather than trying to protect employment through such constructive steps as the implementation of the thirty-five-hour week. He attacked the government for not consulting the unions on what to do and for wasting two months before acting to stem the obvious economic deterioration that set in at the start of 1983.

Although not everyone accepted Maire's position, parts of it were echoed by almost every group on the left: the unions universally felt that they had been left out of consultations on what to do and they reacted quickly to the possibility that the new policies would undermine jobs, while the Communists and the far left in the Socialist party condemned the Delors plan for making concessions to the right once again rather than coming to the aid of the leftist electorate. Possibly Jean Poperen, the number-two figure in the Socialist party, best expressed the sentiments of the far left when he stated that Delors had undertaken "a classical policy of deflation, favoring the entrepreneurs, the patrons, the peasants, who, in all likelihood, shall never rally around the theses of the Socialist party. He demands the greatest effort from the salaried employees, the skilled workers, and the middle level *cadres*, who provided the support and the electorate for François Mitterrand in May 1981."[4]

These were serious accusations, ones that the government had to address. At first, Mauroy and Delors attempted to convince the left that some decline in the standard of living was inevitable and that March inagurated a new era in which the government would "géré les réformes" rather than initiate them. But this realistic approach did not go over very well. By April, Mauroy provided a different explanation of the new, post-March era. First of all, it was not new, but rather a continuation of the policies that the government had pursued since 10 May 1981, policies that in François Mitterrand's words of 23 March "must be maintained." In that sense, the "increased rigor" that the government inaugurated in March was only "transitory," a necessary step to assure the success of its long-term policies, which had no relation to those of the right: "Our policies remain based on the will for social justice and the struggle against inequalities," Mauroy contended. Ticking off a number of reforms that the government had undertaken, from the Auroux laws to changes in the tax system, Mauroy attempted to counter the criticisms made by the unions and the far left, adding the point that his government's policies aimed at achieving such positive goals as the "industrial renewal" of the nation. For these compelling reasons, the prime minister concluded, the government would not compromise on the Delors plan.[5]

But Mauroy convinced no one with his attempt to rally the faithful around the long-term policies of the government. He failed to divert attention from the main issue of the continued pursuit of rigor, entailing the loss of buying power and increased unemployment. With signs of growing unrest in the ranks of the unions and in certain rightist circles, the government finally compromised with its far-left critics in the Socialist and Communist parties by promising to spend more on training young workers, to allocate funds to refurbish nationalized industries in order to employ additional workers, and to rework government programs to insure that unemployment would not increase. In addition, Mauroy promised that he would review the Delors program to exempt as many of the lowest-paid workers from the 1 percent social security tax and the forced loan as possible. For these concessions, the government gained the support of the far left in the National Assembly. The Communists voted for the government program in April 1983, in contrast to 1982 when they abstained over the first phase of rigor.[6]

Mauroy's promise to stem the tide of increasing unemployment came just in time to prevent a possible catastrophe for the government. In April and May 1983, a combination of protests by various elements, ranging from physicians and interns in the hospitals to small merchants and peasant farmers, brought the Socialists to a difficult impasse, raising the specter of a repetition of May 1968. Jean Poperen, overlooking the developing situation in late April, saw the right organizing "un coup du Chili à leur manière." His rightist counterpart, Michel Poniatowski, provided credence for such an unlikely development, when he claimed, "We are entering a period in which anything can happen."[7]

Poperen and Poniatowski notwithstanding, for the most part the April and May demonstrations had very little to do with politics and a great deal to do with French corporatist interests. Beginning in February, medical students went on strike against the new examination requirements that the government had proposed. Fearing that the Socialists wanted to restrict the number of physicians, since the nation already had an oversupply, they viewed this step as part of a weeding-out process. Shortly later, in March, the medical students were joined by interns and physicians in the hospitals, who became concerned over the government's plans to introduce administrative reforms and gain control over medical expenses. By late April, with the medical profession in open revolt, students in the universities turned out to demonstrate against the Savary reform of higher education, which required that they pass an examination before entering the second cycle, or after two years in university. While these urban protests developed, peasants began to riot against Common Market agricultural policies, and the low prices that they received for pork, eggs, and other commodities. In turn, the small merchant and artisan syndicats, seeing that the situation was getting out of hand, called for a 5 May march in Paris to protest Socialist policies on price controls. Finally, on top of all of these disturbances, the Parisian tourist agents also demonstrated against the Delors plan amid accusations by rightist newspapers that the government was creating military camps for vacationers, a sort of Riviera "gulag."[8]

But the sound and fury of these corporatist, and in some cases openly political, interests did not add up to much in the end. For one thing, they represented only a small minority of the population. The largest demonstration, the 5 May march of artisans and small merchants, brought only twenty thousand to the streets of Paris. The student protests against the second-cycle examination proved to be quite anemic; only eight thousand showed up at the largest rally. In fact, the real danger from these protests was not the size of them, but the possibility that certain groups, such as the physicians and interns or the peasant rioters, might be able to paralyze key sectors of the nation or create a snowball effect that would bring more demonstrators to the streets of Paris. To prevent this from happening, the government made major concessions to physicians, interns, and peasants in late April and early May. In short, the Socialists caved in to corporatist interests, retracting or modifying most of the medical reforms they intended to implement and promising peasants that the government would fight hard in the European Community to gain higher prices for French agricultural commodities.[9]

Yet, despite these tactical retreats, concessions made here and there to various interest groups, the government did not scrap the general outlines of the Delors plan. Nor did the right succeed in blowing up corporatist protests into a political crisis, even though leading politicians such as Giscard d'Estaing referred to the spring events as another 1958. Instead, the government stuck to its political agenda, resolutely determined to maintain the general outlines of its reinforced policy of rigor. Delors, Mauroy, and Mitterrand all made timely appearances in the media to convince the nation that the government was united on this policy. At his June press conference and again later in the month in a surprise television appearance, François Mitterrand made clear that the policy of rigor was his policy, that it was the only policy that the nation could pursue in trying to correct the economic imbalances that existed, and that the critics of rigor had no legitimacy. If any doubts existed about the president's stand, and there definitely were some in light of his supposed protectionist position in March, these appearances and his September 1983 press conference provided clear proof that, for whatever reason, François Mitterrand had embraced the Delors doctrine of rigor. When, at his September press conference, Mitterrand called for the reversal of a fifteen-year trend of growing state revenues by demanding that the tax burden for 1985 be decreased by 1 percent of the gross national product, rigor was clearly in the saddle, determining the fate of France.[10]

Overwhelmingly, however, the French remained skeptical about this shift of direction. The vast majority doubted if rigor added up to a coherent policy and by a margin of 51 percent to 21 percent they maintained that François Mitterrand was a tepid convert to the policy, for tactical reasons rather than out of conviction.[11] Jean-Pierre Chevènemnent and the CERES faction within the Socialist party continued to express strong reservations about this policy, agreeing often with the Communists in criticisms of the Delors plan. At times, Chevènement sounded more like an ultra-Gaullist than a Socialist, arguing for the sacred union of left and right to save the nation from ruin, but in his more lucid moments, he hit upon some of the major weaknesses of the Delors plan. For example, in late May 1983, at the national convention of the Socialist party, Chevènement responded to

Pierre Mauroy's appeal for support of the government's policies. Mauroy had argued that the left needed to acquire the "légitimité de gestion" by mastering the crisis. To this, Chevènement replied by asking whether the current policy of rigor was a "parenthesis" or a "virage" in the history of the left in power. If it were a "virage," he argued, then the *projet socialiste* was dead and so was socialism in the ranks of the party leadership, for "the conception on which rigor is based has nothing Socialist about it." He concluded by stating that he believed the party leaders viewed rigor as a "virage" and not as a "parenthesis."[12]

Time and again, during the summer and fall of 1983, Chevènement voiced the challenge he made at the national convention. Under his guidance, the CERES current in the party drew up a motion to present to the October 1983 Bourg-en-Bresse Socialist congress, in which they called the government's deflationary direction "a change of policy and not the policy of change" and argued that the new course called into question the long-term commitments, made at the 1971 congress of Epinay, regarding the union of the left and the anticapitalist position of the party. In public interviews, Chevènement raised the traditional CERES themes of reconquest of the internal market, the use of the state to effect major economic change, and the need for massive economic growth to implement the left's policies of reindustrialization, pointing out that the Socialists had not implemented any of them: "One can—I believe—better utilize the state apparaus, to put more people in the ranks, to make better use of nationalization of the banks and industry, to motivate, to mobilize, to make the principal economic partners work together—I am thinking in particular of the role of the *cadres*—and finally to develop the spirit of enterprise which must not remain the domain of the few." To Chevènement, the Delors plan would accomplish none of these objectives, for it risked increasing insecurity and unemployment for the workers, leading to the disenchantment of the Socialist electorate with the government's policies. Without a clear idea of what rigor should accomplish for the party and the people of France, the right would gain the advantage, encouraging individualism in place of the left's project of collective discipline. Chevènement did not question the need for rigor. The issue was what kind of rigor, for what objectives, for what electorate, and for what ideology.[13]

When the Bourg-en-Bresse congress was held in late October 1983, the confrontation between Chevènement and the vast majority of the party that many had expected would occur failed to materialize. Above all, Jean-Pierre Chevènement was loyal to the party and loyal to its leader, François Mitterrand. Seeing that neither had budged significantly from the Delors plan, Chevènement and CERES accepted a compromise at the congress. In essence, the main outlines of the Delors plan were reaffirmed, including the acceptance of the external restraints of free trade and the basic inability of the French economy to pursue a *relance* on its own. Compared with the Valence congress of 1981, a subdued group of militants ate humble pie at Bourg-en-Bresse. The bold ideas of 1981 had given way to the realism of the Delors plan. The party leaders could offer the rank and file very little in the way of inspirational rhetoric. No doubt sensing this malaise, neither Chevènement nor Rocard spoke at the congress. The militants were left with only one or two major projects from the pre-1981 program: a new press law against monopolies and the long-awaited proposal to unify private and public education under one national system. For better or worse, the government held up this meager, unfinished agenda as the militants' last domain, a poor recompense for accepting the restrictions of the Delors plan.[14]

Despite Chevènement's capitulation at Bourg-en-Bresse, the criticisms he had levied against government policy remained troublesome. Since the March crisis, policy had focused increasingly on the conjunctural problems of controling inflation, reducing debt, and monitoring social security expenditures. With Delors and Bérégovoy in charge of this conjunctural policy, the government succeeded in restricting demand. The budget for 1984 continued and expanded the tough austerity measures that the Delors plan had implemented. The forced loan that had been imposed on the top third of taxpayers in March was replaced by a surtax on the wealthiest 10 percent, while the 1 percent social security tax was extended into 1984. To control inflation, Delors restricted severely price increases by nationalized industries to a maximum of 6 percent, with the exception of the electricity and gas utilities, and he proclaimed that the government would keep salary increases below 5 percent during 1984, almost half the rate of increase during 1983. Although this budget included an increase in taxes as a percentage of gross national product, from 44.7 percent in 1983 to 45.5 percent in 1984, most of the increase would be at the local level and be temporary in scope, if the president's promise to reduce the tax burden by 1 percent of gross national product in 1985 were kept.[15]

By the end of 1983, the results of the Delors plan were beginning to show up, confirming some of the fears that Chevènement had expressed. The buying power of the average Frenchman declined by 0.3 percent during the year, a figure that would have been much higher if savings had not been sacrificed to consumption. The outlook for 1984 indicated a further decline in the standard of living. On the other hand, declining purchasing power had exactly the effect on inflation and the trade deficit that Delors had expected. Inflation remained below 10 percent for the second straight year, registering 9.3 percent compared with 9.7 percent in 1982, while the trade deficit was cut in half, as the current account went from a massive 79.3 billion francs in the red during 1982 to 33.8 billion in 1983. However, the vast deflationary pressures that Delors had unleashed to restrict demand began to affect employment quite seriously by the end of the year. In early 1984, economists began predicting that the French unemployment figure would reach 2.5 million by the end of the year, an increase of over 400,000 above 1983, representing a major defeat for the government's much-vaunted promise to contain unemployment at 2 million or less. Although the economy continued to grow in 1983, its rate of increase was below 1 percent, not enough to absorb the increased number of workers who came into the job market.[16]

By 1984, the government had exhausted most of its palliatives for unemployment. The solidarity contracts, which had been extended greatly in 1981 and 1982, had encountered numerous problems. Intended to allow workers to retire early if unemployed workers were hired to replace them, these contracts placed a heavy burden on the unemployment and retirement systems without reducing unemployment by any significant amount. For the most part, those who opted for early retirement were the best-paid, best-qualified workers, in the most prosperous sectors of the economy. As a result, they cost the unemployment system a considerable amount, forcing UNEDIC, in 1983, to decrease early-retirement benefits under these contracts from 70 to 65 percent of an individual's salary, with a cap on the total. In addition, the system did not get at the heart of the unemployment problem: skilled unemployed workers who were most likely to obtain jobs were the ones most likely to benefit from solidarity contracts, whereas the unskilled remained the ones who were least likely to be employed, whether the contracts were in force or not.[17] Be that as it may, by January 1984 the unemployment system had become heavily burdened by solidarity contracts and other devices to stem the tide of joblessness. To put its house in order before the explosion of 1984 threatened to undermine the system, Pierre Bérégovoy moved to place early retirements, solidarity contracts, and other social conventions under the regular budget, while decreasing unemployment benefits from 80 percent of a workers' former salary to 75 percent and increasing the unemployment insurance levy on employed workers.[18]

While Delors and Bérégovoy were busy wringing excess demand out of the economy and devising plans to save the social security and unemployment systems from the burdens that deflationary policies placed upon them, Laurent Fabius was left in charge of formulating long term economic policy at the Ministry of Industry, at least to the degree that Delors, Mauroy, and Mitterrand would allow him freedom of action. Jean-Pierre Chevènement had resigned from that post under considerable pressure from Mitterrand and Mauroy. In a stormy February 1983 session of the Council of Ministers, Mitterrand warned that there must be no government interference into the workings of the nationalized industries. Only through "autonomie de gestion" will they be able to function properly, he argued. Chevènement protested that he had not interfered, but handed in his letter of resignation anyway, knowing that it would not be accepted on the eve of the March municipal elections and hoping that he would be able to negotiate for his position in the coming cabinet reshuffle. But, in the end he lost out and the more obliging Fabius was appointed to the ministry.[19]

Laurent Fabius brought a new style to the Ministry of Industry as its third occupant in less than two years. More attuned to the forces of the marketplace than either one of his predecessors, Fabius clearly differentiated himself from Chevènement in his first speech as minister. He claimed that "the state does not intend to become a substitute for the role of enterprises and entrepreneurs," adding that "the notions of risk, of profitability, of competitiveness are in no way disreputable."[20] This new spirit of capitalism applied as much to nationalized industries as it did to private industry, in Fabius' opinion. Nationalized industries had to become profitable, they could not continue to rely upon the state to bail them out with subsidies. In that spirit, Fabius opened the way for state-controlled firms to borrow extensively in private capital markets through the use of such devices as *titres participatifs* and *certificats d'investissement*, which had the effect of partially denationalizing some of these firms, as private investors gained certain ownership rights through these devices, although no claim to any present or future control over state industries. During 1983, state enterprises used the bourse to raise 4.05 billion francs in *titres participatifs* alone; in 1984 they would increase that total to about 6 billion.[21]

In taking these steps to change the direction of economic policy, from state control to more independence for individual establishments, Fabius tended to follow Delors's lead. Not until the fall of 1983, at the earliest, did Fabius begin to formulate clearly a policy that would eventually be identified totally with him. In face of the increasing deterioration of the competitive position of large areas of the economy, it became more and more apparent that the government would have to abandon its attempts to save jobs at any cost for a policy that placed primary emphasis on the future. Laurent Fabius became the central figure in that major shift in government policy.

The general outlines of the new direction emerged in Fabius's 11

October 1983 speech before the National Assembly, which he entitled
"To Modernize Our Industrial Enterprises." On that occasion he raised
many of the same problems on which Jean-Pierre Chevènement had
focused, but placed them in a radically different context. Beginning with
the usual litany of economic woes, in which the international context
of the crisis, the responsibility of the previous government, and the
various inadequacies of the French system were pointed out, Fabius
went on to argue that a massive restructuring of French industry was
necessary in order for the nation to master the economic situation. This
meant, as he put it, that the priority must be granted to the future and
not to the past: "we cannot hope to save everything. Enterprises are
living organisms: they are born, they develop, and some perish."[22]
Although the government would do as much as it could to modernize
endangered areas, it could no longer promise as Pierre Dreyfus had
done that no sectors were in danger. Priority would go to those industries
of the future such as biotechnology and telecommunications.
Furthermore, the state could no longer guarantee that it alone could
bring significant change: "It is clear that the state can not do
everything."[23] Instead, civil society must play an increased role; social
dialogue and new cultural attitudes toward industrial production must
be developed among the French to bridge the enormous gap between
the economy and society. To drive the point home concerning the
decreased role of the state, Fabius added:

> There is no way that the State budget can serve as a *voiture-balai* for
> nationalized enterprises, any more than these enterprises could serve as a
> *voiture-balai* for the rest of industry. Those who propose systematically,
> when an enterprise is in deficit, that it be taken under the charge of the public
> sector no doubt fail to understand that this system could not be viable and
> that, if one would follow them, one would render the worst possible service
> to the public sector. The industrial public sector must be identified with
> success and not with deficits. . . . This is why, with the possible exception
> of steel, the industrial groups that were nationalized in 1982 must, at the
> latest, be in financial equilibrium by the end of 1985.[24]

In conjunction with this new, more market-oriented approach to the
nationalized industries, Fabius also called for numerous changes in the
relationship between the state and the private sector for the purpose
of decreasing excessive indebtedness and improving industrial
investment. These included letting the marketplace determine prices,
decreasing social security expenses for firms, and granting state aid to
help enterprises modernize or innovate in new technologies. Finally,
the Fabius plan called for more flexibility in education and research
in order to meet the challenges of the third industrial revolution, and

a new attitude toward Europe, one that would revive the spirit of Monnet, of cooperation for the purpose of modernization on a European scale. To Fabius, the choice for France was "modernization or decline." Everyone and everything must participate in the process: "The success of this modernization depends on mobilization of the French, that is to say their *rassemblement* around the need for industrial renewal."[25]

The theme of modernization also resonated in the government's Plan for the years 1984 to 1988. Approved by the National Assembly in December 1983, the Ninth Plan claimed that it had no total solution to the problems that France faced. Increasingly, it argued, those problems had become international and could only be solved through the concerted effort of the industrial powers, under the leadership of the United States. France could not grow out of the current crisis, as many had believed in 1981, nor could it solve its problems through monetarist policies. Economic health could only be achieved through a carefully thought out strategy for the modernization of France, a strategy that would take into consideration the restraints upon the nation's economy. But unlike Fabius's blunt approach to the subject, the Ninth Plan envisaged modernization without pain. In fact, the Plan maintained, modernization would establish the thirty-hour week and lead toward greater solidarity and reduction of inequalities in society. Yet, despite this simplistic approach, the authors of the Plan saw themselves involved in a life and death struggle to bring the third industrial revolution to France, and correspondingly they placed the highest priority on modernizing industry, introducing new technologies, renovating the educational system to meet the needs of the new economy, favoring research and innovation, and developing such industries as communications. As Jean Le Garrec said in his introduction to the Ninth Plan, it placed high priority on "industrial modernization, education at every level and professional training."[26]

To talk about modernization was one thing; to become involved in the difficult decisions about modernization was another. By late 1983, the hour of decision making had finally arrived. Suddenly, the government found itself faced with failing industries that could not be bailed out very easily, new technologies that required massive amounts of investment, and increasing unemployment in traditional sectors of the economy. Modernization was the answer to all of these difficulties, but what exactly did that entail?

First of all, the problem. By the end of 1983 it was clear that the Socialist plans for coal, steel, and shipbuilding had not worked. For one thing, energy consumption had declined since 1981, endangering the optimistic projections that coal would become a major factor in the nation's energy supply. Despite subsidies of 5.8 billion francs in 1982, the nation's coal industry still lost money, leading the government to consider retrenchment instead of expansion.[27] The steel industry did no better. The 1982 steel plan had collapsed almost as soon as it had been inagurated; projections that total production would reach 24 million tons by 1986 suffered a serious blow when output slipped two years in a row, to 18.6 million tons in 1982 and 17 million in 1983. With losses of 10 billion francs in 1983, the prospect of a 12 billion franc loss in 1984, and pressures from Brussels to reduce subsidies in order to comply with the European Community's steel policy, by late November 1983 the government began to think seriously about more dismissals and lower production plans.[28] Suddenly, with the shipbuilding industry also in total disarray by late 1983, as orders for new ships declined to one-fourth of the nation's capacity, the government was faced with the unwelcome alternative of pouring more money into these declining industries or cutting back on production and employment.

Signs of serious economic collapse also emerged in other areas of the economy during the second half of 1983 and early 1984, exacerbating the government's problems. The nation's paper industry, which had been reduced to one major firm, underwent a restructuring that aimed at eliminating three of its four plants and 1,500 of its 2,100 workers by 1989. But this was evidently inadequate to compete with much more efficient foreign firms and by the end of September 1983, the government was entertaining bids from foreign paper manufacturers to take over the remnants of the French industry. The machine tool industry faced similar problems. The 1982 plan to restructure it did not work, as production declined in both 1982 and 1983, despite government aid of 2.3 billion francs during that period. Between 1982 and 1984, employment in the industry dropped from 17,500 to 15,000, reflecting both the heavy penetration of foreign machine tools into the French economy and the low level of French industrial investment.[29]

As serious as the problems were in paper and machine tools, they paled into insignificance compared with the difficulties that emerged in the automobile industry and the Creusot-Loire metallurgical giant. Between 1979 and 1983, the French share of the European automobile market declined from 30 percent to slightly over 24 percent. Foreign penetration of the domestic market increased each year, reaching 33 percent in 1983. Since the nation's automobile industry exported half of its production and employed, either directly or indirectly, 1.5 million workers, this deterioration implied difficulties for both foreign trade and employment. In July 1983, the long process of returning the industry to profitability began when Peugeot announce that it would dismiss 10 percent of its work force or about 8,000 employees. For the most part, the government and the unions accepted the company's plans, since the majority of those dismissed would be placed on early retirement. But, at the Poissy plant outside of Paris, where immigrant laborers composed the bulk of the work force and where serious disturbances had occurred in 1982, Peugeot's plans were hotly contested. In December 1983, without obtaining union approval, the Socialist government and Peugeot agreed to a plan to dismiss 1,950 workers at Poissy, offering them retraining opportunities or the possibility of obtaining aid to return to their native country. The CFDT and the immigrants protested vigorously: 88 percent of the workers at Poissy had never gone beyond the primary-school level, making it highly unlikely that retraining would help them obtain other jobs, and the vast majority had very little desire to return to their native country under the government's suddenly revived *aide au retour* program. In justifying these actions, Pierre Mauroy spoke of "mutations industrielles nécessaires" at the Poissy plant, adding "we must adapt ourselves to economic necessities while respecting men."[30]

In the spring of 1984, amid projections that the automobile industry would have to dismiss 60,000 or more workers in the next five years in order to become profitable, Citroën followed Peugeot by demanding the elimination of 6,000 positions. Faced with a decline in its share of the French automobile market from 21 percent in 1979 to 13 percent in early 1984, the company wanted to cut the least-qualified workers from its rolls, which meant immigrant workers located primarily at one problem plant, Aulnay, in the Parisian suburbs. The same scenario of union protests, government deals, and immigrant defeat repeated itself at Aulnay. While early retirements made up the bulk of redundancies at most Citroën factories, in August Laurent Fabius agreed to allow Citroën-Aulnay to dismiss 1,950 workers, almost all of whom were semi-literate, unskilled North African immigrants, who were in no position to benefit from government retraining programs.[31]

If the crisis in the automobile industry revealed the change in Socialist policy from protection of jobs at all costs to support of corporate plans for modernization, the Creusot-Loire affair represented a startling reversal from the 1981–82 idea that nationalization was the answer to the problems of French industry to the acceptance of the primacy of market forces. Creusot-Loire, which employed 30,000 workers, began threatening bankruptcy in mid-1983, appealing to the government for some sort of bailout, possibly along the lines of the Giscardian deals with the steel industry or Rhône-Poulenc. Laurent Fabius, as minister of industry, refused to accept any of the company's proposals unless it obtained substantial aid from its stockholders. When that was secured, at least partially, in November 1983, the government agreed to take over two-thirds of Creusot-Loire's failing steel industry, to purchase most of its prosperous nuclear energy sector, Framatome, and to lend it 2.1 billion francs. But, in the spring of 1984, when Creusot-Loire came back once more for state aid, Fabius responded abruptly: "The State is not a sponge for wiping out the errors of management. Favorable to the freedom of enterprise, we estimate that certain responsibilities go with it and that it is not incumbent upon the taxpayers to remedy the insolvency of some."[32] While right-wing journals such as *L'Express* pleaded for a government takeover of Creusot-Loire, the Socialists stood by and allowed the company to go into bankruptcy, the largest such declaration in ten years. On 30 June 1984 François Mitterrand commented ironically on the situation: "I am surprised to see that one turns to the state to pay for one's losses. The very state that is detested, denounced, that one accuses of wanting to go beyond its proper limits."[33]

The shocks that these individual crises administered to the nation, and especially to the people of the left, transformed the vague words about modernization into reality. But nothing brought home the meaning of this new policy better than what the Socialists did in such nationalized industries as coal, shipbuilding, and steel. In all three, the government drew up plans of action without consulting the unions, although it offered ample warning that cuts would be made. As early as November 1983, for example, Fabius outlined a plan for coal that called for shutting down inefficient mines, reducing production from 18 million tons a year to 11 million, and cutting back on workers by 20,000 over a five-year period, while keeping state subsidies constant. When the unions and the Communists protested and the Communist head of the Charbonnages resigned his post, the government did not back off, but pursued the path of modernization through solidarity. As a result, in February 1984, the Socialists issued a master strategy that advocated the use of such devices as early retirement, "congés de reconversion," and "aids à la réinsertion" to insure that no worker would be unemployed because of modernization. The "congés de réconversion" represented a new means of retraining workers; in the spirit of the Socialist motto of "vivre et travailler au pays," the "congés" allowed workers to remain in their own firm for two years of training in a related industrial trade that was located in the region. In conjunction with these measures, the Socialists also called for the establishment of fourteen "*pôles de conversion*" in the areas that would be hurt most by modernization. Industries would receive special benefits, such as exoneration from payment of certain taxes, if they established plants within these poles. To further sweeten the pot, 2 billion francs were to be allocated to the Fonds industriel de modernisation for the sole purpose of investment in the fourteen *pôles de conversion*; 1.3 billion francs were to be given to the Fonds spéciaux de grands travaux for housing, road building, and other projects in these *pôles*; and an extra 1 billion francs was to be provided to the nationalized industries to invest in the adversely affected regions. With these proposals ready for implementation, the government increased the number of redundancies in the coal industry to around 25,000, tentatively estimated that 20,000 or more would be dismissed from steel, and called for cuts of about 5,000 workers in the shipbuilding industry. If everything went as planned, no one would be unemployed as the result of modernization, the social fabric of the affected regions would be kept intact, and new, possibly better jobs would be provided to workers involved in retraining programs as industries were attracted to the fourteen *pôles de conversion*.[34]

While the government's plans were accepted passively by workers in the coal and shipbuilding industries, steel was a special case. In a sense, steel represented the last bastion of the old left, especially the Communist left; it symbolized the struggle between the modernizers and the syndicalists. But steel also symbolized the power of France in the world. The Gaullists had created the modern French steel industry as a part of a nationalist industrial strategy that included the Concorde and nuclear power. To abandon steel was to abandon the nation. But these symbolic factors were overshadowed in the immediate situation by the economic fact that steel was affected far more severely by Socialist modernization plans than either coal or shipbuilding, both of which did not come under stringent European Community rules regarding subsidies and could consequently be allowed more flexibility in carrying out cuts.[35]

Numerous plans had been formulated for steel in the past, but none of them possessed the sense of finality, of giving up the struggle, that surrounded the second Socialist plan on steel. In 1982, the government had formulated its first steel plan with a sense of optimism, believing that now the problem would be solved. François Mitterrand had proclaimed at Longwy, in October 1981, that "the public enterprises, among which figure Sacilor and Usinor, shall be the launching pad for industrial renovation and the battle for jobs."[36] But in 1983, as massive debts accumulated, totalling 10 to 12 billion francs, with prospects for more of the same in 1984 and after, the government decided that it could not continue providing such subsidies. In late March 1984, the Socialists drew up a plan for steel that called for reducing production to 18.5 million tons by 1986, in comparison with earlier projections of 24 million tons, and the closing down of a large part of the Lorraine steel industry. Of the 20,000 jobs that were to be cut, 13,500 would come from Lorraine. Although this move clearly represented the victory of economic realism over political expediency, since the Lorraine steel industry was the least efficient in France, the immediate repercussions were harsh criticism, wildcat strikes, and mass demonstrations against this new plan.[37]

The March–April 1984 steel crisis represented the final major battle in the hard-fought war for modernization. Every element of the traditional left attacked the government's decision. André Bergeron expressed total opposition to the policy of modernization, claiming that it would lead to massive unrest. He demanded a *relance* of the economy to solve the nation's problems. In this he was joined by an unwelcome partner, Georges Marchais, who called the government's decision a "tragic error." Marchais accused Mitterrand of abandoning the common Socialist-Communist accord of 1981—reaffirmed on 1 December 1983—that he maintained supported a "policy of employment founded on a policy of growth," and adopting the mistaken Giscardian policy of retrenchment. In this environment of massive indignation, all of the major French unions—the CGT, the CFDT, and FO—plus a number of minor ones, called for a general strike in Lorraine for 4 April 1984 and a "march on the Elysée" for 13 April.[38]

François Mitterrand reacted quickly to this turn of events. On 4 April he held a press conference in which he confronted the major issue. He began by insisting that his policies had not changed: "It is the same policy with the same objectives, but it comprises different obstacles which require different actions." Because of this, the president called upon his minister of industry, Laurent Fabius, "to assume exceptional powers which will allow him to implement the restructuring plan." As a consequence, Fabius was elevated to the post of super minister of industrial redeployment, confirming the leading role that he had already assumed in the modernization program. Mitterrand's offensive did not end there, however. He attacked Marchais's position and questioned the role of the Communist party in the government. Over and over again he repeated that France had to become competitive in international markets: "Either France shall become capable of holding its own in international competition or it shall be dragged to the bottom." Referring to the Common Accord, Mitterrand informed Marchais that, as president, he was not bound by it, but if he were Marchais should be aware that the accord took into consideration France's place in the international community and the need to adjust the French economy to the rules of that community. Always speaking in a positive sense, Mitterrand pointed out the many restrictions upon French sovereignty that the European Community and international competition created. He hastened to add that within those restrictions the government was doing everything possible to help Lorraine and other adversely affected regions.[39]

More than any other single event, the Mitterrand press conference impressed political observers that the Socialist leadership had undergone a Bad Godesberg experience. They were now convinced that the Socialists would no longer use the nationalized industries to save jobs, that the rules of the marketplace would reign supreme in Socialist economic decision making, that statism would give way to realism in policy matters.[40] The appointment of Laurent Fabius as prime minister in July 1984 would merely confirm this new attitude. Yet, Mitterrand's claim that this policy did not differ from previous policy was closer to the truth than the insights of political journalists. Rigor had been the order of the day since 1981. Modernization was merely another form of rigor, one in which the emphasis was placed on competitiveness, but not without considerable attention paid to the issue of solidarity. Laurent Fabius, as super minister of industrial redeployment, emerged as the most prominent advocate of modernization through solidarity. On top of the numerous plans for industrial redevelopment in the *pôles de conversion* and retraining programs for redundant workers, Fabius added a special proviso for Lorraine: any new jobs created in Lorraine would be exonerated from the payment of social charges for a three-year period, a concession that equaled a staggering 50,000 franc subsidy per job.[41]

Such concessions led some to think that the government was engaged in costly appeasement of the steelworkers on the eve of their 13 April Paris demonstration.[42] Whether one calls it appeasement or solidarity, the effect was the same: the April challenge to the government's policies faded fast. Only 40,000 demonstrators showed up on 13 April. No further strikes of any consequence occurred. The Socialists forced the Communists to vote for a motion of confidence in the government on 20 April after Pierre Mauroy had outlined clearly the policy of rigor and modernization. Because the vast majority of Communist voters still supported the union of the left, the PCF feared that it would lose what little electoral support it still had if it deserted the government. But, these Socialist victories provided little consolation for the rank and file. With unemployment rising in early 1984, the government's popularity plummeted. In a SOFRES poll taken at the height of the steel controversy, between 13 and 18 April, only 26 percent responded that the left could do a better job of handling the nation's affairs than the right could. On who could best deal with the major issues facing the nation, including the issue of who could best defend liberties, the right was perceived as more capable than the left on all but the maintenance of social security benefits.[43]

Despite these ominous signs of disaffection from his government's policies—or possibly because of them—on 10 May François Mitterrand told an interviewer from the left-wing journal *Libération* that the left would emerge from this time of troubles with the reputation of being a party of government, thought of by the electorate as able to resolve the nation's economic problems as well as to implement social justice. Instead of gaining power only on rare occasions, the left would be seen, in the future, as "the permanent guarantee of good government for the nation." Over and over again, Mitterrand referred to his policies as a "third way" between economic liberalism and collectivism. The right, he claimed, wanted production but not redistribution of goods, whereas the left harped on redistribution but neglected production totally. His government, in contrast to these opposed positions, held both production and redistribution to be important. The "économie mixte" was the key to Socialist policy.[44]

Mitterrand's optimism seemed misplaced in the context of May 1984. While the issue of economic modernization seriously divided the left and sapped the popularity of the president's government, the problems surrounding reform of the private-school system posed a potentially greater threat to political stability. With the left bickering over what reform should entail and the right united in opposition to the Savary Law on private education, the Socialist government found itself faced with massive demonstrations against that law and repeated accusations that the law aimed at eliminating freedom of education. What had begun in 1983 as an attempt to appease the party militants, who were upset over the Delors plan and economic modernization, turned into a major revival of the long-standing conflict between the lay republic and the Church, the free-thinking left and the *bien pensant* right.

Yet, there was more to this issue than the rehashing of archaic positions. Educational policy was a central aspect of Socialist ideology. The way to *autogestion* and true socialism was through proper education. Almost half of the Socialist deputies elected in 1981 were educators, mainly professors at the secondary level. Their unions, like the industrial unions, expected the implementation of Socialist policies that would reinforce their values, corporate interests, and security. They formed a crucial bloc of support for the Socialist party, more crucial in some respects than the industrial unions, whose relationship to the party had always been tangential and circumspect. Therefore, the Socialist government elected in 1981 had the dual and somewhat contradictory objectives of implementing socialist educational reforms and protecting the vested interests of its supporters in the system. The question was, would one or the other prevail, or would some sort of compromise emerge between the two?[45]

To oversee this potentially contentious area, François Mitterrand appointed Alain Savary minister of education. This was a peculiar, but potentially brilliant selection. Savary knew virtually nothing about the educational system, but he was a compromiser by nature, bordering on procrastination, extremely cautious and unwilling to act until all the issues had been resolved. Furthermore, Savary could unite virtually all factions within the party. He had become a member of the PSU after breaking with Mollet over the Algerian conflict, but had later patched over relations with the old SFIO leader to emerge as the first secretary of the Parti socialiste in 1969, only to lose that post in 1971 to François Mitterrand. Close to Pierre Mauroy in the party, Savary was more of a social democrat than anything else. At any rate, when he became minister in May 1981, he faithfully took his mission from the 1977 Socialist declaration on education, which called for the abolition of inequalities in the system, increased emphasis on professional training and adult education, decentralization, more contact with those outside of the system, more emphasis on research in the universities, and, finally, the creation of "a public, unitary, and secular National Educational service, integrating by negotiated stages the private establishments that receive public funds."[46]

For the most part, Savary carried out the Socialist program without encountering overwhelming difficulties and with some modest successes. To combat inequalities, he established the "zones d'éducation prioritaire" in 1981 in those areas that were defined as deprived, according to "social, economic, and cultural criteria." These ZEPs were provided with extra funding to carry out educational projects that the schools and outside parties, such as local officials and parents, agreed were beneficial and necessary.[47] To modernize the educational system, especially professional education, Savary inagurated a plan to put a hundred thousand computers in the classrooms by 1988 and he allocated extra funds to aid the technical and professional lycées to purchase modern equipment to train young people in new, high technology jobs.[48]

But these, and other, quiet successes were often overshadowed by the contentious issues that aroused corporatist educational interest groups to protest. For example, when the minister of education's commissioned reports on the *collèges* and the *lycées* appeared, with criticisms of the teaching profession and its pedagogical methods, recommending some radical changes to prepare students better for the new industrial age, the teachers' unions protested vigorously that the government was trying to make reforms solely at the expense of the professors. Nor was the professoriat very enthusiastic about the limited government plans to decentralize the educational system. Many feared that decentralization would lead to more interference by local authorities, parents, and outside interest groups in their affairs. In reflecting on his years as minister of education, Savary told Mona Ozouf that one of the greatest difficulties he faced was that of convincing teachers and their unions that they would have to work in an atmosphere of decentralization and autonomy in the future. The vast majority of teachers opposed any sort of democratization of the educational system.[49] Most had become so accustomed to taking directions from the centralized state that they feared any increase in their own responsibilities. They preferred their special corporatist niche above any change that could potentially place their privileges at risk or increase their duties.

Increasingly, the teaching profession became suspicious of Socialist aims. Modernization and democratization seemed to take precedence in Savary's office over the special interests of the professors. Only at the university level did the Socialists adhere to some of the special pleas of the profession. In reaction to the hotly contested university reforms that the Giscard administration had carried out to increase the powers of the full professors at the expense of the lower ranks and the students, the Socialist government proceeded to reverse totally that situation, providing the bulk of the power in university governance to the lower ranks and the students, even granting tenure rights to all assistant professors. These radical changes, which were coupled with attempts to make university education more professional—that is, more relevant and more democratic—shocked the professorial elite into a massive outburst of letter writing to Le Monde and other journals. When, in the fall of 1983, Savary issued new rules that required professors to teach four hours a week over a thirty-two-week period, in contrast to the old system of three hours a week over a twenty-five-week period, and applied these rules to every rank equally, thus decreasing significantly the work load of assistants and master assistants, the professoriat threatened to strike, claiming that research would suffer as a result of these egalitarian policies. Although no strike occurred, the old guard did obtain one significant victory in this battle of opposing corporatist interests: in January 1984, the Constitutional Council struck down the governance provisions of Savary's law on university education, arguing that only the professors had the right to make final decisions on matters related to research and pedagogy.[50]

For a government of teachers, the educational record by 1984 was not spectacular. Elitism tended to prevail over egalitarianism, archaic notions of pedagogy tended to overshadow efforts at modernization, and corporatist interests took precedence over the general interest. The Grandes Ecoles, which clearly represented elitism, archaic pedagogy, and corporatist interests, were hardly touched by the Socialist reformers, who followed the Communist secretary of state for the civil service, Anicet Le Pors, in opening up admissions to disadvantaged groups, such as trade union leaders, in what posed for egalitarianism but actually represented blatant corporatism and the reinforcement of the elitist, archaic values that these institutions stood for. But not all of these failings could be attributed to the government. In many cases, the minister of education tried to implement reform only to be rebuffed by Socialist unions and educators. By 1984, as a consequence, the government found itself in an awkward position: its key supporters, the backbenchers in the National Assembly and the scores of militant educators in the trenches, began to doubt whether François Mitterrand, Pierre Mauroy, and company were willing or able to implement the party's program. To gain back the confidence of these "républicains jusqu' à la tripe" and "amateurs conviviaux de cassoulet radical et de fanfares SFIO" the reform of private education was moved to the top of the list of government priorities.[51]

The question of the relationship between private and public education was extremely complex and difficult to untangle. Since 1959, the situation had been complicated by the Debré law, which aimed at long-term integration of the two systems. Through that law, two types of contractual relationships were created between private schools and the state. The first, known as the *contrat simple*, gave the private schools great leeway to do what they wanted, but with the understanding that they would come under the second form of contract, the *contrat d'association*, within nine years. The *contrat d'association*, which was widely accepted at the secondary level, allowed the state to examine educational facilities and play a role in the appointment of the teaching corps in return for monetary aid. But private primary schools refused to accept this second form of contract, which they feared would greatly inhibit their freedom. In 1977, the Giscard government passed the Guermeur law in response to this fear. That law changed the *contrat d'association* to place final authority for hiring teachers in the hands of the *chef d'établissement*, who was often a representative of the Church, since most private schools were run by Catholic religious organizations. The law also required that all communes pay the operating expenses of schools that accepted the *contrat d'association* and it made the employment of teachers contingent upon their acceptance and adherence to the *caractère propre* of the school, or the mission of it as defined by the *chef d'établissement*. In short, the 1977 law made it relatively easy for primary schools to accept this second form of contract and enraged the advocates of secular education by granting potentially extensive powers to the Church while relegating the state to the role of treasurer for the private schools.[52]

Alain Savary's job, therefore, was to work out a system that would bring these schools under state control without endangering freedom of education. At least that is what Savary thought his job was, especially since François Mitterrand had insisted that the Socialists would not impose a solution on the private schools but would work in concert with them to reach a compromise agreement. Others, however, had different opinions. The most radical advocates of secular education wanted no compromise whatsoever with the "enemy." The Comité national d'action laïque (CNAL) believed in the slogan "For public schools, public funds, for private schools, private funds." It wanted total state control of private education. The same was true of the Free Masons and the far left Fédération des conseils de parents d'élèves des écoles publiques. As a consequence, when Savary compromised with the Church on the bill, these secular organizations condemned him as a traitor or worse.[53]

After numerous consultations between the minister of education and the private-school leaders, a bill was finally worked out that both sides could reluctantly agree upon. The main obstacle to an agreement had been the demand that all private-school teachers become state functionaries, with all the rights and responsibilities that teachers had in the public school system. In effect, titularization, as this process was called, would bring a large part of private pedagogy under state influence and undermine the powers of the head of the establishment to discipline his staff. In April 1984, a compromise was finally reached on this point. According to it, the Catholic educators agreed to accept titularization of all teachers in a private school, if 50 percent voted for it, in return for the state's recognition of the *caractère propre* of Catholic schools and guaranteed public financing of them.[54] But, almost as soon as the agreement had been reached, both the far right and the far left protested vigorously. When the archbishop of Paris, Cardinal Lustiger, expressed support for the amended bill, Bernard Pons and Claude Labbé of the RPR condemned him as a traitor to the cause of private education. Lustiger stuck to his conciliatory position despite these and other protests until the militants in the Socialist party gained the support of Pierre Mauroy to amend the Savary bill. Those amendments made the bill into a provisional act, with the clear implication that the left would settle this matter once and for all at a later date; declared that private schools would have to accept titularization after eight years or lose state financing; and reinforced the restrictions on founding private maternal schools.[55]

The vast majority of the French reacted negatively to these Socialist caveats. It seemed as though the government intended to destroy private education for ideological reasons and in the process destroy liberty. Polls clearly indicated that the French were not opposed to private education. Quite the opposite was the case: a plural educational system, most thought, was far better than a single, public, secular one. In the case of the ammended Savary law, it seemed that freedom of education was being attacked by the left, not some privileged position or anomaly outside of the law, as the militants in the party proclaimed. Yet, the electorate wanted some sort of reform of private education. For example, when asked whether they favored titularization of private-school teachers, a majority of 65 percent responded positively, as did an even larger majority of 68 percent to the question of whether private schools should be subjected to the same obligations as public schools.[56]

Be that as it may, the Socialists had chosen confrontation over compromise, providing the right with a second major issue to use in the European elections during June 1984. Liberty became as important as economic decline in the attempt to discredit the government completely. The right hoped that a massive defeat for the left would translate into a loss of legitimacy that might bring down the government. Certainly, at no other time during the Mitterrand presidency were the Socialists so vulnerable as they were in June and July 1984. Although the possibility of a coup or even an early legislative or presidential election was not great, the government did run the risk of losing de facto control of the nation if it failed to respond effectively to the increasingly more vehement and believable accusations that the right leveled against it. With both Mitterrand and Mauroy at the nadir of their popularity, the situation looked bleak.

While Fabius's economic restructuring plans and the contentious Savary law created overwhelming difficulties for the government, the European elections provided incontestable proof that the government had lost the support of the nation. Although the Socialists argued that the June elections were not related to French domestic politics but rather to European matters, the election campaign concentrated almost exclusively on the record of the left in power.[57] From the beginning, the left had a difficult time putting its case across. The two leftist parties decided not to run on one united ticket, in contrast to the RPR and the UDF, which combined their slates under the leadership of Simone Veil. Not only were the Socialists attacked by the rightist parties, but they also encountered Communist opposition. Simone Veil gained the offensive very early in the campaign and never relinquished it. In opening up the June television phase of campaigning, she emphasized the motto "Europe, union, liberties," adding that the right would be the "protector against the most unfortunate consequences of socialism." She continued: "For three years, demagogy, incoherence, the incompetence of our government has weakened France and compromised our future." Socialism, she claimed, led to "less work, less security, less liberty."[58]

Lionel Jospin, who led the Socialist electoral campaign, found himself in the awkward position of responding to accusations from the right, without being able to offer any new Socialist policies. In replying to Simone Veil's telling attack, Jospin projected his own dilemma on the right's campaign: "Mme Veil has no concrete propositions to offer on unemployment, industry, social problems, and the problems of security. She rehashes the grand theme of caricature: she strains to utilize totally, for her advantage, a demagogic discourse founded on the difficulties that the nation is undergoing, stirring up discontent."[59] The only issue that Jospin was able to use effectively in the campaign was that of right-wing extremism. He tore apart the united list of the right, pointing out that extreme rightist candidates had been selected in order to attract votes from the National Front, and he attacked the right for playing upon the fears of the French by linking the immigrant population with crime and nurturing xenophobic attitudes among the populace.[60] However, Jospin's critique was easily countered by references to Socialist policies on the press and education. In short, the right had the upper hand on virtually all of the issues.

As expected, the results of the European elections were disastrous for the left. The right gained 57.6 percent of the votes cast as opposed to 35.7 percent for the left. Never before in the history of the Fifth Republic had there been such a gap between the two in an election. In part, the left could blame abstentions for its difficulties: the June election witnessed the lowest turnout of any French election, 56.7 percent. The highest abstention rate came from those who had supported François Mitterrand in 1981: only 59 percent of them voted in 1984, compared with 73 percent of Giscard's backers. In addition, 19 percent of the president's 1981 electorate deserted the left to vote for the rightist camp in the European elections. The Communists were clearly the biggest losers, gaining slightly over 11 percent of the vote. Not since 1932 had the party performed so poorly in a national election. Except for the possible consolation of seeing their rivals on the left discredited, the Socialists gained no solace from these results. With only about 21 percent of the vote, the Socialists saw their dreams of hegemony disappear. The right regained virtually everything it had lost in 1981, including all of the departments in traditional rightist centers and almost all of the various social groups that had deserted to the Socialists.[61]

Clearly the most startling development in the June elections was the success of the extreme rightist National Front party, led by Jean-Marie Le Pen, which gained slightly more than 11 percent of the vote, coming in fourth just behind the Communists. Le Pen's anti-immigrant, openly racist, and xenophobic party had never before gained more than 1 percent of the vote in national elections. Now, in June, it was propelled to a major position in French politics, the first time that an extreme rightist party had gained such visibility since Poujadism swept France in the 1950s.[62]

Inevitably, this unnerving development raised more questions than answers. Why did the National Front emerge from obscurity to challenge the Communist party as the third major political force in the nation? Who had created Le Pen? Was the June victory a fluke or a new reality that French politics would have to live with in the future? To many political activists, the Le Pen phenomenon was simply a reflection of Socialist failure or rightist demagogy. But the evidence indicates that it was a bit of both. Clearly, the Socialists had failed to solve the problem of unemployment, which had been the key issue in the 1981 election campaign. This failure left the radical supporters of Chirac, who had voted for Mitterrand, with a sense of total frustration: where could they turn to if the left and the traditional right had both failed them? At the same time, the government's policy toward immigrants was filled with contradictions, at times seeming to favor immigrant groups, at other times clamping down severely on illegal immigrants and criminal elements. The traditional right, especially Jacques Chirac and the RPR, attempted to take advantage of this ambiguity in Socialist policy by appealing to anti-immigrant sentiments. As mayor of Paris, Chirac established stringent rules for immigrants who used municipal social services and employed police powers to keep close tabs on immigrant populations. In the September 1983 municipal election in Dreux, Chirac's RPR even united with the National Front to gain votes and later form a government. To these developments, the Socialists responded with righteous indignation, while beefing up the police to control the immigrant population and supporting an industrial policy that adversely affected immigrants most of all, especially in the automobile industry, but also in the building industry. Yet, despite government attempts to make the streets secure, to provide a massive safety net for French workers who were made redundant, and to soften the blows of unemployment by dismissing immigrants first, if possible, a small but significant section of the French electorate came to the conclusion that the system had betrayed them, creating insecurity and unemployment for the French while catering to every whim of the immigrant population. Although French public opinion concerning immigrants had not changed at all since 1977, with a steady 61 percent claiming then and in 1984 that there were too many of them in France, the perception of a part of the electorate had changed because of political and economic events that had led them to the conclusion that a new type of political action was needed to solve *their* problems. In that sense, the success of Le Pen in June 1984 was directly related to the failure of Socialist economic policies and the broader failure of the traditional political system.[63]

An analysis of the National Front's supporters tends to confirm that they were not particularly "fascistic" or closely tied to the extreme right, but instead came from the ranks of the *déçus*, whether of Socialism or the RPR. For example, 24 percent of them had voted for François Mitterrand on the first round of the 1981 presidential election, while 27 percent had supported Jacques Chirac and 19 percent had not voted, for whatever reason. On the second round, 29 percent had voted for Mitterrand, which was substantially higher than the 10 percent of the rightist electorate that had switched to the Socialist candidate. In turn, 11 percent of them had previously supported leftist parties and one-third were former RPR voters. Their political attitudes differed considerably from those of the old extreme right as well as from the traditional right. On the issue of abortion, 53 percent approved, which was higher than the national norm of 49 percent and well above the approval level in the traditional rightist parties (40 percent in the RPR, 34 percent in the UDF), while in regard to the old rightist triumvirate of *famille, travail, religion* only 35 percent gave it a high priority versus 47 percent of the RPR-UDF electorate. However, National Front supporters favored more extreme responses to political problems: 27 percent approved of scrapping legality in the effort to defeat the left, as compared with 8 percent and 10 percent respectively for the RPR and the UDF, and 88 percent favored the restoration of the death penalty (versus 71 percent and 61 percent). They were also more skeptical of politicians (72 percent versus 57 percent and 54 percent) and more authoritarian in the home (62 percent versus 54 percent and 49 percent). Overwhelmingly, their vote was a vote against the Socialists: 70 percent claimed that they voted for Le Pen to protest the left's policies. In addition, National Front supporters tended to be concentrated in urban areas, especially in cities with populations of more than a hundred thousand, in which immigrant communities comprised more than 10 percent of the total. In those cities, Le Pen received slightly less than 17 percent of the vote, which was well above his 11 percent national average. Finally, the Front received its highest vote percentage in the cities of the Midi, where high unemployment, large numbers of recent immigrants, and a major *pied noir* population seemed to contribute to its success: in Marseille the vote for Le Pen totaled 21.42 percent; in Perpignan it was 21.52 percent. But this phenomenon should not lead us to neglect the fact that the Parisian basin and other northern urban areas were also major centers of far-right support. In the departments of Seine-Saint-Denis, Val-d'Oise, Yvelines, Hauts-de-Seine, Seine et Marne, and the Val-de-Marne, all of which surrounded Paris, the National Front received at least 14 percent of the vote, with Seine-Saint-Denis leading the list with 15.98 percent.[64]

Yet, despite evidence that the rank and file of National Front voters were probably the *déçus* of the failed policies of both the left and the right, the rhetoric employed by the leader of the party, Jean-Marie Le Pen, appealed to openly racist sentiments. To cite just a few of an almost infinite number of examples: "If this [immigration] continues, France will be submerged by the flood of these immigrants who wish to reduce us to slavery and who consider themselves with pride as the bridgehead of the Islamic-Arab revival." Or, regarding immigrant rights: "Would you recognize any rights for someone who pushed down your door, installed himself in your chair, drank your whiskey and, after having told you to go sleep elsewhere, said to you: 'You know that your wife interests me?'"[65] Or, finally, on immigrants as a "sixth column": "As soon as a word of order comes form abroad (. . .), as soon as Muslim integralism or revolutionary Islam declares war on us for one reason or another, the voluntarily constituted immigrant ghettos will turn against us."[66]

In making these comments, Le Pen reflected the rise of a new mood in France by 1984, a mood that had been either consciously or unconciously abetted by respectable journals and newspapers, which increasingly engaged in analyses of the anti-immigrant mentality, sometimes publishing articles that seemed to justify racism. For example, in early 1984 the nation's most respectable newspaper, *Le Monde*, published an article that commented on polling data that 58 percent of the French believed too many foreigners and naturalized citizens lived in France, that 18 percent thought the immigrants were trying to destabilize the country, and that 17 percent maintained one could not become French by being naturalized. The article tried to explain why these attitudes currently prevailed, arguing that the new wave of immigrants was different from previous ones, since they were heavily concentrated in a few occupations and geographical areas, rather than spread throughout the nation; that the new immigrants belonged to a culture and a religion that was quite alien to most French people, and increasingly so in light of events in Iran and Lebanon; and that most of the new arrivals did not attempt to become integrated into French society as previous groups had done, but rather tried to maintain their cultural identity. An intellectually plausible argument, but totally inaccurate based on the historical record: all immigrant groups in France had committed the sins of "concentration," cultural aloofness, and separatism, but they had not been so easily identifiable as the North Africans were, nor had they been associated with a bloody anti-imperialist war, as the Algerians had been, the most hated of all immigrant groups in France. But the most unfortunate error in this argument was the most believable part of it: far from being an alien religion or an alien culture, Islam was the second major religion of the *French* population, a religion that the French supposedly knew nothing about only because they chose not to, even after hundreds of years of intimate relations between France and the Islamic world.[67]

Whatever the nature of the Le Pen vote, the June European election results sent a clear message to the government that its policies had been rejected by a significant majority of the electorate. The initiative in political debate clearly moved to the right. One week after the left's European election disaster, on 24 June, the largest demonstration in the history of the Fifth Republic occurred in Paris, where 1 million concerned parents, schoolchildren, and their supporters marched all day in protest against the Savary law. The demonstration had been planned shortly after the Socialists amended the law in May, undermining the fragile compromise that Mauroy and the Church had worked out. The largest private school organization, the Union nationale des associations de parents d'élèves de l'enseignement libre (UNAPEL), which counted 800,000 families as members, switched from supporting passage of the law to outright condemnation. UNAPEL's leader felt betrayed by the Mauroy government, as did the archbishop of Paris, Cardinal Lustiger. In an interview with *Le Monde* in early June, the archbishop expressed his outrage that Mauroy had reneged on promises that he had made to the private-school leaders, allowing the passage of a law that threatened the existence of the private-school system. Lustiger and the UNAPEL leaders insisted that they were moderates who had been driven to public protests by government deception and the threat to freedom of education that this law entailed. They did not want their protests to be read as a political statement for the right, but rather as a universal appeal to the principle of liberty, led by the parents of the children in private schools rather than by political groups. To assure that this would be the case, no politicians were allowed to speak at the 24 June demonstration and the Church hierarchy did not participate in the march.[68]

While the Church and the private-education movement painted a convincing picture of government duplicity and clerical moderation in pursuit of freedom of education, Pierre Mauroy countered with crude attempts to depict the demonstrators as far-right pro-Vichy goons who opposed liberties for immigrants and other underprivileged groups.[69] But few believed him. The prime minister seemed incapable of understanding the broad support for private education in France or the degree to which the government had become identified, rightly or wrongly, with liberticide. Interviewed on Radio Monte-Carlo on 24 June, he expressed amazement that the issue of liberty of teaching had been raised in the debate over the Savary law, pointing out that the Socialists had never challenged the principle of freedom of education and adding his opinion that a rightist press, "dominated by money," had been responsible for the distortions surrounding the debate. At no point during that interview, which occurred on the same day as the massive Paris march, did Mauroy respond to the charge that he had broken his word by amending the law to satisfy the advocates of secular state education. Nor did he explain how the rightist press could have mobilized the largest demonstration since World War II or why more than half of the French population supported the demonstrators.[70]

In the aftermath of electoral defeat and antigovernment demonstrations, with the Communists openly condemning Socialist policies for the debacle of the left, the right began challenging the legitimacy of the Socialist government to rule France. The new mood was well expressed by an editorial in *L'Express* on 29 June 1984. Yves Cuau, in analyzing the election, foresaw two "long and difficult" years ahead before the legislative elections. Distorting history to serve his purposes, Cuau argued that the Socialists lacked the heroic grandeur of a De Gaulle, who would have called for a referendum in order to clarify his legitimacy if he had found himself in such difficult circumstances. Directly challenging François Mitterrand, Cuau claimed that the president was now totally stymied by the popular will, that his 1981 mandate was worth almost nothing, and that his legitimacy had been called into question to the point where he must do something dramatic to restore it.

Echoing Cuau's position, the opposition began stepping up its demands for the dissolution of the National Assembly. While that gambit was hardly original or promising, some members of the right pushed the bizarre argument that the left's majority in the National Assembly could no longer claim sovereign power because it had lost the European elections. Sovereignty had passed to the Senate, they reasoned, where the two major victorious rightist parties controlled two-thirds of the seats, which reflected the true will of the nation, in contrast to the lower assembly's discredited mandate. Giscard d'Estaing had given credence to this new constitutional position at an earlier date when he claimed that the right should only accept those Socialist laws that had also passed in Senate. Now, in early July, the Senate acted on this new theory by passing a motion for a national referendum on private education, claiming that this reflected the will of the electorate. At the same time, leading right-wing politicians stepped up their rhetorical attacks on the left. Bernard Pons, one of the RPR leaders, claimed that the nation was in a "revolutionary situation." Jacques Chirac informed the RPR central committee that the government "no longer had the confidence of the people," while the dynamic young UDF leader, François Léotard, informed the nation that Mitterrand must "consult the French" if he wanted to get out of the "political impasse" that he found himself in. By the second week in July the combination of demands for a referendum on the Savary law, calls for new elections to the National Assembly, and the deposition of a censure motion against the government for another of its supposed affronts to liberty—a press law to limit monopolies—created the impression of a major crisis. François Mitterrand had to act decisively to restore his government's credibility, especially since Pierre Mauroy did not comprehend that the issue of liberty was a real issue that the left had to address and not something that the right-wing press had manufactured.[71]

On 12 July, after floundering around for some time, François Mitterrand struck, in a manner that the right had not expected. He accepted much of the right's advice, oddly enough, as he called for a referendum on the issue of public liberties. But he did not call for the referendum that the right had wanted. Arguing, correctly, that the constitution did not allow referendums on issues of public liberty, but only on the institutions of the state, Mitterrand called for a referendum on the referendum—in other words, a referendum that would determine whether the French wanted to change the constitution to allow referendums to be held on such issues as private education. At the same time, he withdrew the Savary law, promising to offer a new bill soon.[72]

Mitterrand's coup totally reversed the political situation: from being on the defensive, the president now emerged as the great protector of public liberty, against a Senate that was suddenly very skeptical of allowing him to define the terms of the referendum in such a way that a "yes" vote in favor of a constitutional change to allow referendums on liberty would reinforce the left's power and not the right's. Now, the opposition found itself in the odd position of opposing a referendum on liberty only days after it had made loud, constitutional appeals based on faulty reasoning, erroneous historical information, and political greed. Mitterrand, not the right, emerged as the defender and most accurate interpreter of the Fifth Republic's constitution. If the Senate opposed him and continued to support its faulty notion that a referendum could be held on the issue of liberty, it ran the certain risk of a smashing reversal of its position by the Constitutional Council, which would undoubtedly rule in favor of the president's interpretation of the constitution.

The brilliance of Mitterrand's political maneuver against the Senate, stymieing overnight the opposition's bold rhetoric about the sovereignty of the upper house and threats to public liberties, was almost overshadowed by the resignation of Pierre Mauroy and the appointment of a new government only a few days later. The two events were closely interconnected and probably thought out in advance by the president. Certainly, François Mitterrand was aware that Pierre Mauroy had fought hard for the passage of the Savary bill. This had been one of his government's key priorities since the Bourg-en-Bresse congress in the fall of 1983. Now, the president withdrew the Savary law, discrediting both Savary and Mauroy, not to mention the scores of militants who had fought so hard for secular education. All illusions were smashed. The left had not only succumbed to modernization, with the Delors and Fabius plans of 1983 and 1984, but also it had now given up its deeply felt, archaic commitment to the lay, secular republic that Savary represented. The elevation of Laurent Fabius to the post of prime minister, replacing the *bon enfant* man of the North, Pierre Mauroy, marked the end of the SFIO, of archaic Socialism, and of all the old ideologies, and the real beginning of social democracy in France. For that reason, more than any other, the Communist party departed from the government in July: the union of the left was officially over with the appointment of the Fabius government. François Mitterrand had slain the dragon by embracing it and he had transformed the Socialist party by showing it that the old archaicisms no longer worked in the modern world. He chose exactly the right time to make his move: at the precise moment that the legitimacy of the left came under severe attack, Mitterrand restored that legitimacy by addressing the criticisms that the right posed. By August, the government could get on with its business, untouched by the challenge from the right, prepared to create a new French socialism that could withstand the challenge of 1986.[73]

4

Changing Ideological Contours:
The Critique of Socialism in Power

By the summer of 1984, after three years of continuous struggle, the Socialists had reached the nadir of their power, demoralized and on the defensive against a rising rightist tide. Since March 1983, when the policy of rigor was established as a state of affairs that would last until the end of hostilities, so to speak, Socialist morale had been kept up by constant references to the "durée" and the Bourg-en-Bresse decision to shift the party's focus to the issue of the secularization of the educational system. But now, in July 1984, the "durée" was rapidly slipping from the hands of the legislature, which had completed two-thirds of its term, and the archaic cause of merging private education with public had been torpedoed by François Mitterrand's astute political maneuvering. Nothing remained, it seemed, except the bleak prospect of modernization. The *relance* had failed, decentralization had fizzled, the economic situation looked bleak. In short, very little appeared to be working for the government.

Increasingly, as the mystery of what the Socialists would do in power became unveiled, the ideological contours of French politics had undergone a transformation. By the end of 1984, that transformation was more or less completed revealing a new environment of antisocialist criticism from every part of the ideological spectrum, from the Communists and the *deuxième gauche* to the new philosophers and the traditional political right. Although antisocialism was often the only common strand to these critiques, the general themes of liberty and antistatism infused all of them in some form or another, reflecting what most observers seemed to think was the most serious flaw of socialism in power, namely the tendency to emphasize the statist, Jacobin tradition as the vehicle for solving the nation's problems rather than the decentralist, Girondin tradition that the party had emphasized so heavily in the 1970s. *Autogestion* may have died in May 1981, before having a chance to be tested, but its death came back to haunt the Socialists by 1984, if not earlier. If nothing else, socialism in power had created the fragile foundations of a new political consensus in France around the theme of more liberty, less state. The problem arose in defining what liberty meant. But whatever it meant, by 1984 the right had captured the initiative by identifying itself closely with liberty, against a divided and confused left.

What the right meant by liberty and how the left responded to the general theme of liberty helped define the issue of *après-socialisme* in terms that were non-Marxist, if not anti-Marxist at times. The shift in ideological direction was definitely toward the right, as the realities of the "durée" made even convinced Communists into partial believers in libertarian ideas. But the most important shifts occurred within the ranks of the Parti socialiste and the traditional right. To understand what this renewed theme of liberty entailed, we shall first outline the changes that occurred on the right, which initiated the theme, and then observe how others responded to the new ideological environment. We shall rely primarily upon a number of leading polemical and ideological works in our quest for the contours of *après-socialisme*.

The victory of the Socialists in 1981 left the right seriously divided, pointing accusing fingers at one another in a simpleminded effort to determine guilt for the debacle. Giscard and the UDF blamed Chirac and the RPR for secretly desiring a Socialist victory, while the Gaullist right countered that the president had lost because of his lackluster record in office. Although this family squabble did not prevent the right from attacking the Socialist government's program, it did create the image that the right had no constructive, consensual policies to offer the nation. By March 1983, however, with the victory of the right in the municipal elections, the third devaluation of the franc, and the continuation of the policy of rigor, the right began to put some of the pieces of a policy together, based partly on the negative experience of socialism, as seen from its perspective, and partly on the foreign models of Reaganism and Thatcherism, which seemed to provide external evidence for the theme of liberty. In moving toward this ideological position, however, the right found itself involved in scrapping its own Gaullist, statist tradition, which aroused some doubts in its ranks about the degree to which liberty should be permitted free reign. In the end, the more extreme aspects of the libertarian, Anglo-Saxon variety were toned down for a responsible form of liberalism, tempered by various aspects of egalitarianism and statism, in the French tradition.

Not until 1984 did the right put all of the pieces of a renewed liberal program together, but in 1983 at least three important tentative steps were taken to begin the process of rethinking. Alain Peyrefitte, the former minister of justice under Giscard, offered the first sustained analysis by a major political figure, while two works by rightist

intellectuals, one from an RPR perspective and another from a radical
libertarian point of view, carried through the necessary criticism of the
right's past and pointed toward some revolutionary possibilities for the
future. The three, taken together, indicate both the confusion and the
new approches to politics that existed in rightist circles at this early point.

Alain Peyrefitte's work is the most political and polemical of the three.
It is also the least innovative and imaginative, rehashing many old themes
from the political wars of the Fifth Republic. Entitled *Quand la rose
se fanera . . . Du malentendu à l'espoir*, the book's thesis is transparent
from the beginning. The victory of the left was a misunderstanding,
Peyrefitte argued. Those who deserted Giscard to vote for Mitterrand
were not voting for the Common Program but rather were voting against
the incumbent. The same thing occurred in the legislative elections, as
the rightist electorate stayed home instead of voting for either side, giving
the Socialists a victory by default. In short, to Peyrefitte the left
possessed no mandate to govern for seven years and thus acted
illegitimately when it carried out nationalization of industries or other
radical proposals, of which the electorate had not approved. Almost
as soon as the left had emerged victorious, the rightist electors realized
their mistake; by the fall of 1981 everyone wanted another election,
which they partly obtained in the four legislative by-elections held in
January 1982, one of which Peyrefitte won. He interpreted the right's
sweep of these elections as an overwhelming victory of 300 to 130 on
a national basis. If any further proof were needed of the left's illegitimate
seizure of power, the January elections provided it, according to
Peyrefitte; another 1958 was clearly in the making if the Socialists
attempted to hang on to power.[1]

The essence of Peyrefitte's argument centered around the issue of
liberty. Everything the Socialists have done, he argued, violated the
principle of liberty. Nationalization, for example, had no real economic
function but did have political appeal to leftist militants, as it increased
their power and influence as well as the power of the state. Similarly,
decentralization was not intended to promote liberty and democracy
for the masses but instead aimed at entrenching the left in power and
increasing the authority of the bureaucracy by extending its grasp to
every level of government. Nor were the Socialist reforms of the media,
the schools, and the judicial system inspired by the principle of liberty:
in all three cases, Peyrefitte argued, liberty was undermined, as the
media was made to conform to Socialist agit-prop, the schools were
transformed into indoctrination centers to create new Socialist citizens,
and the judicial system was modified to increase insecurity among the
citizenry.[2] All of this was due to the nature of French socialism: it
tried to be all things to all people ("La cafetière impossible") by uniting

together humanists, ecologists, animal lovers, and other interest groups, and pursuing contradictory goals that aimed at liberating man while increasing the power of society, at achieving egalitarianism while maintaining social differentiation, at increasing democracy while enhancing the role of the state. Whether they know it or not, Peyrefitte claimed, the Socialists were the Trojan horse for the Communists. At every level, CERES and the Parti communiste française were infiltrating the state, preparing the day for the takeover of power. The Communists, who are masters of the "double jeu," will eventually gain the upper hand, despite Mitterrand's belief that he will succeed where others have failed.[3]

Peyrefitte's extended polemic did not end with a condemnation of the PCF. In outlining six scenarios for the future, he envisaged nothing but disaster for France unless Mitterrand and the Socialists accepted the "give in or resign" scenario that he claimed would win them the eternal gratitude of the French people. Beyond that possibility, Peyrefitte surmised that France had the choice between some variant of "popular democracy" Soviet-style and some form of massive upheaval, neither of which he thought desirable.[4] To Peyrefitte, socialism was simply a disease that had to be overcome: "Par le socialisme, le mal français connait un accès de fièvre—qui peut être mortel, mais dont nous pouvons aussi sortir guéris."[5]

What, then, needed to be done to spur on the healing process? Peyrefitte offered a cure based on political, economic, social, and cultural medicine. In the realm of politics he continued his polemic against the Socialist gulag by calling for an equilibrium between the state and the citizenry, a president who represented the nation and not a party state, a Senate that was equal to the Assembly in power, the extension of the referendum as a check on the state, security for all, and independence for France. His economic prescription included a strong dose of the marketplace: the franc had to be made strong again, the nation's enterprises had to be given more freedom in every area, the nationalized industries had to be privatized, taxes and state expenditures had to be reduced, and France had to accept its place in the international economic community. Similarly, social policy needed to reflect the principle of liberty, making workers into responsible members of their firm by extending stock ownership to them, undermining the powers of unions which did not represent the real interests of the workers, and paring down the welfare state to make people responsible for their own destinies through private welfare schemes. Finally, cultural policy must entail the freeing of all communications from state control, total freedom for parents to educate their children where they wished, the purification of the French language, a renewed emphasis on teaching national history, and the transformation of all immigrants into good French citizens or their expulsion from the nation.[6] Liberty and nationalism, it seems, went hand in hand against the subversive forces for equality and internationalism.

Peyrefitte's vision of Socialist France was not an isolated one. His views were echoed in various ways by the intellectual right in 1983. Michel Massenet, the editor of a series of studies brought together under the title *La France socialiste*, supported the general theme that liberty had been destroyed by the Socialists in their effort to carry out a "rupture" with capitalism. Massenet and other authors such as Annie Kriegel, painted a dismal picture of a France that had fallen under the iron curtain of Communist domination, with the gulag reigning supreme in every area from the economy to politics and culture. Or, as Jean Féricelli put the issue in his article, "Les logiques de l'Etat socialiste," either the Socialist state will move towards a neo-Stalinist model or it will become stationery. Féricelli gave considerable credence to the neo-Stalinist model over the stationary one: everything pointed in that direction, he believed.[7] In general, the thrust of these articles was to deny the legitimacy of Socialist rule by identifying socialism with totalitarianism, a juxtaposition that had become commonplace in France since the mid-1970s.

Not everyone who contributed to Massenet's work provided such a simple Manichean explanation of socialism in power. A number of authors saw the evils of socialism as nothing more than an extension of the misguided policies of the Giscard/Barre government. For example, Pierre Biacabe, in an article on "Les mésaventures du franc," viewed the Socialist problems with the franc as an extension of the previous government's failure to address the issue, although he maintained that Socialist policies needlessly exacerbated the situation. In turn, Roland Granier pointed out that unemployment was a long-term phenomenon that neither the right nor the left had addressed appropriately. Both had used gimmicks such as *contrats de solidarité*, early retirement, etc. rather than attacking the real causes of the problem.[8] However, even though these and other contributors were more realistic, less polemical in their approach to the nation's difficulties, they could all agree with Massenet, Kriegel. et al., that the solution to the nation's time of troubles was less state, more liberty. They concurred with Peyrefitte that the marketplace should have a much wider role to play in a post-Socialist France: denationalization, deregulation, debureaucratization, and dewelfarization ranked high among their priorities for the reestablishment of liberty.

Yet, neither one of these works confronted adequately the issue of the right's responsibility for the statist Fifth Republic. Both of them—

Massenet slightly less than Peyrefitte—created an implausible scenario of a libertarian right versus a statist left. In short, they failed to come to grips with the issue of their own complicity and they did not answer the question of why they had never paid much attention to the problem of statism and liberty until after the Socialist victory of 1981. Until such issues were faced head on, the right's arguments would appear self-serving.

In this context, the appearance of *De la reconquête*, by the appropriately named "Caton," provided the right with a dose of badly needed realism. Caton did not pull any punches: the right created the top-heavy state apparatus that caused the current *crise*, he maintained, and yet the right has claimed that it alone can solve these problems. Rather than facing reality, the right has engaged in sheer hysteria: after the victory of the left in 1981, Jean Cau, in *Paris-Match*, proclaimed that France had been "sodomized by the USSR and the despicable hordes from the Third World," concluding with the battle cry of "Jaurès, never! Blum, never!" If one were to believe Cau and his fellow right-wing journalists, Paris had been occupied by a foreign power, Caton observed, and the press had resorted to writing "*samizdats* that we pass to one another furtively in the metro." Yet all of these shrill analyses failed to recognize that the state that the Socialists "took over" was the state that the right had created and not some Leninist construction: continuity, not revolutionary change, marked the rise of the Socialists to power.[9]

To Caton, Giscard was the one who created the situation that the Socialists inherited. During his presidency the workers gained in buying power while the capital base of the nation eroded and the welfare state exploded to previously unknown heights. Giscard was the one who created massive unemployment benefits and restrictions on firing workers, not Mitterrand. It was Giscard who witnessed the massive increase in the indebtedness of industry and the surreptitious advance of nationalization. Unemployment and inflation increased steadily under Giscard and Barre, the "first economist of France." In fact, Caton argued, the Socialists were engaged in solving the problems that the right refused to face: under Socialist rule, inflation is being conquered, unemployment is being stabilized, and both private and nationalized industries are being rejuvenated.[10]

What, then, must the right do to regain the initiative over the Socialists? First, on the negative side of the ledger, it must quit accusing the left of implementing the gulag in France. Such claims were implausible at best and demagogic at worst, to the vast majority of the population. In a positive vein, Caton insisted, the right has to begin placing its primary emphasis on what the electorate wants, which is the "improvement of their well-being and an increase of their liberties."[11] This means that the right must "get rid of its statist, centralizing, Jacobin characteristics that prepared the way for the Socialists to come to power by helping make our nation into a society of welfare recipients, in the name of liberalism and advanced democracy. This right must disappear: we shall not waste tears over its burial. In our prayers, we call for a decentralized, libertarian right, which will be part of the lives of all citizens, at all levels of life, professional as well as social, daily and familial."[12] But Caton was not convinced that the right had the ability to make this leap. As the right becomes more and more like the old SFIO, incapable of adapting to new circumstances, the Socialist party has revealed an uncanny ability to achieve hegemony through pragmatic actions in every area, from the economy to culture. Whether the right can match this new socialism will depend on the rise of a new generation of right-wing politicians. To Caton, the best thing the old guard could do would be to abdicate power to the Young Turks in their midst, in order to fight the Socialists on equal terms.[13]

While these three works, and others like them, tentatively prepared the ground for the counterattack, not until 1984 did the opposition assume a dominant and confident position in regard to the government. The supposed success of the Reagan revolution came to the aid of the right. The new model could now be identified in real terms rather than in theoretical ones. However, even though some accepted the liberal revolution in the western world with no qualifications, most tempered their enthusiasm for Reaganism or Thatcherism with careful reservations, especially by 1985, when the legislative elections began to loom as a reality. This was particularly true among political figures, as opposed to intellectuals. As polls indicated overwhelming support for the welfare state, the traditional old-guard political leaders on the right began to move away from the more radical aspects of the liberal model.

The appearance of Guy Sorman's *La solution libérale* represented the most serious attempt to place the rightist revolution in an international context. Following on the heals of his popular journalistic account of the American conservative revolution that appeared in 1983, *La solution libérale* offered a panoramic vision of liberalism—that is, Reaganism or Thatcherism—spreading throughout the world in the course of the 1980s. To Sorman, the 1980s marked the age of liberalism after a forty-year period of statist domination in Western Europe. Even the left was aware of this, he claimed: such leftist journals as *Libération*, for example, openly expressed antistatist attitudes. The spirit of 1968 was essentially the spirit of liberalism. But, Sorman argued, true libralism must be sought in the works of Friedrich von Hayek and Milton

Friedman and not in the French political system. France must learn to emulate Great Britain and the United States if it is going to reap the benefits of this revolution.[14]

To begin with, Sorman maintained, liberalism in France must attack the cause of state tyranny, which is the budget process. The New Class of bureaucrats that have emerged in all western nations have a vested interest in increasing the power of the state. To counter their conspiracy, the liberals must introduce massive tax cuts to produce budget deficits that will trigger a call for a balanced-budget amendment to restrict the size of the state. To Sorman, the only purpose behind the expansion of the state was the perpetuation of the New Class. Guided by that sort of vision of the state, Sorman proceeded to argue that the ultimate aim of liberalism was the minimal state, one that provided "law, justice and order." Civil society should take the place of the state in virtually every area: the principles of contract, free enterprise, the free market, direct democracy, freedom of choice in educational matters, complete deregulation, total privatization, and social security under private provision were part of the liberal solution to tyranny. The economic success of Japan, the United States, and Great Britain in the past few years was the ultimate proof that liberalism worked. Unlike France, which had remained mired in a defensive, statist position, these three nations have benefited from deregulation of industry, increased competition, and more exposure to market forces.[15]

Sorman's solution to the nation's economic problems sounded very much like the classical laissez-faire prescription for such matters. But, he hastened to distinguish between what he called the old and the new liberalism:

Old liberalism was the absolute rule of the patron over a mass of undifferentiated workers, in an enterprise which belonged totally to its proprietors. New liberalism, on the contrary, is a collectivity of work, where each one participates and has recognized responsibilities. Old liberalism was economic competition taken to the point where anything that created obstacles to it was excluded, or the disposability of men and enterprises. New liberalism still involves competition, but competition between products, not between men.[16]

Whether Guy Sorman's distinctions between the two types of liberalism were accurate or real, the ideas that he expressed spread rapidly among the various groups, think tanks, and clubs that sprouted like mushrooms in 1984–85. One of these, Printemps 86, which was founded in August 1984, brought together a number of liberals from the private sector of the economy—no technocrats were included in their ranks—for the purpose of planning ways to overthrow the left after March 1986. To them, the state was the enemy; only civil society could bring the profound changes needed to get France back on its feet again. A rightist government in power after March 1986 would have to move immediately to abrogate all price controls, including the Quillot law on rent controls and the 1928 law that placed the petroleum industry under state regulation and control. It would also have to move quickly to end regulation of industry, to dismantle the welfare state, to do away with the minimum wage, to abolish unions in order to establish the principle of contract as the sole basis for relations between employers and employees, and to establish an independent commission to solve the debt crisis in an environment outside of political interest groups. Whether one calls this old or new liberalism, it marked a radical, revolutionary break from the past that represented the right-wing equivalent of the old Socialist saw of the "rupture" with capitalism.[17]

The attack on the Socialists returned repeatedly to the theme of their tyrannical, statist policies, as in Michel Prigent's *La liberté à refaire*, which brought together another group of essays by rightist intellectuals. Beginning with Prigent's preface, in which Mitterrand was depicted as a Leninist, and continuing on through Michel Massenet's postface, in which the nation was found to be in a "pretotalitarian system," the authors engaged in an unrelenting attack upon the "totalitarian" left. Once more, calls for dismantling the state and the creation of "true" democracy, in the form of referendums, popular initiatives, and direct control of politics, emerged from these libertarians. Once more, demands were made to privatize and decentralize the educational system, to make it more democratic and less under union control. Once more, denationalization and the privatization of the welfare state were viewed as urgent priorities. But the authors went further on some issues. Pierre Chaunu, for example, accused the left of pandering to immigrant groups that were "totalement inassimilables" and encouraging an antinatal policy that would eventually destroy the French family. François-Georges Dreyfus blithely demanded that all technical schools should be placed under the control of local businesses, which would determine what kind of education they should provide. Emil-Maria Claassen made a number of radical recommendations about the future of the welfare state, including the requirement that everyone attending university pay for their education because France had more university graduates than it could use and a proposal that everyone should be forced to arrange for their own retirement, without state help, except for the truly needy.[18]

Prigent's collection of essays went beyond a partisan rightist perspective to encompass a position of radical mistrust of the entire political system. In the conclusion to the second part of the book, the authors blamed the state for creating the French civil society that they were trying to reshape: "The result [of this civil society] is consequently not only general impoverishment, but also the creation and reinforcement of a *société bloquée*, that is to say a society which takes refuge in immobilism, afraid to modify a complex equilibrium of multiple privileges." The only answer to this situation was to allow the nonpolitical leaders to take over the job of implementing solutions to these complex problems. Politics, it seems, corrupts; the economists should rule in placing of the politicians. Even though the transition to liberalism will cause a few dislocations—you can't make an omelet without breaking some eggs, so to speak—the end justifies the entire process.[19] Similarly, Michel Massenet, in the postface to this volume, expressed profound distrust of the normal political process. No compromises with the present system can be permitted, he argued: "It is too late to 'reconcile' the plan and the market, nationalization and the spirit of enterprise, political hegemony and liberties. France refuses to work one out of every two days to pay taxes or social levies." But Massenet still feared that the next government might be in the tradition of "fausses alternances," as had been the case in Great Britain after 1951.[20]

The climax of this rightist intellectual renaissance occurred with the publication of Bertrand Jacquillat's book, *Désétatiser*, in 1985, which followed on the heels of Charles Millon's attack on the 1981–82 nationalizations and prepared the way for Jean Loyrette's practical guide on how to privatize state firms.[21] Professor Jacquillat was the quintessential representative of the new generation of right-wing intellectuals. At age forty-one, he had already reached the position of professor at the University of Paris-Dauphine and at the Ecole des Hautes Etudes Commerciales. His experience extended beyond France to the heart of liberal thought, the United States. He had taught at both Stanford and Berkeley and he had published extensively in American and English journals. Influenced heavily by both Hayek and Friedman, he acted as one of the main interpreters of their ideas to a French audience.[22]

Like Hayek and Friedman, Jacquillat viewed the state as the main obstacle to achieving freedom and economic progress. Beginning with the "principe de subsidarité," which stated that everything should be done at the most decentralized point possible in the hierarchy, Jacquillat argued that the state is the least efficient economic actor. Nationalized industries had not succeeded. On the contrary, they were prime examples of the inability of the state to intervene in the marketplace. Regulation of industry, in turn, had created inflexibility and heavy tax burdens that inhibited economic growth in France. In contrast, in the United States the combination of flexibility and low taxes had led to massive economic progress.[23] With those factors in mind, Jacquillat proceeded to call for the dismantling of the state apparatus.

First, he considered the area of denationalization and state economic policy. Using Great Britain as a model and relying greatly upon the ideas of the Adam Smith Institute in London, Jacquillat established one general rule regarding privatization of state enterprises: *"Only that which can not function or exist at all according to a mode of private exploitation, can and must function acording to a mode of public exploitation."*[24] On that basis, he proceeded to divide up enterprises to be denationalized according to a matrix of four categories: profitable societies in the competitive sector; unprofitable societies in the competitive sector; profitable societies in the noncompetitive sector; and unprofitable societies in the noncompetitive sector. The goal was to privatize immediately all enterprises in the first sector, which totaled sixteen, and to move all other firms into that category over time. This meant that firms in the unprofitable, noncompetitive sector, such as the SNCF, would eventually be made profitable and competitive to be sold by the state. The state's role would thus become that of the prime force in privatization. No longer would it attempt to implement industrial policy, which Jacquillat called the "fundamental sin, even the original sin." Jacquillat rejected the arguments for industrial policy that were used to justify the development of nuclear power and the aeronautical industry. He thought that these industries would have developed eventually through civil society, which would have made better use of the resources that the state had usurped in the name of the public good.[25]

With the ruthless logic of the marketplace Jacquillat extended his analysis to state regulation and social policy. In every case, he concluded that civil society functioned better than the state, whether it be in determining the minimum wage or the price of rentals or basic health care and educational facilities. Borrowing from his familiarity with the United States, Jacquillat called for "educational vouchers" to allow parents to choose freely the school they wanted their children to attend, advocated the use of Health Maintenance Organizations as the solution to increasing health costs and freedom of choice in medical matters, and proposed the privatization of pension plans as the proper response to the crisis in state expenditures for the aged.[26]

The final objective of Professor Jacquillat's reforms was the restoration of the maximum amount of liberty to the individual. This included the right of the individual to determine precisely what his or her tax money should be used for. As much as possible, taxes should be collected and used by local government, where individuals can see and control the process. But this individual freedom did not extend to the business firm: participatory decision making did not work in business, Jacquillat argued; only the Bourse should be allowed to determine the efficacy of a firm, not the individual workers and certainly not the state. The entire solution to France's problems resided in less state, more civil society. The proof of this, to Jacquillat, is that economic growth since 1945 had come solely from civil society and not from the state, which created obstacles to growth that prevented France from going beyond the level of "simple survival."[27]

Clearly such intellectual right-wingers as Massenet, Prigent, and Jacquillat had good reason to fear, as Massenet had argued, that their radical libertarian revolution might falter on the tricky shoals of the "alternance." Their plan was truly revolutionary. No politician could possibly win election on the basis of a program that aimed at dismantling the welfare state. Every major party endorsed—in fact, embraced—the Socialist acts that implemented the thirty-nine-hour week, five weeks of paid vacation, a higher minimum wage, improved old-age pensions, and retirement at age sixty. These *acquises sociales* could only be tampered with at the risk of encountering electoral oblivion. So therefore it is not surprising that the more realistic political figures who ventured an opinion an *après-socialisme* were less willing to espouse total laissez-faire. Freedom remained their ultimate objective, but freedom had to be tempered by the need for security.

Both Raymond Barre and Valéry Giscard d'Estaing took this cautious approach to the new liberalism. They found it much easier to espouse the goals of increased freedom of speech, education, and culture than those that embraced the total liberation of civil society from state control and regulation. They both believed that the state had played a major role in creating the prosperity that France had experienced since World War II, even though they now maintained that the state had overextended itself. They both hastened to make clear that such overextension did not apply to the welfare system, which they pledged to keep intact. Nor did they think that the state should denationalize everything it controlled. In certain areas, such as high technology, state intervention would remain crucial to the nation's effort to compete with other advanced economies. In short, Giscard and Barre may have gravitated toward more liberal ideas, but they also maintained a strong dose of pragmatism.[28]

Of the two, Raymond Barre was probably influenced the least by the new liberalism. Although he soundly condemned the Socialist program as bankrupt, attacking its decentralization policies for increasing bureaucratic control and its nationalization efforts for being more political than economic, he offered a very familiar Barrist analysis of the situation. Social justice, he argued, could only emerge from "economic growth and gains in productivity," and not from egalitarianism. But he reserved his major concern for the debts that the Socialists had accumulated: "Socialist policy has been financed by credit. The result is that France is indebted heavily in every area: the state, public enterprises, private enterprises, and externally. Neither individuals nor enterprises nor the government nor the nation can live durably on credit."[29] No new program emerged from this analysis. Instead, Barre offered the policies that he had pursued while in office: defense of the franc, a balanced budget, and lower taxes on business. Nor did he move toward the new right's liberalism: over and over, Barre reiterated that the state had to intervene to assure the "general interest" above particular interests. As he told François Furet in an interview in *Le Débat* in September 1983, he was not a neoliberal but rather a Tocquevillian—that is, someone who was concerned about the overextension of state power but not convinced that the destruction of the state was the best means to achieve liberty.[30] Raymond Barre's *Réflexions pour demain* reads more like reflections on the past. Except for a passing nod to the "new freedoms" in education and the media, for example, his vision remained fixed on technical economic issues.

In contrast, Giscard's perspective embraced the "new freedoms" with enthusiasm, although it included little of the neoliberal position on the economy. However, this perspective owed more to Giscard's perception of his *septennat* than to the ideas of the right-wing intelligentsia. Giscard believed that his election in 1974 represented a mandate for change, a mandate that he fulfilled until 1978 when the opponents of change gained the upper hand in rightist ranks. Since then, change had been thwarted. France became engaged in a struggle between the forces of renaissance and decadence, which must end with the triumph of the former. To Giscard, the renaissance involved the rebirth of Europe and France's place in it, the rebirth of liberty, and the rebirth of the spirit of enterprise. Aside from some vague references to a European defense, European sovereignty, and the election of a European president by universal suffrage, Giscard focused the bulk of his analysis on the rebirth of liberty, with passing mention of the spirit of enterprise. He pointed out that the French referred to two types of liberty, liberty from the encroachments of the state and laisser-faire. The second type had helped to discredit the idea of liberty among the French and consequently Giscard rejected it totally. Liberty must be tempered by solidarity, he claimed. The individual must be seen as part of society. In this context, Giscard spoke of "libéralisme conscient" or a "conscience sociale libérale."[31]

With that clear restriction on liberalism, Giscard outlined a radical program to promote pluralism in every area of French life. Pluralism, he argued, was the key to liberalism and the opposite of socialism. Pluralism could be partly guaranteed through such devices as total freedom for television and radio, but the key means of entrenching pluralism in France was through a careful separation and balancing of powers that would avoid the instability that existed under the Fifth Republic. To achieve this, Giscard enumerated a number of necessary political and constitutional reforms. First of all, the president should be divorced from day-to-day politics, which would become the preserve of the prime minister. Foreign affairs, defense, and matters of state would become the president's area of authority. He would be above parties and politics, acting as the representative of the nation. Power would be increasingly decentralized under this system. Citizens would be given extensive rights to use referendums to counterbalance government actions. The powers of such ministries as education, sports, culture, and agriculture would be placed in the hands of local officials. Economic liberty would also be extended, as enterprises would be freed from extensive regulations, taxes would be reduced, state spending would be carefully monitored, and planning would be eliminated. Solidarity and contractual negotiation would take the place of the state in a decentralized system that would bring workers, cadres, and entrepreneurs together for the achievement of common goals in the enterprise. Social cooperation would replace class struggle. The state would only intervene in extraordinary situations.[32]

The net result of the acceptance of liberalism, Giscard argued, would be the "Historical Reconciliation of the French," as he entitled chapter 12. This would be accomplished by making France into a nation of small-property owners through encouragement of home ownership, the privatization of nationalized industries, and other means. The "groupe centrale" would be the main support of this reconciliation. These were the two out of three French citizens to whom Giscard believed his program appealed. They were part of the new high-technology, computer generation that defined itself as much by its new mentality as by its economic position. With its rise to power, the rebirth of France will be achieved, with liberty the dominant motif, the class struggle relegated to oblivion, and the spirit of solidarity and cooperation supreme.[33]

The cautious neoliberal positions that Barre and Giscard outlined in their treatises were echoed by those who were close to Jacques Chirac in the published deliberations of the Club Participation et Progrès, which contained a short preface by the RPR leader. The authors spoke in great detail about possible models that the nation could follow. The recent economic policies of Japan, the United States, and the United Kingdom were all discussed in this context. Although the authors found something good about each one, they were very skeptical of applying any of these to the French economic system. A. Bonnafous attacked the problem realistically in an article entitled "L'expérience américaine est-elle transposable en France?" He pointed out that the American *relance* of 1983 could not be replicated in France for it depended upon massive foreign indebtedness, which France could never afford to incur. But he was more receptive to American policies on privatization and deregulation, which he thought would be generally beneficial to the French economy. And he praised the supply-side economists for revealing the perverse effect of high taxes on the economic system, although he did not believe that France could afford massive tax cuts because of its high public debt. In short, Bonnafous left only the barebones of Reaganism for the neoliberals to chew on.[34]

While the Club Participation et Progrès supported such neoliberal economic changes as privatization of nationalized industries, deregulation, and limited tax reform to encourage investment, its members said nothing about scrapping the welfare state. Taxes had to be limited to 40 percent of gross national product, they argued, while social security expenses had to be controlled rigidly, the state debt had to be pared back to a reasonable level, and waste in state welfare programs had to be eliminated. These economic measures were to be accompanied with solidarity and worker participation in the workplace. Every worker would be provided with a guaranteed annual salary that could be used for any purpose, from starting a new industry to taking a sabbatical. Such liberation would also be extended to the factory floor, where workers would be able to participate "in the results, the capital and the functioning of the enterprise." Unlike the Socialists, who had increased the power of the state at the expense of participation, the right in power would unleash the forces necessary to overcome the *crise*.[35]

By 1986, the neoliberal critique of socialism had provided the right with a new program. Liberty was its dominant motif, although not liberty without solidarity. The attack on the welfare state that some neoliberals espoused was quietly dropped and forgotten. Reform replaced revolution. The more extreme Reaganite and Thatcherite models were modified to fit the supposed limitations of the French economic system. Although entrepreneurship was extolled, security was still valued highly. Above all, however, the idea of liberty dominated political rhetoric. The neoliberals capitalized on a mentality that identified the Socialists with statism and egalitarianism at the price of liberty.

Contributing strongly to this mentality were various groups that had more or less identified with the left. The new philosophers' group was one of these. After the 1981 elections, their leading spokesmen became vitriolic in their criticism of the Socialists in power. They argued that the inclusion of the Communists in the new government constituted definitive evidence that the Socialists intended to create the gulag in France. Jean-Marie Benoist, who was never friendly to the left, spoke of the "occupation" of France by the Marxists. He called on the right to issue a manifesto on liberty to counter "Marxist-Leninst totalitarianism." Weekly, in editorials written for *Le Quotidien de Paris*, Benoist carried on his scurrilous attack, labeling nationalization as the first step toward the Sovietization of France, claiming that Munich was an "act of resistance" compared to Socialist policy regarding Poland, calling upon the "nation to rise up" against the totalitarian policies of the left, and accusing Mitterrand of allying "with the forces of darkness" in order to gain power and marrying France "with death." Terror, insecurity, irreligion, Satanic forces, death, destruction, totalitarianism: these were the marks of Socialist France.[36]

The extremism of Benoist's critique of Socialism was not an isolated occurrence. As he claimed, his cause was the same as that of such intellectuals as Castoriadis, Lévy, Barthes, and Foucault, all of whom were united together against the Marxists.[37] The simplistic connections that the new philosophers had made between social democracy and totalitarianism had transformed them into uncritical advocates of "liberty" at all costs. Bernard-Henri Lévy, the guru of the cause, whose political ties were with the left, engaged in unrelenting criticism of the Socialists, in contrast to his passive acceptance of the right during the 1970s. In his introduction to the collected chroniques that he wrote for *Le Matin* in 1981 and 1982, he identified the Socialist program with pre-1914 nationalism and anti-Semitism. Nationalization of industry, he maintained, had to be understood in light of Drumont's *Vers un capitalisme national*, a work that was infused with anti-Semitism. Lévy claimed that the Socialist state was "the most authentically *reactionary* state that we have experienced since Vichy." The French Socialists were engaged in creating a French form of socialism that would mimic the Soviet Union, just as Pétain's fascism had mimicked Nazi Germany. To Lévy, the only legitimate form of socialism had its origins in the 1968 tradition that was inspired by the ideas of Althusser, Lacan, and Foucault. This was the 1968 of "an authentic anticommunism of the left," which formed the basis for the ideas of the new philosophers.[38] Like Benoist, Lévy found the Socialist alliance with the Communists to be the source of all evil, for it revealed that the French Socialist party opposed true liberty and true socialism in favor of the road to the gulag. In that light, Lévy attacked most of the Socialist program, including *autogestion* and decentralization, which he equated with totalitarianism:

"a man is reputed so much 'freer' if he 'participates,' as it is claimed, in the chains that bind him.''[39] But unlike Benoist, Lévy discovered some redeeming characteristics in the Socialist government: he had high praise for Robert Badinter, the minister of justice, who belonged in the category of "The True Left.''[40]

While the positions taken by Benoist and Lévy could have been predicted, based on what they had written prior to the Socialist victory of 1981, the antisocialist attitudes of André Glucksmann and Jean-Paul Dollé, two new philosophers who had been revolutionaries in 1968, were less certain. Glucksmann had been openly sympathetic to the Socialists prior to 1981, but the inclusion of the Communists in the government and Socialist attitudes toward the Third World turned him into a rabid critic of the totalitarian left in power. To Glucksmann, Europe was the last remaining bastion of democracy and freedom in a world of servitude. Yet, the Socialists had developed no coherent policy to defend it against communist threats. The Socialists were ashamed of their European origins, Glucksmann argued; they sympathized with the oppressed of the Third World rather than with democratic Europe.[41]

Similarly, but with slightly less vituperation than his colleagues, Jean-Paul Dollé chastized the Socialists for their antidemocratic policies. Dollé pointed to his impeccable credentials for offering such criticism: in 1968 he had been a Leninist and an outspoken opponent of free enterprise, which made him better-qualified than others to understand what democracy and entrepreneurship entailed. Like many converts, Dollé was more Catholic than the pope, extolling the virtues of decentralization and capitalism, while condemning the Jacobin left and nationalization. To Dollé, the victory of the left in 1981 marked a regression, as the spirit of 1968 was overwhelmed by statism. Yet Dollé believed that the Socialists could still redeem themselves if François Mitterrand comprehended and implemented his message. In that spirit, Dollé addressed the president, informing him that democracy entailed the existence of "a State which is limited by the law and requires the autonomous activities of citizens, creating on their own the entities of the economy and knowledge.''[42] Or, to put the matter in a slightly different way: "The role of the democratic State consists, then, to safeguard the rules of free debate, of cohabitation between disparate interests, and to protect citizens against internal and external violence. That is all, they demand nothing more.''[43] Dollé presented a nightwatchman conception of democracy that reinforced his faith in entrepreneurship, which he believed was "the only modality of action," the "only form of free action and free thought.''[44] Dollé hoped that his long voyage from Lenin to Hayek, from statism to libertarianism, would also be completed by the Socialists. To him, the spirit of 1968 was closer to Adam Smith than to French socialism.

Whatever the spirit of 1968 might be, the Socialists were accused of violating it by virtually everyone. The utopias that the May revolution had created in the minds of the French did not match the reality of day-to-day politics. The neoliberals and the new philosophers were especially quick in their rush to judgment on Socialist policies, condemning strongly the statist, antilibertarian element in them. But the *deuxième gauche* was not far behind these libertarians in offering similar evaluations. A curious consensus emerged that seemed to unite opposites behind the concept of liberty. As the hopes that the Socialists had raised in 1981 faded, variations on the idea of liberalism emerged to take their place. But exactly how liberalism would be implemented remained very vague, an issue that only a few addressed, usually providing the old political answers of compromise and incrementalism that the intellectual critics of the state rejected.

Whether the *deuxième gauche* should be included in this new wave of liberalism is debatable. Certainly it rejected totally the more extreme proposals of the neoliberals, and clearly it identified its ideas on *autogestion* and decentralization with the Socialist party and not with the right. But, the failure of the Socialists to implement many of the *deuxième gauche*'s concepts led some to join the ranks of the critics of the left, taking up themes that were very close to neoliberalism or that condemned party politics for civil society in such a way as to join the neoliberal camp by default—that is, for lack of any better vehicle to use for changing society.

Among those who deserted the Socialists for a form of neoliberalism was Jean-Marie Domenach, former editor of the journal *Esprit*, member of the PSU in its formative years, and an enthusiastic advocate of *autogestion*. Domenach took up the new philosophers' critique of socialism as the road to the gulag, criticizing socialist language for serving as an "alibi for the most monstrous mass crimes; in its name millions of men have been exterminated and thrown in the camps, and millions of others are forced to flee their country."[45] He saw the Socialists compromising the ideals of humanity everywhere: in Poland, in signing the Siberian gas agreement, in selling arms to right-wing governments. But the greatest sin that the Socialists committed was the rehabilitation of the French Communist party as a democratic force. In doing this, the Socialists hid "the reality of Communism" and lost their honor and "the confidence of the people."[46]

Still, Domenach thought of himself as a man of the left, as one who sought a way out of the "système actuel" by inventing "other relations, another culture, another language."[47] The Socialist alternative would not do, for it had corrupted reality: "the left, as part of the political system, erects itself into an absolute norm, into a totalizing concept, and through that turns itself against its own ends by becoming intolerant, deceptive and inegalitarian . . . , by blocking change, by preventing the democratic spirit from opening up to dialogue and from creating new practices and institutions.''[48] The true left, the Rocardian, CFDT-PSU left, had been destroyed by its 1974 union with the Parti socialiste, which used this *deuxième gauche* for its own purposes, without ever intending to carry out its program, as became evident once the Socialists came to power. The aim of the true left must remain *autogestion*, Domenach believed. By this he meant the right of everyone to decide their own destiny, free from state control. Basically, Domenach agreed with Hayek's criticism of the state: the state should not be allowed to decide arbitrarily who should be privileged and who should not, nor should the state be allowed to compensate some on the grounds of social justice while penalizing others. The state cannot determine who is rich and who is poor, what is fair and what is not. ''It is not justifiable, it is not tolerable that the State decides on the orientation of my studies, on the nature of my leisure time, on the number of channels on my television set.''[49] Civil society must replace the state as the final arbiter in politics.

Domenach's conclusions on *autogestion* clearly revealed the thin line between it and neoliberalism. Although Domenach protested that he was not a liberal and even condemned liberalism for being nothing more than another aspect of socialism, in real terms it would be difficult to make significant distinctions between Domenach's *autogestion* and Hayek's liberalism. Nor was this problem overlooked by the leading advocates of *autogestion*. Pierre Rosanvallon, the CFDT intellectual leader, whose *La crise de l'Etat providence* dominated much of French political and social thought in the early 1980s, attempted to respond to this convergence of *autogestion* and liberalism by offering a historical explanation of the problem that would clarify the relationship between the two ideologies.

To Rosanvallon, the *crise de l'Etat providence* was a recent phenomenon. Beginning around 1973, with the first oil crisis and the economic slowdown of the capitalist economies, the welfare state exploded in relation to economic productivity. Taxation in France went from 36 percent of gross national product in 1973 to 44 percent in 1983, due almost entirely to the expansion of *l'Etat providence*. In contrast, between 1959 and 1973, taxation had expanded by only 3 percent of gross national product. As long as productivity increased at approximately the same rate as demands for welfare, the contract between the capitalist state system and the citizenry remained intact, but as soon as disparities began to emerge, the crisis of the modern state occurred on every level, from the political to the social and economic. The demand for *autogestion*, for the breakup of bureaucracy, emerged as a direct result of the *crise de l'Etat providence*.[50]

Rosanvallon viewed *l'Etat providence* as a stage in history that could be dissected and analyzed. In the Foucault manner, which so heavily influenced the new thinkers in France, Rosanvallon located the origins of this system in the seventeenth century, with the rise of the *Etat protecteur*, or the modern state as Locke and Hobbes had defined it. The state had been created to protect the individual, which meant the protection of private property, in a capitalist world in which insecurity was omnipresent. With the democratic revolutions of the eighteenth century the *Etat protecteur* was replaced by the *Etat providence*. In the transition, the marketplace supplanted corporatism, the state replaced religion as the new faith, and statistical certainty made it possible to integrate Providence and the State. Crises, especially world wars, reinforced the power of the providential state. Wars made society revert to its origins, whether consciously or unconsciously, and thus forced society to rethink its contract, with each rethinking leading to a more profound level of expressing *l'Etat providence*. With the most recent period, the 1980s, *l'Etat providence* reached a point of nonrenewal. Unable to remake the social contract, its enemies on the left and right challenged it, with the left pointing out that the providential state was a mechancial, cold means of reaching a theoretical form of equality—*"solidarité mécanique"*—and the right doubting whether equality should be the final end of society, as the providential state seemed to indicate.[51]

With those preliminary remarks to set the stage, Rosanvallon proceeded to demolish the accepted wisdom on the welfare state. Contrary to the idea that *l'Etat providence* had been the victim of its own success, he argued that it had failed because of its undefined, and probably undefinable, objectives, namely those of "bonheur," "besoin," and "égalité." Although equality can be realized rather easily in civil and political matters, it was problematic whether the same could be said about economic and social relations. At any rate, the providential state did not increase solidarity, as it claimed to do. On the contrary, individualism and statism were the two supporting pillars of this state. The total individualism that the marketplace and *homo economicus* created led to the breakdown of solidarity and the eventual creation of the false solidarity of welfarism to fill the vacuum that was left in the social contract.[52]

Pierre Rosanvallon realized, however, that there was a major problem in this kind of attack on the modern state: it left the way open for neoliberalism to emerge as the answer to the crisis. Yet, the liberals were the ones who had created the crisis in the first place! Always, from the very beginning of liberal thought, the state had been ill-defined, if defined at all. The state could be everything or nothing to a liberal; no clear demarcation of the boundaries of the state emerged in liberal philosophy. The arguments for less state were counterbalanced by the idea of welfare or the Benthamite principle of utility, which could justify any form of state from a libertarian one to totalitarianism. However, in America, Rosanvallon argued, contemporary liberal thinkers addressed this problem by espousing the principle of anarchy as the proper response to the providential state: Robert Nozick's *Anarchy, State and Utopia* was a perfect example of this. Nozick's state was the *Etat ultra-minimal*, one that exercised a monopoly over the use of force and nothing else. John Rawls's *A Theory of Justice* was another great modern anarchist treatise against the welfare state. Rawls went beyond the idea of redistribution to the idea of distributive justice. Rather than correcting inequalities, the objective should be to allow everyone the right to begin at the same point. Educational vouchers for every child and a guaranteed minimum revenue for everyone were the primary means of achieving distributive justice, not welfare and redistribution of income.[53] To Rosanvallon, these two theorists were formidable opponents, for their ideas dominated neoliberal thought and bore some resemblance to *autogestion*. But, their thought led to a perverse end: "*individualisme radical*." It rejected "even the idea of 'social context.' The individual is for them 'a perfect and solitary whole,' to use Rousseau's expression in the *Contrat social*." Sympathy was totally rejected by these thinkers as a basis for society or government or psychology; self-love and indifference to others were the ultimate aims of justice, individualism, and society. The neoliberal universe was a bleak one in which politics eventually became meaningless as narcissistic individualism increasingly dominated all.[54]

When Rosanvallon turned from criticism of liberalism and the *Etat providence* to solving the problems of the modern age, his arguments became less plausible. First of all, he argued, the new society required that we abandon archaic ways of thinking, such as the Manichean division of the world into capitalism and socialism, inequality and equality, market and state. Once that was accomplished, the three objectives of "*socialisation*," "*décentralisation*," and "*autonomisation*" could be implemented. These entailed the gradual shift of power from the bureaucracy and the state to the local level, to the citizens, to civil society. The central problem was to reduce the demand for the state, not by anarchistic abolition of it but rather by increasing the power of civil society. But this could not be done *through* the instrument of the state, for that would only reinforce the state at the expense of civil society. The solution seemed to lie in the expansion of free time for the individual, which would lead to new forms of sociability, association, and liberty.[55] Yet, in the final analysis, this solution was not convincing. It remained a utopian construct, vaguely sketched out, based upon the supposition that the cultural crisis of the post-1968 era was a crisis of the *Etat providence*, which civil society would resolve in accord with Rosanvallon's specifications.

Feeling more at home in the realm of analysis than in prophecy, Rosanvallon concluded with a recapitulation of his critique, with slightly different emphasis. The *crise de l'Etat providence*, he emphasized, began before the economic crisis of the 1970s with the attack on the state in 1968 and went beyond economic factors to challenge the order of things: relations between "men and women, directors and directed, State and regions. . . ." The neo-Keyneseans tried to explain and resolve these new developments, but they failed, discrediting the social democratic model of the state, opening the way for the liberal offensive, and raising the possibility that no positive solution to the crisis could be reached. Quite possibly, Rosanvallon feared, the end result would be the emergence of "a bastard society in which the reinforcement of the mechanisms of the market will coexist with the maintenance of rigid statist forms and the development of a partial social corporatization."[56]

Not surprisingly, Rosanvallon found the Socialists incapable of instituting the sort of social contract that he believed to be necessary. Political expediency had guided their austerity program and not the general good. Thus, they raised the TVA rather than income tax, they forced the youngest workers to bear the largest share of the burden of unemployment since they had no real political influence, and they cut unemployment compensation rather than raising taxes on the employed to help finance the system. But Rosanvallon was aware that the Socialists were only part of the problem: most French men and women would rather see unemployment rise than experience a decline in their standard of living through a program of solidarity with the least fortunate. In short, the civil society that was required to create *autogestion* was lacking in France. The only hope for *autogestion*, it seemed, was the CFDT. Combining Christian socialism, Fabianism, antitotalitarianism, and the spirit of 1968, Rosanvallon argued, it alone had not compromised the ideals of the movement.[57]

The same sense of despair over the Socialist record emerged in the work of André Gorz, whose 1983 book, *Les chemins du Paradis*, repeated most of the themes that he had outlined in the 1970s. To Gorz, the left's answer to the *crise* was nothing but outdated Keynseanism. As he put it: "The socialism of the future will be postindustrialist and antiproductionist or it shall not exist." Both capitalism and socialism have been proved incapable of solving the world crisis; both "are destroyers of limited natural resources and of necessary equilibriums that are needed for the continuation of life."[58] The Third World has been devastated by the policies of First World governments, which have refused to accept an ecological solution to the earth's problems, but instead have pursued futile *relances* of their economies and maintained the lie that full employment at full pay could be achieved for everyone. In reality, new technologies were destroying work, creating a dual working class of secure and precarious workers, while capitalism had evolved into a system of technocratic control, whether under leftist or rightist political leadership. The great question of the 1980s was whether western societies would become totally technocratic and programmed or free in the sense that Marx envisaged "in which the necessary production of necessities occupies no more than a very reduced portion of the time of each and in which *work* (paid labor) ceases consequently to be the principal activity of each."[59]

The answer, to Gorz, was quite simple: the only way to avoid totalitarian rule by a technocratic elite, of either the left or the right, was through a system of division of work, with reduction of individual working time, and a guaranteed lifetime salary. The industrial imperative of work must be transcended by the realization of the pleasure principle. To accomplish this, the working life of the individual would have to be set at about twenty thousand hours, which roughly equaled the amount of labor needed to produce necessities. All nonessential goods would be produced in a workers' free time, under a system of "activities that were autonomous, self-determined and optional."[60] Although this system would not overcome the division of labor, which Gorz maintained could never be totally eliminated, it would attenuate that burden by extending the amount of free time that each individual possessed. Autonomy, consequently, became the central focal point of Gorz's concept of freedom: "For me, autonomous activity is really such only if it is neither an obligation that is imposed on us in the name of moral, religious or political principles, nor a vital necessity."[61] Unfortunately, this definition leaves us with no clear understanding of autonomy. To Gorz it is a negative: it is *not* the division of labor, it is *not* the realm of necessity, it is *not* an imperative of any sort.

In the end, Gorz abandoned *autogestion* as the final answer to the problem of autonomy: "*Autogestion* is an aspiration whose sphere can be quite large, but it is not a solution to everything."[62] The solution to everything seemed to be the individual. As Gorz stated in a rhapsodic review of Edgar Morin's *La vie de la vie*, "The 'grand confrontation' of our era shall not pit humanity against the super brains of extraterrestial beings; it is already pitting individuals against the super brains of the States, 'cyclopean monsters, coercive and bloody, who are as foreign to us as people from outer space.' "[63]

While disillusioned leftists such as Domenach, Rosanvallon, and Gorz moved toward the individual and civil society as the answer to the riddle of the modern age, rejecting the party or any institutional structure, others in the second left embraced more traditional ways of reaching the goal of *autogestion*. Regionalists, such as Robert Lafont, continued to emphasize cultural and linguistic groups as the key, while the *autogestionnaire* camp within the Socialist party placed primary emphasis on the leading role of the party in creating *autogestion*. Both presented critical assessments of the government's programs, but neither one was pessimistic about the future of *autogestion*. Unlike Domenach, Rosanvallon, and Gorz, they remained true believers despite the disappointing record of the Socialists in power. On the other hand, they and their more skeptical comrades—as well as the neoliberals—reached a broad consensus over the imperative to decentralize power, to dismantle the state.

Robert Lafont, the nation's leading spokesman for regional decentralization, found the Socialist record seriously deficient. The great marriage of *autogestion* with Jacobin socialism had been perverted by the perceived imperative of modernization. The Socialists had turned into technocrats and capitalists, revealing themselves to be true adherents of the Gaullist Fifth Republic. The spirit of 1968, which the regionalist movement embodied, was threatened by the Socialist government's use of decentralization for the purpose of advancing the cause of modernization, the so-called Third Industrial Revolution. The net result of this movement toward modernization was the disillusionment of the nation with its political leaders. The National Front evolved directly out of this, Lafont argued.[64] The status of immigrants in France was closely related to modernization and regionalism. Capitalist modernization brought them to France to serve as a reservoir of cheap labor and subjected them to racist and assimilationist pressures. In contrast, a regionalist policy would provide to them, and to all other groups living in France, "le droit à la différence." To Lafont, the only solution to the immigrant problem was to open up France to all cultures, to accept the autonomy of every community that existed within the nation. "Either the nation transforms itself or it cracks under its old form."[65] This transformation required not only the establishment of regionalism, which Lafont hoped would be realized in 1986, but also the withdrawal of the nation from the international capitalist system, which was responsible for modernization and alienation. Unfortunately, Lafont pointed out, neither the right nor the left was capable of moving toward this necessary anticapitalist, anti-internationalist position. The left wanted to talk about modernity and archaic nationalism, whereas the right chose to emphasize laisser-faire and anti-immigrant attitudes. Between neomodernism and neofascism, Lafont chose the humanist alternative of regionalism.[66]

In choosing humanist regionalism, Lafont claimed that he opted for a dialectical perspective over a structuralist one. Structuralism was capable of comprehending the Other, but could not transcend this to understand the relations between the Other and us. Structuralism was a philosophy of the center that could never move from that position to the periphery. It was part of the movement toward modernization that had dominated France since 1958 at the expense of the periphery. In contrast, the dialectic comprehended and accepted the periphery as a legitimate counterforce in society. From a dialectical perspective, the existence of the periphery led to alienation, which emerged out of the clash of "two socially unequal cultures." This alienation could be overcome, however, through the creation of the "droit à la différence." Through it the rights of each culture and the rights of each individual within a given culture would be recognized. A new concept of citizenship would emerge from this, one that went beyond the eighteenth-century definition of the nation state. Pluralism would prevail over uniformity. The new citizenship that would emerge out of this late twentieth-century struggle would destroy modernity and create the "ultramodern man," whose existence was necessary for the creation of a new Europe, a Europe of the peoples rather than a Europe of modern capitalism. A new Treaty of Rome would be signed, with the region as the base of European federalism. The homogenization of culture that capitalism had created would be reversed by the diversity of regionalism and a new stage in the history of civilization would emerge, that of "l'après-socialisme et le post-capitalisme."[67]

Lafont's profound sense of alienation from the world of the Fifth Republic made him into one of the most utopian of the second-left thinkers. Such was not the case with Les Gracques, the group of leftist thinkers who published, in 1983, a very negative appraisal of the Socialists in power. In fact, of all the second-left thinkers we have considered, Les Gracques come closest to being pragmatic politicians. Their complaints about Socialist policies centered around the same themes that other second-left critics raised, but their solutions were profoundly practical rather than utopian or revolutionary. *Autogestion* was their objective, but one that could be reached within the confines of the system by carrying out reforms. For example, Les Gracques argued that more democratic powers had to be granted to the workers and to decentralized entities in order to realize the true aims of *autogestion*. The Socialists failed to extend such rights far enough. Nor did they carry out the necessary educational reforms in order to create the new autonomous human beings who must be at the heart of *autogestion* if it were going to work effectively. The system had to be opened up to more dialogue, to more outside influences. In turn, mass culture had to be encouraged. Not the mass culture of television, but rather the mass culture that existed prior to the industrial revolution, when everyone from the elite to the popular classes participated in the same cultural events. The Socialists needed to decentralize culture as much as possible, to place it in the hands of the outsiders, to encourage the development of a popular culture separate from any sort of statist control or commercialization.[68]

Les Gracques never lost sight of their primary objectives in arguing for *autogestion*. First of all, they conceived of *autogestion* as a Socialist policy, one that would lead to Socialist hegemony in France. Therefore, they warned the government to make sure that its programs did not reward the opposition in any way. Wherever decentralization might give power to the right, it should be circumscribed by the state. To Les Gracques, *autogestion* in its pure form was the mass mobilization of society from the base up to support the general interest against the particular interests of the right. But such a pure form did not exist and consequently the state had to intervene to protect the general interest and to encourage social experimentation at the local level. Although the authors opposed *dirigisme*, they thought that a certain amount of Parisian control was necessary until the culture of *autogestion* was firmly implanted in the nation.[69]

Finally, in contrast to a Lafont or a Gorz, Les Gracques conceived of *autogestion* in productivist terms. To them, *autogestion* would unleash the latent, unused productive forces of the nation. Workers would be mobilized, through *autogestion*, to make firms work: "If we want the nation to revive, it is necessary to use all of our powers to convince the workers to assume their responsibilities in the life of the enterprise, going so far as to become concerned about its future and its strategy."[70] Time and again, the authors returned to this theme, as though the key goal of *autogestion* was the creation of a Japanese-style system. For example: "the *autogestionnaire* society is capable of creating unsuspected increases in productivity." Or: "Technical progress penetrates properly only as the result of a social compromise, itself disengaged through dialogue and participation." At times the authors expressed their belief in *autogestion* in quasi-religious terms. *Autogestion* would solve the riddle of social relations, they maintained; it would be the great experiment that would make France a leader; it would increase employment; and it would lead to the withering away of the centralized state, which would be replaced by civil society, contractual relationships, dialogue, and so forth.[71]

Our final band of critics of Socialist policy, the so-called hard left, roughly concentrated around the Communist party but including elements of the CERES group, offered a slightly different perspective on the leftist experiment. By considering the work of Alain Lipietz, Anicet Le Pors, and Pierre Juquin, we can obtain some idea of what their concerns were and how they related to the criticisms of others.

Of the three, Alain Lipietz presented the most analytical and dispassionate hard-left critique of Socialist policy, but also the most traditional critique, which made him into something of an anachronism in the era of second-left ideas on *autogestion* and decentralization. An economist employed by the state scientific research agency, the CNRS, Lipietz belonged to no political party, although he claimed to be a lifetime leftist. To Lipietz, France had been part of a Fordist, social democratic economic system since 1945. However, at no time did France adapt well to this environment and beginning with the 1973 crisis, Fordism quickly became discredited and irrelevant for solving the nation's economic and social problems. The right attempted to replace the Fordist system with a monetarist one in which profits took precedence over the social contract with the workers. By 1981, when the Socialists took over, the nation was in a disastrous economic position, as monetarism had led to massive capital flows abroad and deindustrialization at home, which created unemployment, inflation, and a decline in the nation's balance of payments. The *relance* was an attempt to deal with this situation, although a faulty one.[72] The left that took power in 1981 was incapable, ideologically, of dealing with the crisis of Fordism. To Lipietz, the Common Program offered only a technocratic solution to the crisis and the second left presented a vague, amorphous interpretation of the ideals of 1968 that coincided with capitalism more than it did with the traditional left. In turn, the *relance* was succeeded by a deflationary policy of Saint-Simonist, technocratic origins. By 1982, consequently, the Socialists had forsaken leftist ideals for a neoliberal, capitalist approach to the economic problems that had been bequeathed to them. In Lipietz's view, the second left, with its suspicious ties to the new philosophers, libertarians, and others in the captialist camp, was primarily responsible for this accommodation with the marketplace. With the events of March 1983, the victory of these elements was completed. The government opted for an economic approach that promised austerity, the decline of worker buying-power, and an emphasis on investment and savings.[73]

To Lipietz, the March 1983 decision to remain in the Common Market's monetary system was totally wrong. Far from solving the nation's problems, the Common Market exacerbated them, increasing the need for further austerity measures, which, in turn, increased unemployment. Instead, the Socialists should have withdrawn from the European monetary system, indexed prices, resorted to protective tariffs as allowed under the Treaty of Rome for emergency situations, set up import quotas, followed the policies of such countries as Sweden, Norway, and Switzerland in regard to social justice rather than the reactionary policies of the Common Market, and united with the Third World in a protectionist policy that would provide social justice and economic progress to both France and its trade partners. In short, Lipietz wanted to see the implementation of a policy of solidarity, justice, and development instead of one that emphasized the liberal economic agenda of investment, austerity, and rigor. The antistatist ideas that dominated leftist circles in the 1970s were the enemy to Lipietz. Such second-left thinkers as Pierre Rosanvallon and André Gorz, who attacked the Etat-providence as the source of alienation when the real source was capitalism, had contributed greatly to the rightist course that the Socialist government pursued unconditionally by March 1983. In Lipietz's opinion, the left needed to return to its traditional values if it wanted to create a society based on equality and social justice.[74]

While Lipietz adhered to a straightforward, Marxist view of Socialist rule, one that CERES could have supported without difficulty, the two Communist commentators on the Socialist experience embraced some aspects of the new-left, *autogestionnaire* agenda. Anicet Le Pors, who served in the government as minister of the civil service, offered a defense of the state as an instrument of reform, against the neoliberal attack upon bureaucratic institutions. Although Le Pors also borrowed from the second left, merging *autogestion* with bureaucracy, like Lipietz he harbored deep suspicions of all the "new" movements of the 1970s, viewing them as part of a massive liberal movement in favor of economic individualism, the marketplace, and inequality. To Le Pors, Pierre Rosanvallon, in particular, epitomized this liberal apologetic for capitalism in the name of socialism.[75]

For the most part, Le Pors's work concentrated on defending what he called, in the title of his book, *L'Etat efficace*, pointing out the positive role of the state in achieving economic progress, the introduction of new technologies, the extension of social justice, and other matters. To promote these goals, Le Pors had worked hard to provide security for civil servants, against the neoliberal desire to establish a spoils system in the bureaucracy. He defended this position on the basis of the fundamental right of everyone to be guaranteed employment:

It is only the simple recognition of what must be considered an elementary right, fundamental to all human beings: the right to work. Yes, there is something scandalous here, but it is not that the bureaucrats want to be total citizens; the scandal is that in French society the right to work is not recognized for millions of persons, while millions of others live poorly in economically developed France.[76]

In addition, Le Pors maintained, bureaucrats must be granted as much security as possible in order to immunize them against the pressures of the bourgeoisie, who controlled the state. Similarly, in regard to *autogestion* and decentralization, Le Pors argued, it was essential to extend worker control, that is union control, as extensively as possible before the right returned to power with an agenda to take over and pervert the reforms of the left. The problem with the Fifth Republic, Le Pors philosophized, was that the opposition could reverse democratic reforms, overriding the general will for the purpose of promoting private interest.[77]

In essence, Le Pors still accepted the idea of the dictatorship of the proletariat. Although he used Gramscian language in discussing how the left would assume power (the hegemony of the bourgeoisie would be replaced by the hegemony of the proletariat), his arguments remained thinly veiled Leninist constructs. He conceived of *autogestion* as nothing more than another means for the working class to seize total power. In this light, Le Pors supported unconditionally the resolution passed by the twenty-fifth congress of the PCF, which called for "a representative power of the people favoring popular intervention at all levels and permitting the working class to have access to the highest responsibilities and to exercise a leading role."[78] However, Le Pors's grasp of hegemonic politics led him to conclude with a broad definition of what democratic decentralization must entail: "the creation of productive jobs, the reinforcement of the internal market, the development of each region, the establishment of infrastructures and necessary public facilities. Decentralization will succeed only if it is the concern of everyone; it is the condition for the union of social efficacity with the will to 'live, work, and decide *au pays*.' "[79]

In contrast to Le Pors's orthodox position, Pierre Juquin stood on the fringes of French Communism, offering his so-called *Autocritiques* of the party. Little that Juquin said, however, differed from normal Communist party positions. Although he criticized the party for its failure to "modernize," he placed such criticism in the context of enduring Marxist-Leninist values that had to be adjusted to changing historical circumstances. Juquin's autocritiques quickly turned into an apologia for Stalinism, spiced with a few references to the errors of the past, and a scathing criticism of liberal democracy and the social democratic alternative to capitalism. Intellectually, the total bankruptcy of Juqin's supposed "dissent" from the mainstream of the party left little doubt that the PCF would have difficulty emerging once again as a viable political alternative on the left. His analysis offered little more than clichés and warmed-over Leninist solutions as answers to the problems that the party faced. While aspiring to be "modern" by borrowing from the mainstream of French intellectual discussion— the *Annales* school, for example—Juquin's work failed to integrate these ideas into the mainstream of his self-criticism, which never moved much beyond a reluctant admission that the party's image had been damaged by association with the gulag. Despite Juquin's protests against this connection, which included the claim that he and the party were in the humanist tradition, in favor of the rights of the individual and *autogestion*, in the final chapter he reaffirmed the primacy of the class struggle as the essence of capitalist society and maintained the necessity to transform *autogestion* into another means of achieving the hegemony of the proletariat or the debourgeoisification of French society for the purpose of creating "true" individualism. Only the already converted, the true believers, could be convinced by Juquin's claims that the PCF represented the spirit of 1968.[80]

Yet, in fairness to Juquin and the PCF, every group in France attempted, in some way or another, to coopt the spirit of 1968 for its cause. Such ideas as individualism, *autogestion*/decentralization, liberty, and their various offspring, on either the left or the right, had become common parlance by 1984. It was virtually impossible to avoid the new rhetoric, although its meaning varied to fit different contexts ranging from the utopian to the cynical political manipulation of people. But, assuming that most of those who employed the rhetoric of *autogestion* were sincere, serious structural and institutional obstacles to its implementation existed in French government and society. In addition, the problem of the impossible and indefinable objectives of the spirit of 1968 had to be surmounted. Behind the rhetoric, or rather within it, there existed an irreducible and constantly changing utopianism. Built into the dialogue on decentralization/*autogestion* and liberty were objectives that could lead to disillusionment and cynicism, for they could never be fulfilled by real politicians and citizens. Despite all the claims made by new philosophers and other offspring of 1968 that teleological concepts of history had been discredited and buried, the evidence indicates strongly that such was not the case. Virtually all of the writers we have discussed had a narrow vision of liberty and individualism, one that was defined by their particular social, or economic, or political perspective, and one that was circumscribed by various criteria, often arbitrary in nature, that defined the final goal of history. But very few of these thinkers offered a historical and structural analysis of the problem. Living in a postdeterminist intellectual universe, or so they thought, total voluntarism, within self-prescribed limitations, served in place of rigorous historical and structural analysis, even for a Jean-Marie Benoist, who should have known better. Or in the case of the hard-left Communist party members, voluntarism and individualism were attached to a determinist conception of history without much concern for the contradictions. In the end, 1984 becomes more and more appropriate as the year in which liberty became the clarion call of the intellectual/political class, for by 1984 liberty had been so distorted, so confused, so intellectualized and fragmented, that it no longer had any clear meaning. Paradoxically, 1984 represented the climax of the ideas of the libertarian 1968 generation. Those ideas had become so widely accepted and commonplace that they could be labeled "hegemonic," but only in the sense that they were all-pervasive, part of the "zeitgeist," and thus ultimately indefinable.

Nevertheless, in the confusion that the nation endured in trying to comprehend such concepts as liberty and individualism in the 1980s, some offered a broader perspective that did include historical and structural factors. Such thinkers as the sociologist Michel Crozier, the economist Alain Minc, and the intellectual guru François de Closets provided long-term analyses that transcended pure party politics or intellectual fashions. Their responses were not encouraging, for they discovered a France that could not be transformed easily from statism to voluntarism, from bureaucratic rule to individual inititative, from Parisian decrees to the autonomy of civil society. Perhaps Alain Minc's work, *L'après-crise est commencé*, best stated their position. Although Minc was an economist who dealt primarily with the economic problems the nation faced, he grasped clearly the noneconomic factors that made up the problem. Rejecting all utopian solutions, whether they be the liberal one of supply-side economics or the Socialist one of industrial reconquest, Minc presented a bleak picture of economic scarcity for the future. The *crise*, to Minc, transcended traditional economics, which was too theoretical, to embrace Braudelian proportions. The *crise* included social institutions, structures, and mentalities as well as the economic system. After accepting the place of France in a market economy, as Braudel had shown to be the case since the middle ages, and revealing the severe external and internal constraints upon the French economy in the recent situation, Minc turned to the question of what had to be done.

First of all, Minc argued, France had to overcome its archaic corporatist and rentier mentalities. This meant, among other things, the elimination of closed professions, the various *positions acquises* that existed everywhere, which François de Closets exposed unmercifully in *Toujours plus*! As a corollary of this, dynamic risk capitalism had to be promoted over the premodern, patrimonial capitalism that dominated the nation. Borrowing from Lionel Stoleru's division of France into protected and exposed sectors, Minc insisted, along with Closets and Stoleru, that corporatist entities always attemped to solve their problems at the expense of other groups through the use of the state. But, in conjunction with the powerful arguments of Michel Crozier's *On ne change pas société par décret*, Minc did not advocate or believe possible that this situation could be changed through bureaucratic initiative or state directives. Speaking in the name of 1968—a treacherous thing to do, as we have seen—Alain Minc placed most of his confidence for change in civil society. Since 1968, civil society had played an increasing role in promoting such non- or anti-institutional movements as ecology, homosexual rights, feminism, *autogestion*, and the *droit à la différence*, which more or less encompassed everything. To take just one of these, *autogestion*, Minc argued that it was "a libertarian aspiration in the organization of the city," and not a specific political or institutional movement. In short, to Minc the *après-crise* would resolve many of its problems through civil society and not through any institution or according to any preconceived or foreordained agenda. This did not mean, however, that the state would disappear. Far from it. The state in the après-crise would continue to play a role in the mixed society that France was, which Minc thought resembled a sort of combination of Japan and Italy, or Colbert and the market working together. Because of the weakness of French industry, Minc could conceive of no other solution to critical investment in such areas as nuclear energy or the aeronautical industry than continued state intervention. But the state must not monopolize the marketplace or prevent the development of civil society where it can replace the state, or else France will suffer severe consequences, such as loss of economic productivity. Here Minc offered a timely example about the welfare state, in light of Pierre Rosanvallon's criticism of it. To Minc, the only answer to the crisis of the welfare state was the privatization of certain parts of it, those parts that subsidized the middle class to the detriment of the poor. However, the final outcome of the *après-crise* would not be any particular reform program, but rather a new stage in the historical development of society, which Minc called the polymorphous society. Such a society would not be a utopia; on the contrary, it would be filled with conflicts and contradictions. The polymorphous society would be the counterweight to the top-heavy state structure that was necessary for industrial productivity in certain key sectors; it would be decentralized, as close to civil society as possible, and totally divorced from institutional, central control, not because of changes made by the state, but rather as the result of forces originating in civil society itself. To Minc, the polymorphous society was not a mental construct, but the direct result of historical, social, economic, and cultural factors that had been at work in France and Western Europe since at least 1968.[81]

Although both Closets and Crozier might differ with parts of Minc's analysis of the problem, the spirit behind that analysis was pragmatic, open-ended, non- (if not anti-) utopian. Better than most thinkers who attempted to reconcile liberty and authority, civil society and the state, Alain Minc provided a plausible analysis of the historical and structural problems involved in moving toward the realization of the spirit of 1968. Although he treated politics as a secondary factor in this process, he did not disdain politics in the name of some higher technocratic agenda. On the contrary, technocracy was limited by Minc to a very narrow function in a state system that was necessary but not the central factor in the *après-crise*. Instead, civil society assumed the central role and with it the chaos that would inevitably be connected with a more libertarian, anti-institutional milieu. For, if Minc was correct in his historical assessment, since 1968 France had evolved away from the state as creator of civil society to a more Tocquevillian position of civil society as an independent entity, shaping itself in an ad hoc fashion, in accordance with the *droit à la différence*, in effect sui generis. No party, no union, and no interest group had the right to monopolize this process in the name of some higher cause or right. No one had the right to place a teleological meaning on it. Liberty and civil society were ends in themselves and not means toward some higher goal of socialism or liberalism or nationalism. And that was the meaning, above all, of the *après-crise*, for the après-crise was *après*-socialism, *après*-liberalism, *après*-politics as usual.

Assuming that Minc was correct in his analysis, did the Socialists understand the new environment that had emerged by 1984? The answer, quite clearly, is no. For the most part, the party was bewildered by the events of the early 1980s, incapable of comprehending why the intellectuals had turned against them—as witnessed by Max Gallo's call for the intellectuals to rally around the party—or why their policies were condemned for undermining liberty, a value that the party held dear. Those Socialists who rushed to print to analyze the Socialist experience in power generally offered apologias and poorly digested material. No major work of political philosophy emerged from Socialist ranks to deal with the crisis that the party was clearly going through by 1984. Many of the works that did appear, such as Max Gallo's *Troisième alliance pour un nouvel individualisme*, were filled with repetitious clichés, which did not prove helpful for understanding the problem.[82] Others merely repeated old positions or engaged in tired conspiracy theories. For example, CERES and its leader, Jean-Pierre Chevènement, engaged in a critical evaluation of the second left, condemning it for leading the party into the impasse that it faced in the 1980s. Under the collective name of Jacques Mandrin, CERES issued a broadside against the generation of 1968, accusing the intellectuals of that generation of creating a "new Holy Alliance of the liberals and the libertarians."[83] CERES claimed that all of the "new" movements were part of the same hegemonic process of rightist thought and political practice. The only answer to this threat was to reaffirm the values that CERES had outlined in the 1970s. Beyond this and a reaffirmation of support for the *Projet socialiste*, CERES had nothing to say. The problems that the government faced in the 1980s were totally the fault of the second left.[84]

Reluctantly, some within the party began to engage in a serious analysis of its shortcomings. The party's main intellectual organ, *La nouvelle revue socialiste*, moved toward recognizing the need to integrate parts of the liberal critique of socialism into the party's and the government's programs.[85] The journal talked less and less about the rupture with capitalism and more and more about the need to modernize the economy.[86] But, for the most part, the party found itself incapable of responding intellectually to the numerous accusations leveled against it and resorted instead to following the pragmatic leadership that François Mitterrand provided through his keen sense of political realism. With the appointment of Laurent Fabius as prime minister, the Socialist government moved rapidly toward a more centrist position, taking into consideration some of the criticisms that the opposition had levied against it. With that change in direction, the ideological debate in the party came to a virtual halt. Not even CERES had much to say after the summer of 1984.

Finally, when the dust had cleared on the "battle of the eighties," one could claim that it was much ado about nothing. Liberty was hardly endangered by the Socialist government and much of the rhetoric that came from opponents or critics was overblown, bombastic, or barely believable. Yet, in another sense this battle was unlike any other that France had fought. It marked the end of an era, the era of the post-1958 generation in politics. The right, which had been staunchly committed to state intervention, with some exceptions, converted to libertarian values, while the left—at least the Socialist left—reluctantly shed itself of the statist, hard-left option. Although these transformations did not lead to a centrist alternative, they made such an alternative more plausible. Class struggle, the dictatorship of the proletariat, hegemonic politics, the rupture with capitalism, and other leftist shibboleths were seriously challenged in the course of the 1980s. As a result, both CERES and the Communist party lost support. If the Socialists were to hold their own in such circumstances, they would have to adjust to the new environment rapidly. Since no new political ideas emerged on the left in response to this crisis, Mitterrand's pragmatism became the only alternative for the Socialists. Whether that would be sufficient to hold off the liberal rightist threat remained problematic. The great danger was that in the process of moving to the right for the purpose of maintaining power, socialism would lose its identity. But the alternative of political annihilation was even worse. In the end, the party would reluctantly move toward the center, *faute de mieux*, and eventually end up embracing *cohabitation*.

The case of Paul Quilès offers one striking, representative example of this change of course. In 1981, Quilès had been one of the key advocates of radical change, being labeled by the right as "Robespaul" for his shrill statements at the Valence congress. But Quilès was a loyal Mitterrandist, so loyal that the president appointed him to the politically sensitive position of minister of defense in 1985 when Charles Hernu was forced to resign for his role in the sinking of the Rainbow Warrior in New Zealand. In other words, Quilès could be trusted to put the lid on this bothersome matter, which he did promptly. No one would have called Quilès a party intellectual, much less an intellectual, but he chose the occasion of his rise to the Ministry to publish a slim volume on politics, with the revealing title of *La politique n'est pas ce que vous croyez* (*Politics is not what you think it is*). The thesis of this work was quite amazing: Quilès claimed, without any reservations, that the Socialist party's ideology, since 1968, had been that of the modernization of France, in line with the ideas of Pierre Mendès-France. Thus, he explained the defeat of Michel Rocard at the Metz party congress in 1979 as the defeat of an erroneous strategy for gaining power, rather than a reversal of Socialist ideology. Rocard's ideas on modernization were in the mainstream of the Socialist party, but his refusal to ally with the Communist party in order to gain power was the wrong strategy. Like Rocard, Quilès wanted to go beyond politics in order to reach consensus around the themes of "modernity, responsibility, efficacity." He believed that the Socialists were best suited for achieving such consensus; they were the most "consensual" of all parties in France, as demonstrated by their program since 1981. Hardly mentioning nationalization, which he had supported strongly in 1981, Quilès responded to rightist criticisms that the Socialists had increased state power by pointing to the government's program of decentralization, its encouragement of individual initiative, and its emphasis on civil society. He embraced totally the notion that the power of the state needed to be checked, although he rejected liberal demands to dismantle it. He ended his brief journey into politics with the belief that after 1981, France "entered modernization and ... took control of her future."[87]

Such would be the "ideology" of the Socialist party of 1986, totally divorced from any hint of revolutionary change, desperately involved in the struggle for electoral victory. The views of Paul Quilès were the mainstream of the party by then and not some bizarre centrist deviation from the tripartite strategy of *union de la gauche, front de classe*, and *autogestion*. The effects of the *durée* and the hostile intellectual environment of the 1970s and 1980s had made their final imprint on Socialist ideology by March 1986, shaping it in ways that Pierre Mendès-France would approve of. The Modern Republic had prevailed over the Socialist Republic in every faction of the party, including CERES.

5

"*Moderniser et Rassembler*":
The Long March toward *Cohabitation*,
July 1984–March 1986

By mid-1984, the main outlines of the Socialist program had been implemented by the Mauroy government, yet the rupture with capitalism appeared less, rather than more, possible. Although socialism as a reform movement had succeeded in implementing virtually all of the 110 propositions outlined by François Mitterrand in 1981, socialism as a revolutionary movement, dedicated to creating a new society and a new citizenry in place of "decadent" capitalist society and the proverbial "economic man," had failed in its objectives. The abrupt change of government in mid-July 1984, which entailed the breakdown of the Socialist-Communist alliance and the repudiation of the archaic SFIO holdovers in the Socialist party, represented the beginning of a new ideological course based on the vague concept of "modernization." But it also represented a political coup for François Mitterrand. By scrapping the Savary law, calling for a referendum on the right of the French to hold referendums on questions of basic liberties, and breaking with the Communists, he succeeded in squelching the opposition's criticism that the government represented a threat to the nation's liberties. Yet, such a masterstroke of political opportunism, entailing cataclysmic ideological mutations, could only be absorbed over time. Exactly what the blitzkrieg of July 1984 meant for the left and for France would only become clear by March 1986.

Be that as it may, many close observers of the political scene viewed the July changes as part of a long-term process and not as a sudden change of direction by François Mitterrand. Thierry Pfister, who served as Pierre Mauroy's personal councillor at Matignon, concluded that the prime minister and the president began to move in different ideological directions in early 1984, when Mitterrand placed emphasis on modernization at the expense of employment, refusing to allow Mauroy the necessary funds to increase the government's commitment to early-retirement and job schemes. Through industrial restructuring,

Mitterrand, Fabius, and Delors believed, the "canards-boiteux" of the economy could be eliminated in one rapid stroke. The right would be caught off guard by the new Socialist position and the party would reap the political and economic benefits of a successful modernization policy.[1] From the beginning, Mauroy was uncomfortable with this policy, and when Mitterrand repudiated the Savary law, the prime minister concluded that he could no longer serve in a government that totally rejected what he stood for.[2]

Mauroy's departure provided Mitterrand with the opportunity to change direction completely by appointing a fellow modernizer, Laurent Fabius, as prime minister. Consciously or unconsciously, Mitterrand followed the path that previous Fifth Republic president's had pursued by selecting a close associate to succeed a prominent political figure in the prime minister's office.[3] However, this represented the first time that a Socialist president had acted in this manner and, more importantly, the first time that the ideological position of a government was transformed radically by the choice of a new prime minister. The selection of Laurent Fabius startled almost everyone. No political pundit had imagined that Mitterrand would make such a choice. As the journal *L'Express* concluded: "Rarely has a prime minister been replaced by a successor who is so different from him. The old warrior of the SFIO bows out to the representative of the post-Epinay generation. The party man bows out to the President's man. The 'socially concerned' man to the technocrat. The prolo to the bourgeois."[4]

Laurent Fabius was not known for his deeply held socialist views. He had joined the party in 1974, for reasons that remained obscure. Soon thereafter he became an economic advisor to François Mitterrand and in 1976 was appointed Mitterrand's *directeur de cabinet*. An Enarque, a *sur-douée*, and a very wealthy man, Fabius was not even representative of the Socialist elite. Mitterrand had appointed him to the first Mauroy government to check the more radical tendencies of people like Chevènement. Then, in March 1983, he assumed the CERES leader's post of minister of industry and research, which he used to inaugurate the first aspects of the new policy of industrial restructuring and modernization. By July 1984, Fabius was prepared to carry that policy to its logical conclusion. When the Communists bargained for posts in the new government, Fabius insisted that they endorse without reservation the Socialist policy of rigor and modernization, a condition that they refused to accept.[5]

Despite heavy emphasis on modernization, the Fabius government was not based on a narrow modernizing faction within the party. All three currents paticipated in it, revealing the extent to which Mitterrand commanded the respect of different factions and the degree to which the policy of modernization had become, by 1984, the only viable one that the party possessed in its effort to restore the economic health of the nation. Jean-Pierre Chevènement committed his CERES current to modernization by joining the government as minister of education, just a little over a year after he had condemned the Mauroy government for violating Socialist objectives by pursuing the policy of the "pause."[6] Chevènement justified his decision on the basis of solidarity and electoral politics. In turn, Pierre Joxe joined the government as minister of the interior, bringing one of the most vocal advocates of the union of the left into the government, while Pierre Mauroy's closest political associate, Michel Delebarre, assumed the important post of minister of work, employment, and formation and Michel Rocard remained the lone representative of his current at the Ministry of Agriculture. Beyond those crucial appointments, the Mitterrandists colonized most of the remaining major posts in the government, the most important of which, the Ministry of Finances, went to Pierre Bérégovoy, who replaced the volatile Jacques Delors, who was selected to be president of the European Commission (effective in January 1985), a promotion intended to appease him for not receiving the prime ministership. With the reappointment of old stalwarts such as Gaston Defferre, Georgina Dufoix, Edith Cresson, Yvette Roudy, Claude Cheysson, Charles Hernu, Robert Badinter, and the PSU and Radical party ministers, the Fabius government united every element of the non-Communist left behind a policy of rigor and modernization.[7]

On 24 July 1984, Laurent Fabius presented his government's program to the National Assembly in a speech entitled "Moderniser et Rassembler." He began with a clear commitment to pursue those objectives—"To modernize and to unite: these shall be the priorities of the government that I lead"—and proceeded to define in detail what they meant. To modernize meant, above all, to increase employment, even though in the short run that might entail an increase in unemployment. The choice, to Fabius, was an either/or one: either modernize or decline. Thus, in terms of the economy, the goals of the Ninth Plan had to be carried to fruition: massive support of research, investment, and education were essential for modernizing the nation's economic system. In addition, Fabius argued, social relations had to be transformed. This required that the state encourage industry and civil society to expand their areas of competence: "The State has encountered its limits. It must not go beyond them." Decentralization, social dialogue, the realization of the Auroux laws, and other aspects of civil society had to be promoted in order to achieve thorough modernization of social relations. But modernization by itself was not sufficient for achieving the nation's goals. If modernization were carried out in a divided society, little would be accomplished. For this reason, Fabius connected modernization with the imperative to unite, to "rassembler." This entailed, above all, union behind the objective of liberty. The Socialists had already accomplished a great deal on this score, Fabius thought, but it was necessary to go further, to unite the nation behind liberty for the schools and to allow the people the right to determine what their liberties should include through the vehicle of the national referendum. In addition, unity had to be achieved in the struggle against insecurity and in regard to foreign affairs. If consensus triumphed on all of these fronts over the divisions that currently existed, the future of France would be glorious indeed. "Moderniser et Rassembler" was, to Fabius, "Le coeur du futur."[8]

Very little that Fabius said was new. He had stated his centrist, modernizing position on a number of occasions since he had been elevated to minister of industry and research in March 1983. But, on this occasion, he committed a Socialist government to a program that hardly mentioned equality, except the old-fashioned republican notion of equality of opportunity, that eschewed all of the rhetoric of the union of the left, from the "rupture" to class struggle and *autogestion*, and that embraced such centrist themes as liberty, civil society, entrepreneurship, education, unity of all French people, and modernization as the keys to the new socialism. As the right-wing journal, *L'Express*, commented, the opposition had been caught off guard by Fabius's address and the events of July, which made its objections to the left's archaic leadership and objectives seem irrelevant.[9] At the same time, however, the left began to doubt whether it had any distinctive program of its own. Laurent Joffrin, in his *La gauche en voie de disparition*, argued that the Socialist party was in total disarray after discovering that its policies were impractical and incapable of being implemented in a democratic society. He predicted that the country would move toward some form of Thatcherism in the aftermath of the inevitable Socialist defeat in March 1986.[10] Such staunch Socialists as Christian Pierret, deputy from the Vosges and a Mauroy follower, stated bluntly: "We can no longer hide behind our texts. The exercise of power has changed us. It has become as old fashioned to speak of rupture with capitalism as it is to speak of abolition of salaries." In a more combative vein, but still realistic, Claude Estier, the director of *l'Unité*, proclaimed: "We have existed on some rather simplistic ideas. The rupture cannot occur as we had envisaged in a society which remains and shall remain predominantly capitalist, a society which is totally linked to a capitalist environment." However, the most thoroughly revisionist analysis of the situation came from the Rocardian deputy from the Indre, Michel Sapin: "Socialism is a road. One never arrives at the socialist end. The rupture or the hundred days, which is the same thing, is a total myth.''[11]

Divorced of rhetorical flourishes and the mystique that inevitably accompanies the rise of a new, unknown personality to the prime minister's office, the Fabius program embodied no grand reforms no major changes in policy. It was, instead, a program that recognized what many had concluded were the facts of life. Delors's "pause" and "rigor' were now accepted as policy. The mixed economy moved from the realm of a vague idea to that of a concrete objective. The Mauroy reform program came to an abrupt end. The government, henceforth, would engage in management and not in reform. The status quo, with minor modifications, would be the way of the future. This meant tight budgetary controls to reduce inflation, the trade deficit, and the national debt for the purpose of reinvigorating both private and nationalized industries. Wages had to be kept roughly equal to inflation and profits had to increase substantially in order to achieve the government's modernization goals. No massive state intervention, no grand projects were envisaged in this scenario, except for the grand republican idea of improving education to meet the needs of a modern society and the technocratic notion that the state must intervene to spur on research and development of high technology in a society that is incapable of advancing such projects because of the weakness of capitalism and the lack of an entrepreneurial spirit. The formula that Fabius came up with brought the Socialists very close to the notion of a liberal state, without, however, the neoliberal antiwelfare state mentality. It was an uninspiring formula, lacking in vision and charisma, but structured according to the order of things, necessary for reviving the economy and winning the March 1986 elections.

Laurent Fabius struggled hard to place his program in the best possible light. In an interview with *Le Nouvel Observateur* in its issue of 30 November 1984, he presented what was probably the most convincing justification of what his government was trying to do in pursuing "la modernisation et la rassemblement." He began by blaming the Giscard/Barre government for the nation's precarious economic situation: its neglect of key sectors of the economy had created numerous problems for the Socialists when they took power, requiring them to invest heavily in certain areas such as computers in order to save entire industrial sectors from collapsing. In addition, the newly elected Socialist government had to carry out a cultural revolution to change the attitudes of the French toward industry, international competition, the idea of profits, and the need for social dialogue between workers and management. Unlike the quick-fix Keynsean program followed by the United States, which France could not have pursued without suffering catastrophic economic consequences, the Socialist program required time to take effect. This was especially true, Fabius thought, in the area of education, which was the key to his government's policies. Not only was better education necessary for modernization, but also it was the sine qua non for the achievement of true freedom—that is, for the creation of an educated populace, able to decide on its own about the issues of science, bureaucracy, media, politics, and so on. Furthermore, this "Jules Ferry II" had to be carried out in the context of Europe, not just in terms of France alone: "the liberty of France through a European dimension, the liberty of the individual through a sharing of knowledge" were the ultimate goals of the Socialist program. But, unfortunately politics and long-term changes did not mix well. As Fabius put the matter: "the period of economic, social, and cultural mutation that we are in the process of managing is a long-term undertaking; the period of political accountability is short-term. Will we be able to explain this?" Consequently, to Fabius, the politiical issue for 1986 was, very simply, which party could best manage France in the 1980s to achieve the long-term goals that he had outlined. Yet, after this lengthy explanation of his government's program, the interviewers for *Le Nouvel Observateur* asked Fabius to be specific about what the Socialists still had to accomplish. The prime minister's answer revealed considerable irritation that his interlocutors had not understood his position: "We are not going to remake the nationalizations, the program of decentralization, or the Auroux laws each year just 'for the principle of it.' You can't storm the Bastille all the time." True, but many on the left could not understand this technocratic Socialist manager and his appeal to the "longue durée."

While Fabius's rhetoric clearly established the idea that structures had to be transformed to achieve the government's goals, his government's actions were concentrated primarily on short-term economic objectives. By the summer of 1984, it was clearly established that the minister of finances, through the annual budget procedure, controlled the main outlines of government policy, and not such ministries as industry and research or the plan (now basically defunct), which had attempted in the past to implement some form of long-term industrial or national policy as the key to Socialist rule. As a result, the actions of the Fabius administration can be best approached through an analysis of what the 1985 and 1986 budgets intended to achieve rather than through an analysis of long-term structural reforms.

Although much of the 1985 budget had already been determined by Jacques Delors before the July coup, its general thrust corresponded completely with the managerial mentality of the Fabius administration, confirming the continuity that existed with the last year or so of the

Mauroy government, in which Delors, Fabius, and Bérégovoy controlled economic policy. While the 1984 budget had inaugurated a policy of budgetary austerity, the 1985 budget promised more of the same plus the implementation of François Mitterrand's promise to reduce government expenditures as a percentage of gross national product by 1 percent. This entailed granting individual taxpayers a 20 billion franc cut in taxes and businesses a 10 billion franc respite while reducing the number of state employees (by about five thousand), paring back on subsidies to private industries, and controlling rising medical costs. But this scheme also entailed hefty increases in petrol and telephone taxes to make up for much of the reductions in direct taxes. In effect, the new budget promised that taxes would not increase, but offered no guarantee that they would decline. For individuals, however, the budget promised a 1.6 percent increase in buying power, which would go primarily to the wealthiest taxpayers, as the result of the elimination of the surcharge that had been established in March 1983 on income tax payments of 20,000 francs or more.[12]

Given such major restraints on public spending, the 1985 budget inevitably meant cuts in most departments of government and less emphasis on solidarity with the poor. Only four or five administrative areas received real increases in revenue as the result of this budget: research, industry, education, culture, and *grands travaux*. All other departments were forced to economize. For the poor, this meant lower than cost-of-living increases in basic welfare and pension benefits, both of which were boosted only 4 percent for 1985. The SMICARDS, in contrast, received cost-of-living increases in the minimum wage, but this was a far cry from the massive real gains of 1982–83. As a consequence, the 1985 budget looked like the world turned right side up, after having been turned upside down. It was a budget to encourage industry to invest, the wealthy to consume, and the poor to tighten their belts. Although it was hardly Reaganesque, it came closer to Reaganism than any previous Socialist budget had. Through this budget, Fabius and company committed themselves to modernization, but the idea of *rassemblement* was lacking, if not missing.[13]

By 1985, when the budget for 1986 was drawn up, the economic situation had not changed appreciably, but the government understood more clearly what *"moderniser et rassembler"* meant. Once again, the minister of finances offered the nation an austerity budget, with an increase in spending of only 3.6 percent. Once again, this meant major cuts in various departments of government. However, this time Fabius's policy of modernization was applied fully to nationalized industries. With the exception of steel, Renault, and coal, subsidies to nationalized industries were cut drastically—by 25 percent in the case of shipbuilding—and most of them were required to show a profit in 1986. The minister of industry's budget was slashed 16 percent, as aid to nationalized industries went from 11.3 billion to 8.8 billion francs. Savings from such cuts contributed to funding the prime minister's policy of bolstering certain key ministries involved in modernization and *rassemblement*. For example, the minister of the interior received a 22 percent increase to modernize the police force, the Ministry of Justice obtained 9 percent more for modernizing the prison system, the minister of research gained an additional 8 percent for research projects, and the minister of education garnered an additional 7 percent to modernize the educational system.[14] In light of Laurent Fabius's July 1984 speech to the National Assembly, all of these increases coincided with Socialist policy, the first two with the policy of *rassembler*, by improving security for all French people, and the last two with the policy of *moderniser*. But, in terms of what Socialist ideology meant traditionally, even in regard to the 1982 budget, an observer would be correct in arguing that these increases represented capitulation to rightist electoral pressures and pragmatic centrism, as we shall see in more detail later on.

With the addition of measures to aid business in the 1985 budget, namely the reduction of the corporate tax rate from 50 to 45 percent and a further 10 percent cut in the *taxe professionelle*, the Fabius government made clear that the ideal relationship between the state and industry was one in which the state intervened primarily for the purpose of establishing the general business environment, rather than to create a comprehensive industrial policy. Although the Socialists still maintained certain sectoral policies in regard to textiles, electronics, and other areas of the economy, as well as general rules for the operation of nationalized industries, the Jean-Pierre Chevènement idea of close state tutelage of industry had been totally scrapped by 1985. Nationalized industries were encouraged to go to the *bourse*, not to the state, if they wanted funding for projects, and with that advice these industries moved further away from ministerial supervision and closer to a form of privatization, through the use of *titres participatifs* and *certificats d'investissements* to gain capital funds in the private sector. As one former rightist minister of finances, Jean-Pierre Fourcade, said of the new direction in 1985, "The essential point is to abandon the old social democratic conception of systematic aid to enterprises that are in trouble and to favor, through fiscal measures, those that are profitable." He could have added that the social democratic notion of the welfare state was being gradually abandoned also: in 1986, according to the Fabius budget, welfare spending would increase less than inflation.[15]

In the midst of this passion for modernization, *Le Monde's* presidential watcher, Jean-Marie Colombani, said of the Fabius administration: "Like a distant echo of Guizot's famous 'Enrichissez-vous,' the time of Mitterrand's 'Modernisez-vous' has finally arrived."[16] Perhaps. At least the evidence we have seen so far would indicate that to be the case. But the Socialist party was broader than the government and its concerns were often closely tied to the quotidian needs of its constituents, among whom were an increasing number of unemployed. As the party leader, Lionel Jospin, put the matter, modernization had to be accompanied by social justice. The Mauroy current within the party, which was represented in the government by Michel Delebarre at the Ministry of Labor, supported this general position against the budget-cutting priorities of the Mitterrand current. Taking up where Mauroy left off, Delebarre quickly emerged as the principal government official concerned about rising unemployment. During the summer of 1984, independent economic forecasts estimated that 3 million would be unemployed by the end of 1985, which would represent more than a 50 percent increase over 1981, when the Socialists came to power. Already, by August 1984, unemployment was approaching 2.5 million, an increase of 300,000 over December 1983, representing a reversal of Socialist efforts to contain the problem. In this deteriorating situation, Delebarre took the initiative, proposing four ways to deal with unemployment. Three of the four were more or less long-term, involving training, retraining, and the expansion of higher education , all of which coincided with the general policy of "*moderniser et rassembler*." None of these was particularly new or promising as a solution to the problem. But the final option provided a novel compromise between the modernizers and the advocates of solidarity, one which offered a quick fix without costing the government much of anything. It called for the hiring of unemployed youths, between sixteen and twenty-one years old, to work on socially useful public service jobs at the local level for eighty hours a month at a salary of 1,200 francs, which was below the minimum wage, but slightly above the unemployment benefit level. Both Mitterrand and Fabius were enthusiastic about this new idea. Consequently, by the end of September 1984, the plan was ready to be put into operation, with the objective of hiring 500,000 young workers by the end of 1985.[17]

The TUCs, as they were called—Travaux d'utilité collective—proved to be both successful and controversial. They helped salvage both the conscience of the Jospin–Mauroy left and the party's electoral hopes by contributing to keep the unemployment rate well below the predicted 3 million mark for the end of 1985. Unemployment, by early 1986, was barely above the level it had reached in August 1984, around 2.4 million, a level that had remained more or less the same since March 1985. Much of this stability was due to TUCs, which had employed some 135,000 young workers by the end of June 1985.[18] But the TUCs were not appreciated by the unions, who feared that they would set a precedent for cuts in the minimum wage and pave the way for other kinds of savings at the expense of the working class. Union fears were well founded. During 1985, the number of part-time and precarious jobs created by French firms increased by 134,000 and 78,000, respectively, over 1984. As a consequence of this and the related phenomenon of the very low increase in the number of full-time jobs, French workers lowered their expectations dramatically: between 1982 and 1985, the percentage of those looking for work who said they would accept only full-time employment decreased from 57.6 to 39.5 percent.[19]

The success of the TUCs encouraged the Socialists to come up with similar measures to cut unemployment. In February 1985, the government unveiled a scheme to subsidize the hiring of part-time workers by private industry. Neither the unions nor the patrons welcomed the prospect. At the same time, the government attempted to obtain consensus from the unions in support of measures to allow flexibility in the work place. In late 1985, after failing to gain union support on job flexibility, the government unilaterally introduced a bill that legalized weekend work, part-time work, and the payment of overtime work through days off if desired, all aimed at achieving greater freedom of choice in the workplace. Although the rules on overtime hours, dismissals, and the length of the work week were maintained and even reinforced in favor of the workers in some cases, all of the unions except the CFDT opposed this bill as an attempt to undermine working-class rights for the purpose of improving productivity. With help from the Communists, they attempted, unsuccessfully, to block it from passing the legislature before the March elections.[20]

With very few exceptions, the unions were losing all of the key battles in their attempts to protect workers against the pains of the policy of modernization. Public opinion had shifted against the unions since 1981. With that went a series of negative developments: a consensus had emerged among the non-Communist political parties in support of part-time work and flexibility of employment, workers' wages and benefits had stagnated or declined since 1981 despite the government of the left and the unions, unemployment benefits had decreased as the result of the crisis of the system, and those unions that were closely associated with the government had experienced a sharp drop in support in elections to such bodies as the comités d'entreprise and the social security councils. Not surprisingly, union membership dropped. For example, the CFDT, which was the only union that published accurate membership counts, had declined to only 737,000 paying members by 1983, which was 12 percent below its 1977 peak. Worker apathy and cynicism made the unions' task harder: despite rising unemployment throughout the early 1980s, strike activity declined every year, reaching its lowest rate in twenty years during 1985. Even though CFDT leader Edmond Maire lashed out at the government's short-sighted economic policies and CGT head Henri Krasucki accused the Socialists of "weakening the union movement," the rank and file remained mired in the lethargy that the Fabius government helped create. "*Moderniser et rassembler*" did not seem to include them in its plans. If social democracy were in the process of being created in France, it was over the demoralized acquiesence of the very people it supposedly represented.[21]

But "*moderniser et rassembler*" was not social democracy. It was, quite simply, a pragmatic economic policy based on the failures of previous Socialist policies and aimed at correcting the worst problems before the March 1986 elections. The unions were irrelevant to the success of this overall policy, which aimed at reducing French indebtedness, defeating inflation, improving productivity, and increasing industrial investment, as the primary means of solving the long-term problem of unemployment. Although the nationalized industries continued to be at the center of this policy, their role had changed from that of saving French jobs to the modernization of the nation's economy. Given that new function, those industries could proceed with the plans that had been set in motion during the spring of 1984, without giving much concern to questions of employment, which were now resolved through such devices as TUCs and early retirements at much lower cost and without endangering industrial productivity.

The 1985 and 1986 budgets continued this process of redefinition of the role of nationalized industries. Out of these emerged two kinds of state-controlled industries: those that were too weak to stand on their own, for whatever reason, and those that could and must compete on their own in the marketplace. In the case of the former category, which included steel, coal, shipbuilding, and, eventually, Renault, the government's strategy was to continue subsidizing them until they were either nourished back to economic health or phased out. There was no doubt in the minds of those who determined government policy that jobs would have to be cut, sometimes drastically, in all of these sick industries. And cuts would be made no matter what the unions or Socialist party members wanted, because modernization required them, which often meant the Common Market required them, a convenient subterfuge for avoiding responsibility. In the case of the latter category of state industries, the government basically made them into self-sustaining enterprises, with little supervision over their affairs, except the imperative to realize profits, invest in new technologies, and become world-class operations in their fields. Even though they received some indirect government aid, they were allowed to act much the way that private industry acted in France: *bonnet blanc, blanc bonnet*, for essentially it made little difference whether they were state-controlled or private, given the French system.[22]

A few examples of what happened to both types of nationalized industries under the Fabius administration will be helpful for understanding this transition from the CERES model to eventual privatization under the right.

By the end of 1984, the government could proclaim success in regard to most of the newly nationalized industries in the competitive sector, which included CGE, Saint-Gobain, Pechiney, Rhône-Poulenc, Thomson, and Bull. They had total earnings of 2.07 billion francs during that year, marking their first profitable year since 1980, when they earned 663 million francs. The results of restructuring these industries were beginning to be felt, although the cost proved to be quite high in terms of plants closed, jobs lost, and monies invested. By the end of 1985, however, all of these industries had been recentered on their traditional sectors: CGE was recentered on the telephone and electric energy sector, Saint-Gobain on glass manufacture and public works, Pechiney on aluminum, Rhône-Poulenc on drugs and related chemicals, and Thomson and Bull on electronics and computers. The cost, to the state, had been about 10 billion francs above the expense of purchasing these industries. In 1984, the year of mass dismissals, these competitve industries reduced their work force by 2 percent, primarily through early retirements and retraining. Dismissals became commonplace even in these relatively successful sectors of the state-run economy. As a consequence, by 1986, the workers had no real personal stake in these industries, which many of them viewed as giant monopolistic enterprises intent upon establishing French presence in the industrial world rather than engaging in dialogue with their employees and creating new forms of citizenship, in the spirit of the Auroux laws.[23] Pechiney, for example, placed over two-thirds of its investments abroad, mainly in Canada where energy was cheap, while CGE invested 2 billion francs in the American market in an effort to become a world-class telephone firm, contributing to a cut of 8,000 jobs in its French operations during 1984 and 1985.[24] The CERES-inspired idea of reconquering the internal market no longer applied in the new environment of modernization.

In regard to these state-run industries, Socialist nationalization served as the French means of protecting and restructuring the advanced competitive industrial sector during the crisis of the early 1980s. Everything else was secondary. This required the Socialist government to be very pragmatic in treating these industries, even to the point of using the *bourse* to underwrite their capital. By the end of 1984 they had raised almost twice as much capital through private means as through the state. In pursuing this path, the government did not seem to be concerned that the success of its policies would make these nationalized industries extremely vulnerable to privatization once the opposition regained power. However, it would be incorrect to conclude, as the Communists did, that the Socialists were secret capitalist agents: they acted toward these industries in a Colbertian or Saint-Simonist sense. They did not hesitate to intervene directly to obtain contracts for firms or to encourage takeovers or mergers. Thomson, the electronics and computer giant, was given lucrative state contracts to sell computers to the French schools, and the chemical industry was subjected to extraordinary government pressure to restructure itself according to Socialist plans. The marketplace was neither disdained nor accepted at face value. A guided economic system, subject to market forces, was the Socialist model for competitive nationalized industries.[25]

With steel, coal, shipbuilding, and Renault, however, the mixed economy did not work well. All of these lost vast sums of money in the early 1980s, accounting for 80 percent of the government's subsidies to nationalized industries, or about 40 billion francs by the end of 1984. As we have seen, the modernization program of early 1984 aimed to stop these *trous* by dismissing vast numbers of workers and closing plants, marking a complete reversal of previous Socialist policy, which aimed at saving jobs first. Unfortunately, these plans did not work well. With the exception of the coal industry, which managed to break even by the end of 1984, thanks to 3.4 billion francs in state subsidies and a 10 percent cut in the work force, both steel and shipbuilding remained major problems, while Renault, which was not included in the 1984 plan, went from being a firm in some difficulty to the position of a fourth *trou*. Steel absorbed 40 percent of all state subsidies to nationalized industries in 1985. Despite this, the government had to close down steel plants at Fos, in Bouches-du-Rhône, and Trith-Saint-Léger, in the Nord, alienating two of the most important Socialist leaders, Gaston Defferre and Pierre Mauroy. Yet, the animosities between the two state-controlled steel firms, Sacilor and Usinor, were so great that government plans to merge them, in order to achieve economies of scale and more efficient management and planning, could not be carried out. No resolution of the steel crisis was in sight by 1986. The same was true of shipbuilding. Massive subsidies of 400,000 francs per worker failed to reverse the fortunes of this industry, which built only 165,000 tons of ships in 1984, far below the 270,000 tons envisaged in the modernization plan. More dismissals, to the point where the industry would virtually disappear, seemed to be the only solution.[26]

While everyone expected problems in these three traditional ailing sectors, the crisis at Renault stunned the nation. In reality, however, the Renault crisis had been building since 1980. Delays in research and development of new models, combined with the disastrous decision to enter the American market by purchasing control of American Motors in 1979, led to increasing annual losses throughout the early 1980s. In October 1984, under pressure from Fabius, the head of Renault, Bernard Hanon, presented a plan to dismiss 15,000 workers in an effort to regain profitability. But, in January 1985, preliminary estimates showed that Renault would lose a record 7 billion francs in 1984, or 5.5 billion francs more than its 1983 losses. As a result, the government appointed Georges Besse to replace Hanon on 17 January 1985. Immediately, Besse drew up plans for massive cuts, including the dismissal of up to 25,000 workers in the course of 1985–86 and the sale of Renault's electronic equipment subsidiary, Renix, to the Allied group. In addition, he kept salary increases down to only 1.5 percent for the first half of 1985. The response of the working class to these drastic proposals was one of almost total apathy and despair. The CGT's attempts to carry out strikes in the Renault factories during the fall of 1985, ended in total defeat within the course of a few days, despite the fact that the union was the dominant force in the state automobile industry. At Le Mans, where the CGT hoped the strike would be most successful, 70 percent of the workers voted against it. At Billancourt, two-thirds of the work force returned to their jobs within half a day. According to one poll of salaried workers, taken in the fall of 1985, the CGT's image had deteriorated greatly among them, going from 38 percent favorable in 1981 to 21 percent in 1985. In the 1985 poll, only 6 percent responded that the union was democratic, while 57 percent called it politicized, which meant that they thought it was under the influence of the Communist party.[27] The evidence suggested that Fabius's policy of *"moderniser et rassembler"* had not led to a revival of the far left, despite working-class apprehensions about that policy. Whether because of fear or grudging acceptance of Socialist pragmatism, the modernization program of 1984 prevailed in the toughest constituency of all, Renault. France had moved a long way from the patronizing attitude that one should not discourage the workers at Billancourt! They had the right— the duty—to be discouraged along with everyone else.

Any final assessment of the Socialist experiment in nationalization inevitably must consider the political biases of those who are judging the situation. As we have seen, these biases range from extreme laisser-faire advocates to ardent defenders of the state. But possibly Jacques Delors offered the most reasonable, balanced assessment of an experiment that he had been deeply involved in, belying the usual wisdom that actors lack objectivity. To Delors, the problems with nationalization began with Socialist perceptions of what state control meant. In 1981, no one was aware of the precarious financial position that most of these firms were in as the result of years of keeping dividends high and capital investment low. The Socialists did not know that they would have to spend money and time in restructuring and infusing vast sums of needed capital into the newly nationalized sector. Second, Delors argued, the Socialists wasted much needed funds by nationalizing at 100 percent rather than by assuming majority control. In that context, Delors proceeded to evaluate the success of nationalization. In his estimation, the six newly nationalized industries in the competitive sector had done about as well as their private German counterparts in modernizing, restructuring, and overcoming the crisis of the 1980s. But, no social revolution had occurred as a result of French nationalization, in part because of the enormous energies that went into saving the national patrimony. For the most part, the nationalized industries were run along the same lines as they had been prior to the state takeover. After considering the enormous difficulties that he had encountered in straightening out the financial chaos of the nationalized banks—something he had not expected to be the case—Delors claimed that it was impossible to say whether nationalization was an economic success because so many variables clouded the picture: the *crise mondiale*, the *vieillissement de l'économie française*, and the problems of *étatisation*. However, Delors was quite certain that the nationalized industries "do not have a prophetic mission to fullfill in either the economic recovery or in achieving social progress."[28]

The same cautious perspective seems appropriate in evaluating the success of the Socialist economic program. Clearly, by the end of 1985, problems such as inflation, the trade balance, capital investment, and productivity seemed to be on the way toward being resolved successfully. Inflation declined steadily from 1983 on, reaching a low of 4.7 percent in 1985, with projections of a 2.5 percent rate for 1986, reversing the double-digit level of the early 1980s. The trade deficit, which had reached massive proportions in 1982, as the result of the failed *relance* and the international economic conjuncture, dropped percipitously. The current account deficit declined from 79.3 billion francs in 1982 to 265 million in 1984, with 1985 achieving a slight surplus. As the result of Socialist policies to revive the private sector and investment, French capital investment began to increase in 1983 after a long period of decline. Yvon Gattaz, the head of the CNPF, praised the Socialists on this score when he pointed out that the level of industrial self financing had gone from 48 percent in 1982 to 62 percent in 1983. The OECD's economists also pointed to the improvement of company profit margins, which returned to their 1979 level in 1984. At the same time, industrial productivity increased at a respectable average rate of 2 percent a year during the period 1981–85.[29]

As encouraging as these improvements were, problems still remained. Although the struggle against inflation had reduced the French rate to a little below the European average, which was an improvement over the 1970s, it remained above West Germany's, the nation's main trade partner, and it was achieved through a decrease in individual buying power during 1983 and 1984 (by 0.3 and 0.2 percent respectively). To maintain their standard of living, the French dipped into their savings, which dropped from about 16 percent of total income in 1981 to less than 14 percent in 1984. But those who lost the most, the unemployed, were probably unable to take this course; their buying power plummeted by 13 percent between 1981 and 1984, due to cuts in benefits. Only the lowest-paid workers, the SMICARDS, received significant increases in buying power under the Socialists, and those came in 1981–82. From late 1982 on, however, they received only cost-of-living raises. The domestic solution to inflation was thus based on a policy that penalized the weakest, those who were most susceptible to being unemployed. This included restrictive budgetary and monetary policies, the scrapping of the post-1968 contract that productivity increases would be automatically translated into wage increases, and the abandonment of the indexing of wages and prices, all of which affected the weakest among the working class most severely.[30]

Some critics of the Socialist government have argued that inflation declined primarily as the result of an international economic movement toward lower prices, and not because of Socialist policies. In part that is true, but clearly the Socialists mustered all of their resources to realize this goal and they achieved better than average results, which they needed to do in order to stop the foreign trade deficit from increasing. Lower internal demand, achieved through deflationary policies, contributed to reducing the high trade deficits of 1982 and 1983. But, to many observers, the lower trade deficits of 1984 and after were outweighed by the fact that the nation's external debt increased about five times under the Socialists. Still, the nation's net foreign debt equaled only 230 billion francs on 30 June 1985, which was quite low in comparison with France's trade partners. This was also true of the internal debt, which had also increased greatly under the Socialists. Despite this ominous development, in 1985 it was the lowest state debt—by a large margin—among the great capitalist economies.[31] More important, however, the improvements in foreign trade hid important structural difficulties that had existed for at least a decade and which neither the right nor the left succeeded in resolving. These were: weak investment abroad, in comparison with the nation's trade partners; lack of any dominant international industrial sector in the French economy; heavy reliance upon the Third World for export markets; constant and increasing deficits with Common Market countries, especially West Germany; and heavy dependence on short-term factors such as exchange rates. All of these had been major problems in the late 1970s when Christian Stoffaës warned about them in *La grande menace industrielle*. As Alain Vernholes commented in *Le Monde*, the problem with the French economy was that it could not expand at a rapid rate without encountering severe balance of payments problems. Any attempt to exceed the growth rates of its European trade partners would lead to massive imports, as had occurred in 1981–82, which ended in the crisis that the Socialists spent the next four years trying to solve.[32]

Finally, on the negative side of the ledger, improvements in productivity and investment were directly related to increases in unemployment and restrictions on wage increases. Although the Socialists intended to stop the tide of deindustrialization, they actually contributed to it. In this respect, the continuity between the Giscard years and the Mitterrand ones is again evident. By maintaining a high minimum wage, relative to the nation's trade partners, the Socialists pushed industrialists to replace jobs with machines or to otherwise increase productivity at the expense of the workers. Increased investment for the purpose of achieving greater productivity led to increased unemployment and fewer high-paying industrial jobs. Salaries as a percentage of the added value of an average firm dropped from 70 percent in 1981 to 64.8 percent in 1984, while profits went from 22.1 to 30 percent during that same period. Industry as a percentage of the total gross national product dropped from 21.2 percent in 1980 to 19.8 percent in 1984. Industrial jobs continued to decline in number under the Socialists, as 300,000 were eliminated between 1982 and 1985. The number of unemployed increased as a result, going from slightly under 2 million at the end of 1981 to 2.5 million by 1986, despite government schemes to contain the problem. The areas most affected by deindustrialization remained the same under the Socialists as they had been under Giscard: Lorraine, Franche-Comté, Champagne Ardennes, and Nord-Pas-de-Calais led the nation for the largest drop in industrial employment between 1976 and 1984. Despite decentralization of power and attempts to revitalize the regions, Paris and the Ile-de-France remained the most vital economic part of France, with the lowest unemployment rate—at 8.1 percent in 1984—and the highest percentage of tertiary employment. Again, the Socialist programs failed to reverse deep-seated structural trends. Deindustrialization continued, Paris remained the dominant economic region, Socialist strongholds such as the Nord and Provence experienced some of the highest unemployment rates in the nation, and the tertiary sector remained the only growth sector in the economy, all under Socialist rule.[33]

Structural limits to Socialist reforms existed in every area of the French economy. Without a thoroughly radical program of change, such limits could never be overcome. But radical change required vastly greater state spending over a long period of time and major changes in the tax system, neither of which occurred between 1981 and 1986. Despite the massive increase in outlays in the 1982 budget, the real increase in state expenditures under the Socialists came to about 10 percent, as the budget stagnated after 1983, when Delors's austerity program was launched. Even though certain areas, such as research, adult education, and culture, doubled or tripled their allocations, in constant francs, by 1986, most departments remained at about their 1981 level of funding in real terms. This was true of defense, agriculture, housing and urban development, and transportation and communications. While they stagnated, increasing amounts had to be allocated to service the growing national debt and to contain unemployment: funds for them more than doubled in size under the Socialists.[34]

Furthermore, the Socialists did not attempt to change the structure of the tax system. Regressive taxes not only remained the order of the day under socialism, but they also increased as a percentage of the total taxes collected. Between 1982 and 1985, the income tax as a percentage of total taxes collected declined from 21.8 to 19.7 percent and taxes on corporations fell from 10.4 to 9.5 percent, while the regressive TVA tax and social security charges increased. The former went up by 0.9 percent, reaching 44.3 percent of taxes collected in 1985, and the latter, which is technically not a tax, surpassed the total national tax revenues for the first time, going from 18.5 percent of the gross national product in 1981 to 20.3 percent in 1984, before falling to 19.9 percent in 1986. By comparison, total national taxes declined from 18.6 percent of gross national product in 1981 to 17.9 percent in 1986.[35] Although the Socialists may have saved the Etat-providence from destruction, they did so in a very regressive and unimaginative way. The tax and social security burden continued to fall most heavily on industry and the working class. The demands for fiscalization of the social security system—either partial or total—received virtually no hearing from the left in power. Once more, the structure prevailed over the reformers.

The Socialist policy of modernization did not change profoundly the nation's economic position, any more than the *relance* did or the Giscard years. Modernization merely represented the Socialist government's recognition of the deep-seated problems involved in any reform of the

French economy. In addition, the *rassembler* part of the Fabius government's guiding slogan represented a turning away from pure economic solutions to other alternatives. In that sense, the new government continued the party's Bourg-en-Bresse position, which deflected attention from the economic structure and emphasized the theme of liberty. Nowhere was the spirit of Bourg-en-Bresse more apparent than in the Fabius government's policies on education, which combined both "*moderniser et rassembler*" in an effort to create consensus behind noneconomic solutions to the nation's economic problems in an area with which the Socialist reformers were intimately familiar, in contrast to the treacherous shoals of the economy. Under the Fabius administration, the minister of education rose to a position of prestige and importance that no one had anticipated, given the ignominious reputation of that ministry following the resignation of Alain Savary. Under the astute leadership of Jean-Pierre Chevènement, however, the Socialists rediscovered the Third Republic's educational radicalism, minus anticlericalism, repackaged as the key to the French problem of the 1980s. Or, as one wit put it, Chevènement was "Jules Ferry en kimono."[36]

Soon after taking office, Chevènement defused the issue of merging public and private education by reasserting Mitterrand's position on the Savary law. When the Senate rejected Mitterrand's demand for a referendum to make constitutional the holding of referendums on matters related to liberty, the last contentious aspect of the issue was laid to rest and the minister of education could proceed to rebuild the system. First of all, Jean-Pierre Chevènement cleared up all of the outstanding problems concerning relations between private and public schools by repealing the 1977 law on the subject, which left the far more "republican" law of 1959—the so-called Debré law—on the books. Although this meant that titularization and financial control of private schools had to be scrapped, it did provide the minister with the opportunity to enforce the Debré law's provisions on freedom of conscience and independent rights for teachers in private schools, as well as provisions on job security for teachers and the right of the state to oversee the finances of all private schools. In addition, the new regional-planning mechanism required private schools to adhere strictly to its directives, thus undercutting some of the independence that these institutions had possessed in the past. No merger of the private and the public occurred, but Chevènement obtained as much oversight authority as he could out of the Debré law. The net effect was the implementation of much of what Savary had envisaged without the threat of state usurpation of the rights of private schools to exist as independent entities or the public protests that Savary had encountered.

By late 1984, the issue of private versus public schools had been laid to rest, this time with good prospects that it would not be conjured up again.[37]

But the main thrust of Chevènement's tenure at the Ministry of Education was not to fight the old battles. Rather, he envisaged himself on the front lines of the economic struggle for survival, creating a French educational system capable of competing successfully with the "Nippon-American technological condominium." As he put it: "those who shall not be capable of profiting from the considerable productivity gains that are contained in the diffusion of new technologies shall lose their footing and fall into decadence."[38] To accomplish this formidable task, Chevènement raised the old themes that Jules Ferry and the Republicans used in the nineteenth century, but he placed them in the modern context of Fabius's program of *"moderniser et rassembler"* by proclaiming that "national education must be the *fer de lance* of modernization."[39] No longer were nationalizations placed in this forward position, as they had been under the Mauroy government. Instead, education would provide the miracle solutions that state ownership had not been able to achieve.

In pursuing educational modernization, Chevènement relied heavily on traditional ideas. In his September 1984 press conference on the occasion of the school *rentrée*, he called upon the elementary schools to place greater emphasis on French history, French geography, and civics. Once those basics were learned—once solid values of republican citizenship had been inculcated—students at the college level could begin the task of learning about the new technologies. Clearly, Chevènement believed none of the literature about the failure of the school system to overcome class inequalities. Like Jules Ferry, he thought that society could be remade through the schools and that in the process the struggle for modernization would be won somehow. To encourage this in concrete terms, Chevènement allocated vast sums to improve technical education in the schools: he provided 1 billion francs for purchasing modern machine tools, he bought 100,000 computers for students to use, he inaugurated a program to train 25,000 teachers a year in the use of computers, and he created closer ties between industry and education. In addition, Chevènement also reformed the university system along practical, technological lines: he instituted a degree in new technologies, he reoriented the first cycle to include more emphasis on languages and new technologies, he provided students with orientation and career opportunity meetings to help them plan their course of study in relation to the job market, and he encouraged the universities to open up to industry and new technologies through training more skilled researchers and considering the practical needs of business. To

Chevènement, the final goal of these reforms transcended mere economism or technocracy, to embrace higher matters relating to citizenship, as he stated to a conference on the subject in November 1984: "The workers of our country, no matter what the level of their training and responsibility might be, must know why they are working and that their own personal success cannot be the end of their ambition, for in the difficult circumstances we face, definitive success does not exist, outside of the *collective success of the nation*."[40]

Even though Edmond Maire openly criticized Chevènement for supporting elitist, even conservative educational ideas, and despite the fact that little evidence existed to support the minister's egalitarian beliefs about education, the nation was overwhelmingly enthusiastic about this new educational direction. A poll of the teaching profession, carried out on the eve of the 1985 *rentrée*, revealed that Socialist teachers were the least enthusiastic about Chevènement's reforms, while those who supported the opposition parties expressed massive support for them. On individual issues, however, the minister of education had overwhelming support for most of what he had done: 82 to 11 percent on the introduction of computers into the classroom; 84 to 10 percent on the rapprochement between enterprises and the schools; 84 to 11 percent on the new professional degrees; 93 to 2 percent on the reintroduction of the teaching of French history and geography at the primary level; and 86 to 7 percent on the teaching of civics. By the end of 1985, a SOFRES poll on the schools discovered that the overwhelming majority of the French—74 percent—had confidence in the educational system. In the *bourse des professions*, instituteurs came in third, with an 80 percent approval rating, behind firemen and physicians. To the public, confrontation and ideological conflict no longer described the schools; instead, they thought of them in terms of competence, success, and individual accomplishment.[41] In less than a year and a half, Chevènement had rallied the nation behind the old idea of the republican school system. Whether he had solved the problem of modernization, however, remained to be seen.

The popularity of Chevènement's educational policy was not matched by other areas of the government. In general, however, the policy of *"moderniser et rassembler"* worked effectively in creating a new Socialist image, one that highlighted consensus and reconciliation in place of the divisiveness that prevailed in July 1984. This meant that few ambitious or controversial projects were initiated during the last two years of Socialist rule. Most new governmental proposals resembled Chevènement's educational reforms—that is, they were based on past experience and aimed at gaining the support of the center of the electorate.

The issue of immigration and insecurity was one of the problems that was addressed in this manner. Anti-immigrant activities increased in 1984 and 1985, along with popular antiracist movements such as SOS-racisme. Concurrently, some elements within the police force moved close to Le Pen's position on insecurity and immigration. The resultant polarization called for a response by the government, even though the Fabius administration would have preferred to ignore the matter. Without a great deal of publicity, the ministers of the interior, justice, culture, and education inaugurated a series of reforms to address the situation. Most dramatically, Pierre Joxe, the minister of the interior, proposed a 5.34 billion franc program to modernize the French police over a five-year period, representing a 50 percent increase in spending on the police force. This crash program entailed the introduction of modern techniques, including computerization, the training of police in new technologies, and the purchasing of new vehicles and weapons. At the same time, in June 1985, the government implemented a law that allowed first offenders who had committed petty crimes to serve sentences of six months or less in public-service jobs. Since young immigrant delinquents would benefit most from this change in sentencing, the minister of justice, Robert Badinter, attempted to deflect a middle-class backlash by tripling the amount of aid for victims of crimes in a 5 July 1985 law. Later, in the fall of 1985, Badinter introduced legislation to restrict the use of preventive detention and insure that the rights of suspects were better protected. In addition to these measures, the minister of culture, Jack Lang, revived his proposals for teaching regional languages and cultures in the schools, including Armenian, Jewish, Arab, Gypsy, Vietnamese, and Berber languages and cultures. Unfortunately, this program of reinforcing law and order on the one hand and encouraging civil and immigrant rights on the other was implemented after the government had issued decrees that virtually prohibited immigrant families from regrouping in France. The spirit of *rassembler* stopped at the French frontier.[42]

By refusing to take difficult stands, this new Socialist policy inevitably put off major decisions until after the March 1986 elections. Fabius did not see it that way, but when he defined *rassembler* on the first anniversary of his government, he came very close to such a position. To Fabius, *rassembler* was an attitude as much as it was a policy, for it required the government to listen to the people, to avoid sectarianism, and to create a consensus for change: "less fighting, more debating, fewer vague ideas, more concrete ones, fewer simplistic solutions, more knowledge of the complexity of problems, less demagogy, more truth."[43] But, in reality this meant that such concrete accomplishments as those that had occurred in women's rights, decentralization of government, and reform of social security were put on hold until some later date. *Rassembler* led to inaction rather than action. For example, Yvette Roudy, the minister of women's rights, spent the last years of her tenure in office attending international meetings and administering the reforms that had been inaugurated in the period 1981–84. These reforms had been substantial, but divisive, since they led to the creation of abortion and contraceptive clinics, a clearer definition of women's rights in the workplace, and a reform of French textbooks to eliminate antifemale biases.[44] In turn, decentralization was put on hold until the March 1986 regional elections, to be held at the same time as the legislative elections, and Pierre Joxe spent most of his energy at the Ministry of the Interior trying to sort out problems with the police. Finally, Georgina Dufoix at the Ministry of Social Affairs played a caretaker role, raising patient charges for drugs to balance the budget, implementing the long-awaited hospital reforms, and making sure that the system showed a slight surplus at the end of 1985, even if this required putting off some expenses to the 1986 budget, which would have a 10 to 20 billion franc deficit, depending on whether one used an optimistic or a pessimistic set of assumptions.[45]

Although the policy of "*moderniser et rassembler*" effectively checkmated both the left and the right, reducing expectations and undermining support for radical proposals, it failed to take into consideration all contingencies, especially in relation to the periphery of French society, where the promise of Socialist government had not yet reached. The hopes that had been raised by the left's regionalist ideology remained one of the great unfulfilled aspects of the Socialist program in 1984, leaving a simmering residue of discontent in areas such as Corsica, the Basque country, and the overseas territories and departments. The Corsican independence movement increased its sometimes violent activities under the Socialists, despite the granting of an autonomous regional government to the island, while Basque independence movements regained momentum in 1984 after three years of waiting, in vain, to see the government's promises for the Basque region implemented.[46] But these were relatively minor developments compared with the crisis that occurred in New Caledonia in late 1984. The repercussions of that crisis would be felt eventually throughout the DOM-TOM and would contribute to the development of the shadowy Rainbow Warrior affair in 1985.

The Socialist program of 1981 promised a great deal for the outcasts of French society. Indeed, that program was predominantly an outsiders program: the provinces, the oppressed, and the poor were to be the main beneficiaries of it. But, as we have seen, problems soon emerged to prevent major parts of this program from being implemented.

Nowhere was this program implemented less than in the overseas territories and departments. In the debate over the 1986 budget for the DOM-TOM, the Socialist deputies were unanimous in pointing out the failure of their program for these areas, where unemployment had climbed to 20 percent or more, the dual society of wealthy bureaucrats from France and impoverished local citizens had not been changed, and the dismal export record of the DOM-TOM with the outer world remained mired at 10 to 25 percent coverage of total imports. Aimé César, the president of the Parti progressiste martiniquais and mayor of Fort-de-France, chastized the Socialists: "The situation is intolerable and politically inadmissable. You have to assume responsibility for a debacle."[47]

The problems in New Caledonia were directly related to this failure of Socialist policy. Beginning in 1981, the natives of New Caledonia, the Kanaks, expected that the new government would fulfill the Socialist party's 1979 promise to allow them to decide their own fate. At the very least, they believed that this meant reform of the economic, social, and political system to correct the injustices that the French settler population had perpetrated against them. When violence occurred in the territory during the fall of 1981, the Socialists drew up plans for economic and political reform. Even though these were quite timid, they encountered massive opposition from the French inhabitants of New Caledonia, who did not want to give up any power to the natives. Consequently, the Socialists were very reluctant to challenge the political power of the French residents in New Caledonia. When elections to a new territorial assembly were finally held on 19 November 1984, the French settlers were allowed to maintain their dominant political position. The Kanaks received only a vague guarantee that a referendum would be held on the issue of independence by 1989. Under those conditions, the Kanak separatists boycotted the elections, which brought the total number of abstentions to almost 50 percent and produced an overwhelming majority for the French settler population. Within a week after the election, the separatists had set up barricades throughout the island, which the French settlers countered by organizing their own armed force. In this potentially bloody situation, the government found itself forced to act and appointed Edgard Pisani as its special delegate to New Caledonia on 1 December, with the mission of drawing up proposals to expedite the process of self-determination.[48]

Pisani's mission was not easy. Numerous bloody incidents occurred in December 1984 and January 1985, prompting the declaration of a state of siege in the territory. But Pisani did size up the situation rapidly, returning to France on 20 December 1984 with three fundamental principles for a solution to the problem: "the recognition of the sovereignty of New Caledonia, respect for the interests of the non-Kanak population and respect for the interests of France in this region of the world." If Pisani prevailed, New Caledonia would become an independent state associated with France. But there were powerful interests opposed to this outcome. *Le Nouvel Observateur* revealed, as early as November 1984, that it looked upon independence with considerable skepticism despite its new-left leanings. Not only did New Caledonia have vast nickel deposits, the journal pointed out, but also it controlled 40 million square kilometers of sea, which was more than all of Europe possessed. Furthermore, if the French pulled out, what would happen to the non-Kanak population? Would another Cuba emerge as a result? What would be the effect of independence on Australia, or the rest of the South Pacific? The journal conjured up all of the fears of the colonizer: the loss of imperial power, the loss of economic resources, the victory of alien ideologies in French territory, and the possibility of a domino effect if France left.[49] *Le Nouvel Observateur* found itself agreeing with much that the political right would say about the Pisani principles.

To a degree, the Socialist government was also skeptical of Pisani's position. When the Council of Ministers finally approved the new constitutional arrangements for New Caledonia, it postponed holding a referendum on independence-association until 31 December 1987, well after the March 1986 legislative elections. Pisani had recommended an immediate vote on the matter. However, the council did support the recommendation to hold elections to four regional councils in New Caledonia in August 1985. Each council would have full powers within the region it controlled, which meant that the territorial assembly would be relegated to the role of a debating society. Under these conditions, the Kanak population could gain control over as many as three of the four regions, while the French settlers would be assured of maintaining control over the wealthiest part of the island, around the city of Nouméa. To overcome the economic and social inequalities between the European and Melanesian communities, the council also called for a major reform program that included economic aid, protection of native languages and cultures, and land redistribution.[50]

Finally, on 29 September 1985, elections to the regional councils took place, ending in victory for the Kanaks in three of the four regions. By that point, however, the left had lost its desire to liberate the wretched of the earth, while the right proclaimed loudly that they would reverse this situation after March 1986. The New Caledonian affair had gotten out of hand, as far as the policy of "*moderniser et rassembler*" was concerned, as no consensus seemed possible. Furthermore, the domino effect that *Le Nouvel Observateur* had feared seemed a reality by late

1985. Corsican separatists quickly made the equation between freedom for the Kanaks and the lack of freedom for the Corsicans. In Guadaloupe, the separatist movement used the New Caledonian matter to demand similar rights. And, in the South Pacific French interests were increasingly challenged by Australia, New Zealand, and the Greenpeace movement.

While both the Corsican and Antilles problems were contained without major disruptions,[51] the situation in the South Pacific evolved beyond the issue of New Caledonia and the Socialist program of regionalism and autonomy to the issue of *raison d'état*. To counter the South Pacific Forum's call for independence for New Caledonia and an end to French nuclear testing in the region, the government concentrated on building up the nation's military presence there. Charles Hernu, the minister of defense, visited the area in May 1985, to discuss the prospect of such a buildup. But this was soon overshadowed by the spectacular news that the Greenpeace ship, the Rainbow Warrior, which had been deployed in the area to disrupt French nuclear testing, was sunk by members of the French security force while at anchor in the Auckland, New Zealand harbor. At first, the government attempted to cover up the affair, but the arrest of two French agents by the New Zealand government and the zealous reporting of the French and foreign press made this impossible to do. With the publication of *Le Monde*'s account of the affair on 18 September 1985, in which Charles Hernu was seriously implicated, the minister of defense was forced to resign and the government made public its final version of the Greenpeace/Rainbow Warrior incident, just a little over two months after it had occurred.[52]

As fascinating as the details of this international intrigue might be, for our purposes the most important aspect of the Rainbow Warrior affair was the degree to which it revealed the Socialist government's conversion to a policy of *realpolitik* in regard to the South Pacific and the acquiescence—even complicity—of the right in that policy. Overnight, the opposition greeted Hernu as a national hero for implementing this plan. Without any debate, the rightist parties refused Fabius's open invitation to undertake a parliamentary investigation of the affair. Giscard d'Estaing undoubtedly spoke for many on the right when he said, very early in the development of the matter, "Whether right or wrong, it is my country." *Le Monde*, which had been a major force in uncovering the more unsavory aspects of the operation, backed away from challenging the government further on 25 September, in two major editorials. One, entitled "Apaiser Wellington," argued that no one, except hard-core ecologists, wanted to pursue the issue to the bitter end, for to do so would hurt France, whose interests had to be protected in the South Pacific against challenges to its control over New Caledonia and its rights to carry on nuclear testing. The second, written by the nation's leading diplomatic correspondent, André Fontaine, reiterated the same themes.[53]

Although there were some rumblings within the government about the tactics employed in the Rainbow Warrior affair, these were soon overcome by the massive wave of chauvinsim that swept the country. In its wake, the second left, the ecology movement, and the regionalists were swept aside in one of the many archaic appeals of the slogan of *rassembler*. François Mitterrand himself took an active part in encouraging this mentality, challenging the legitimacy of the Greenpeace movement by claiming that it was engaged in "political agitation hostile to the French presence in this region of the world," rather than in purely ecological matters. Implying that Greenpeace was part of an obscure plot to undermine French power, he ordered the reinforcement of the French military presence in the South Pacific, especially in New Caledonia.[54]

Finally, "*moderniser et rassembler*" served as the basis for a European policy, centered around the Eureka project and closer Franco-German cooperation. Through Eureka, France hoped to create a counterweight to Star Wars by developing a peaceful European high-technology sector to match the Japanese and the Americans. Through closer cooperation with West Germany, the government hoped to establish a new military strategy to replace the ailing NATO alliance at some future date. By 1986, however, neither one of these grandiose projects had borne fruit yet. Both were beseiged with major obstacles to implementation. Although it would be wrong to judge them failures by March 1986, they had accomplished very little that was concrete by that date. Relying increasingly on the international development of high-technology and military means to implement its policies, the government virtually abandoned its pre-1981 Socialist perspective on Europe for a technocratic, republican one, with hardly any debate on the subject. For the most part, François Mitterrand established the agenda on these matters, with only minimal consultation with anyone else. "*Moderniser et rassembler*" was, after all, the President's policy as much as it was his prime minister's.[55]

The March 1986 Legislative Elections

The ultimate objective of the Fabius administration's policy of "*moderniser et rassembler*" was victory in the 1986 legislative elections. If that were not possible, the policy hoped to achieve *cohabitation*, or the coexistence of the left and the right with Mitterrand as president and a right-wing politician as prime minister. In either case, the Socialists aimed at achieving the best possible political outcome for the purpose of protecting the reforms that they had implemented since 1981. But, as we have seen, this political course entailed the acceptance of more limited final objectives than those adopted by the *Projet socialiste* and the Mauroy government. The Fabius administration sought consensus, not division. It incorporated many of the criticisms of the right in its program, much to the dismay of the Socialist militants who protested the moderate nature of the *équipe* in power. Increasingly, however, the rank and file in the party accepted the new course, whether out of necessity or conviction. Although much of the Socialist election campaign would be consumed by a struggle within the party over its ideological direction, that struggle never threatened the unity of the party and it concluded the long factional conflict in the party with a decisive victory for the moderates. The March 1986 elections were the first in which the Parti socialiste offered no blueprint for massive reform. Instead, the party sollicited votes on the basis of the government's ability to manage the system effectively, allowing the right to assume the role of radical reformer.

Party unity behind a moderate electoral program emerged as the major issue for the Socialists to resolve in 1985. Michel Rocard, whose position in the party as leader of the modernizing element was seriously eroded by the rise of Laurent Fabius, threatened this search for consensus from the right, while the rank and file behind the Socialist party leader Lionel Jospin, threatened it from the left. In a struggle which lasted from April until the end of the year, the moderates prevailed, although at no point was their victory in jeopardy. The reasons for this were simple. Rocard had no intention of undermining the moderate course of the government; he merely wanted to gain control over it. Jospin had no alternative to the moderate course of the government; he merely wanted to call it something else for electoral purposes. Nevertheless, by the end of 1985 both men had won partial victories for their version of the moderate course: Fabius had been discredited by the events of the year, leaving the political stage open for Rocard and Jospin to take over if Mitterrand stepped down. To see how this came about, we need to look at the Jospin–Fabius conflict over control of the election campaign, the role of Rocard in the party, the Toulouse party congress, and the rise of Mitterrand as the party's leading political campaigner by the end of 1985.

With the exception of François Mitterrand, few within the Socialist party viewed Laurent Fabius favorably. His revisionist brand of socialism irked many who wanted to reaffirm the central principles that the party stood for in the legislative election campaign. In June 1985, at a political rally in Marseille, Fabius once again offered his standard fare of *"moderniser et rassembler."* Although there was nothing offensive in what he said, he implied that the Socialists should rally the center and the left around a program of government, leading Jospin to protest vigorously that the prime minister was attempting to shape the election campaign according to his own priorities, leaving the party out of the matter. Simply put, the issue centered around what attitude to take regarding the Communists and the center, with Jospin arguing for a union of the leftist vote behind the Socialists and Fabius for a republican *rassemblement* behind the government slogan of *"moderniser et rassembler."* The conflict was one of socialism versus social democracy or the union of the left versus the republican front. François Mitterrand wisely chose both sides rather than opting for one over the other. In a speech delivered in Carcassone at the end of June, he called upon the French to rally behind modernization, attacked the Communists for not pursuing this course of action, and embraced solidarity with passion as the crowning objective of his administration.[56]

In the end, however, Fabius was forced to back down and allow Jospin to run the election campaign. The prime minister was granted control over explaining his government's program, but only that. Still, this outcome did not change dramatically the party's ideological position. As the journal *L'Express* commented, the affair revolved more around personalities than around issues. Everyone within the Socialist party was trying to gain the upper hand for the post-Mitterrand scramble for control. Thus, the odd alliance of Jean-Pierre Chevènement, Michel Rocard, Pierre Mauroy, and Lionel Jospin against Laurent Fabius! Furthermore, in the wake of the Jospin–Fabius dispute, a number of leading Socialists commented on the party's moderate direction, basically accepting it as a necessity. Jean-Pierre Chevènement, for example, told *Le Nouvel Observateur* that the union of the left was dead. When challenged with the accusation that he had acquiesced in the rightist drift of the Fabius government, he responded, somewhat cryptically, that winning elections did not change society.[57]

Despite the Jospin–Fabius squabble, the party was almost unanimous on the need to rally behind the moderate course that the government had followed since July 1984. Michel Rocard was the one exception to the rule, although an exception that proved the rule. In early April 1985, Rocard resigned from the government over its decision to implement proportional representation as the method for electing the next legislative body. Rocard presented his decision as one of principle, arguing that proportional representation would undermine democracy and reinstitute the instability of the Fourth Republic, but most political observers believed that he left the government in order to carry on his own political offensive against it. When, in June 1985, he announced his candidacy for the presidency in 1988, such speculations seemed to be confirmed.[58] Later, in August, he refused to sign the majority text for the Toulouse congress of the party, claiming that he wanted the party to clear up the confusion that existed between its archaic position during the period 1981–84 and its current modernizing one. In turn, Rocard demanded that the party draw up a "contrat de législature" for the post-1986 period, in order to guarantee that it would not revert once more to its old habits. As the Rocardian Gérard Fuchs put the matter: "We must recognize the economic errors committed from 1981 to 1983. We must recognize that we have changed our strategy: we no longer dream of a brutal rupture with capitalism, nor of the union of the left, such as certain individuals have imagined it over the years."[59] In short, the Protestant Rocard wanted the party to undergo a form of repentance to rid it of the sins of the past. To him, it was not enough to state a new policy, as the party faithful had done in line with Fabius; it was necessary to eradicate, root and branch, the archaic errors of the Mauroy years. And in the process, the *correct* form of *"moderniser et rassembler"* would emerge supreme—that is, the Rocardian form.

No wonder that the party leadership viewed Rocard with extreme suspicion. André Laignel proclaimed that Rocard was trying to divide the party, while Pierre Mauroy stated bluntly: "Rocard left the SFIO, he left the PSU, and he will leave the PS."[60] Most believed that Rocard's text for the Toulouse congress aimed solely at advancing his own presidential ambitions, possibly outside of the party if he were rebuked. Many wondered, either publicly or privately, why Rocard had not raised his objections earlier, at the 1981 Valence congress or at Bourg-en-Bresse in 1983, since he opposed the Mauroy *relance* from the start. Nevertheless, Rocard's position had to be listened to, as his current in the party gained almost 29 percent of the votes in party elections, which translated into 38 delegates at Toulouse, compared to 20 in 1983. All other currents in the party suffered losses as a consequence: the Mitterrandists went from 66 to 56, CERES from 23 to 19, and the Mauroyistes from 22 to 19.[61]

The party needed Rocard, but Rocard also needed the party. As a result, Toulouse turned out to be one of the most amicable of recent Socialist congresses. To be sure, Rocard made his points: in addition to his condemnation of the 1981 *relance*, Rocard accused the party of deviating from its *autogestionnaire* base by pursuing an elitist, technocratic path in power. In rebuttal, Pierre Mauroy informed Rocard that he could have resigned from the government at any time. But the tone of the congress was set by Lionel Jospin, who played on the themes of *"moderniser et rassembler,"* appealing to the moderates, accepting the possibility of a union with the center after the March elections, embracing the notion that the Socialist party had changed in power, and proclaiming that the party was pragmatic rather than narrowly ideological in nature. Compromise, not confrontation, was the order of the day. The final resolution passed by the Congress combined the Rocard text with the majority. While Rocard abandoned the idea of a "contrat de législature" and gave up on his attempt to gain open repentance for the sins of the past, he forced the party to modify its language on the *relance*, to view nationalization as a "respiration" rather than as a "force de frappe," and to be more realistic about the future. Much ado about nothing? Possibly. But the party emerged from Toulouse resembling social democracy or French radicalism rather than the Socialist movement of the pre-1981 period.[62] The March 1986 elections would be fought on the basis of realism. No gimmicks, no grandiose promises, no total justification for the Socialist record in power came out of Toulouse. The Socialists would appeal for votes on the basis that they were the party best qualified to run the nation, to take it into the twenty-first century in relatively good shape, *because* they understood the need for compromise and pragmatism as the result of their experience in government.

To the journalists who covered French politics, Fabius and Jospin came out on top at Toulouse, even though Rocard had scored important points. Rocard's enigmatic behavior, his refusal to play the game according to party rules, continued to make him an outsider, although an extremely important outsider. But Toulouse was not the only factor in determining the fate of the players and their ideas. Shortly after the conclusion of the congress, Laurent Fabius confronted Jacques Chirac in the first debate of the election campaign. For Fabius the debate ended in disaster. In trying to adhere to a strict formula of *"moderniser et rassembler,"* he committed the ultimate sin of abandoning principle for political advantage. When the question of the immigrant population was broached, Fabius did not challenge any of Chirac's strident anti-immigrant statements. Like Mauroy in the summer of 1984, Fabius failed to understand the importance of principles in French politics. Soon after the televised debate, Fabius's popularity plummeted and his standing in the party collapsed. At the November National Convention of the Socialist party, Fabius's name was not mentioned, as the party reaffirmed its position on immigration and other issues in an effort to distinguish itself from the right. In December, when Fabius compounded his earlier error by publicly criticizing François Mitterrand for meeting with the Polish leader, Jaroslav Jaruzelski, his fate was sealed. He was no longer useful as either the prime minister or as a leader of the election campaign. François Mitterrand, at this critical juncture, made two major decisions: Fabius would be kept on, to avoid the embarrassment of dismissal at this late date, and he would be relegated to a minor role in the election compaign through the elevation of the president to the post of the standard-bearer of the Socialist cause.[63] After the events of early December, the March elections became, in part at least, a referendum on François Mitterrand's presidency.

While, for better or worse, the Socialists stood almost alone as the party of the left in the March election campaign, the right remained seriously divided. Although rightist politicians originally agreed on some sort of Reagan/Thatcher-type program for regaining power, by 1985 many leaders of the opposition began to have doubts about such a radical direction. Beyond ideological uncertainties, the right was also divided over the issue of *cohabitation*. Raymond Barre opposed it totally, demanding that the right refuse to form a government under a Socialist president if it won the legislative elections, while Jacques Chirac favored the idea, primarily because he believed that his chances to win the 1988 presidential election hinged on a successful tenure as prime minister, given the fact that Barre had gained a massive lead in public opinion polls. Finally, the right had gained a new bedfellow by 1985, the National Front, whose extremist policies on immigration, in particular, threatened to radicalize the opposition or take votes away from the mainstream rightist parties—or, worst of all, do both. Although none of these major problems would disappear or be resolved totally before the March elections, the traditional right did succeed in drawing up a program of government that its candidates generally supported. That program needs to be examined carefully in order to determine the degree to which the right had become radicalized by the Socialist experiment or the extent to which it had accepted what the Socialists had done.

While intellectuals on the right continued to make outlandish demands on the RPR and UDF, the politicians moved increasingly toward the center, attempting to neutralize the Socialist attempt to depict them as opposed to the welfare state. As a result, the right accepted all of the Socialist social reforms, such as the increases in SMIC, the thirty-nine-hour week, five weeks of paid vacation, and increases in old-age pensions. None of these was called into question. Instead the right proclaimed, as the Socialists had done, that no further social reforms would be implemented and that better bureaucratic management would be used to salvage the welfare state from financial insolvency. Neither the Socialists nor the UDF-RPR opposition advocated increased taxes on workers and industry as the solution to the problem. Both believed that industry had to be relieved of the heavy tax burden that the state had placed upon it, although the right went further than the left did in advocating tax reductions and budget cuts. Still, the Socialists had begun the process by implementing lower corporate tax rates, restraining state spending, and reducing the total tax rate as a percentage of gross national product. The differences between the two camps were more evident in the right's proposals for changes in the social contract: price controls would be eliminated by a rightist government, as well as state control over firing workers and some parts of the new laws on working-class participation in industrial firms. But, even here the differences were not insurmountable. The Socialists had already eliminated most price controls, state control over dismissals had never been very effective, not even under the Socialists, and the vast majority of the so-called Auroux laws on working-class participation were embraced warmly by the opposition, even though the right had originally viewed them as infringements on property rights. The same sort of reversal took place in the right's attitude toward decentralization: by 1986 the right accepted all of Defferre's reforms, even though it had opposed them vehemently when they were first introduced in the legislature.[64]

The major differences between the two camps resided in their attitudes toward the Socialist nationalization program and the broad area of security, civil liberties, and immigration. Yet, even here there was room for some compromise on the first contentious issue. Although the right began with a sweeping proposal to dismantle virtually the entire nationalized sector, by 1986 it had confined itself to the banks, insurance companies, and profitable, market-oriented state industries that the Socialists had nationalized since 1981. Clearly, the Socialists did not accept this rightist position. But, as we have seen, the Mitterrand governments had carried out partial denationalization, through various devices to sell shares in nationalized industries on the bourse, and many within the Socialist camp, including Jacques Delors and Michel Rocard, saw little advantage in government control of the banking system or the insurance industry. At the Toulouse congress, Michel Rocard also succeeded in changing the Socialist position regarding the post-1981 nationalizations from "force de frappe" to a "respiration." And such leading Socialist intellectuals as Lionel Zinsou could write, in 1985, that privatization would make little difference in the long run, since Socialist nationalization had succeeded in restructuring the industrial sector to meet the challenge of international competition in the 1980s.[65]

In essence, therefore, only one major issue divided the two camps completely, that of security, civil liberties, and immigration. The reasons for this can be discerned most clearly by looking at public opinion polls.

By 1985, electoral attitudes had changed profoundly from what they had been in 1981, although the issues of employment and economic security remained, by a large margin, the ones that concerned the French the most. An October 1985 SOFRES poll, for example, which asked respondents to list the top four priorities confronting France in the near future, discovered that 84 percent believed the creation of jobs was most important, while 56 percent gave top priority to getting the economy back on its feet and 42 percent pointed to the need to maintain the buying power of the French people.[66] But this presents a misleading sense of continuity between 1981 and 1985, for the electorate had changed its mind on the means to implement these priorities. Numerous polls taken in 1985 revealed that French voters had moved to the right since 1980 or 1981: two SOFRES polls, one taken in 1980 and another in February 1985, discovered major changes in how the French responded to certain key words such as profit, liberalism, socialism, unions, nationalization, and planning. In 1980, 37 percent responded favorably to the word profit; in 1985, 47 percent did so. For liberalism the figures were 52 to 63 percent, while socialism went from 56 percent to 45 percent, unions from 55 to 45 percent, nationalization from 40 to 33 percent, and planning from 43 to 37 percent.[67] In turn, other polls indicated that more French people identifed with the right than with the left by 1985: in 1981, according to a *L'Express* poll, 42 percent identified with the left and 31 percent with the right; by October 1985 the figures were 34 percent and 36 percent, respectively.[68] By February 1986, this close margin had barely changed: 36 percent on the left, 37 percent on the right. In addition, on the eve of the elections, left and right were viewed as almost equal regarding their ability to make the economy function well, compared with a wide margin in favor of the left in 1981.[69]

As we have seen, both the left and the right related to this new mood through such programs as *"moderniser et rassembler"* or pale imitations of Reaganism or Thatcherism. By doing so, they eventually arrived at a reluctant consensus on what should be done about the economy and the welfale state, primarily because they were both more interested in winning elections and governing than in pursuing ideological confrontation for its own sake. The center, not the extremes, determined the programs that would be implemented in these crucial areas. Any electoral party that wanted to govern had to pay close attention to this centrist mentality, for it was the key to victory. In contrast, however, the polls revealed exactly the opposite regarding immigration, security, and civil liberties. Although some potential Socialist voters were concerned enough about these matters to support Le Pen and the National Front, they remained a tiny minority compared to the massive support that Le Penism received from disillusioned rightist voters. As a consequence, the traditional right played heavily upon themes of law and order and anti-immigrant attitudes in order to bring the National Front vote back into its camp. Ironically, the right found itself confronted by many of the same problems the Socialists had faced in their former love/hate relationship with the Communists. As a consequence, the Socialists could play the role of defender of civil liberties and freedom against a right that needed to appease its extremist faction in some form or another. In polls taken in late 1985 and early 1986, the Socialists came out on top on all issues related to defense of liberties and tolerance of others. In contrast, in 1981 the right had been viewed more favorably on these matters by the electorate.[70]

Yet the differences between left and right on the issue of liberty did not present a major obstacle to possible *cohabitation* between the two after March 1986. The left had compromised its generally positive record on immigration by supporting massive increases in funding for the police, by placing severe restrictions on immigration, and by encouraging immigrants to return home. Of course these measures did not go so far as the RPR-UDF program for government did in advocating changes in the law on citizenship to discourage immigrants from settling in France. But, for the most part, the traditional right merely took Socialist measures and extended them to their logical conclusions. For example, the right advocated more surveillance of the immigrant population, more incentives to induce immigrants to return to their native lands, and more police powers to carry out identification checks on immigrants.

With the exception of the immigrant question, however, the 1986 elections were notably lacking in fervor or ideological conviction. Both left and right narrowed in on the economic issues that were foremost in the minds of the electorate. This meant, above all, unemployment. Yet, when the electorate was asked in January 1986, in a *Le Point-IFOF-RTL* poll, whether the elections would make any real difference in how the major economic and social issues would be resolved, about 40 percent responded consistently that no matter who won not much would change regarding inflation, unemployment, social conflicts, and buying power. If one combined the "no opinion" answers with those that foresaw no appreciable change, over 50 percent of those polled viewed the elections as relatively unimportant for resolving what they thought were the major problems of the day. As a result, it is hardly surprising that these same voters supported *cohabitation* by a 39 percent to 29 percent margin, with 27 percent proclaiming that they were indifferent to the matter.[71]

In this environment of apathetic consensus, the rewards would go to those who could best mobilize the vote. For the Socialists this meant two things. First, the party had to energize the militants, from the Communists to the left-wing Socialists. Second, and paradoxically, it had to praise the virtues of consensus and modernity, painting the Socialist government as the true vehicle for accomplishing the difficult tasks that confronted France. To achieve the first objective, the party called on François Mitterrand. To carry out the second, it relied heavily on Lionel Jospin. Fabius played a minor role in the campaign and Rocard played virtually no role, the first because of his previous gaffs, the second because he chose to wash his hands of the inevitable defeat in order to be better prepared to assume the leadership of the party in the role of "healer" or "savior."

As it turned out, the party's strategy was quite effective. To a great degree this was due to the favorable economic statistics that began to appear around January 1986. As we have seen, employment improved slightly, inflation dropped dramatically, the trade deficit almost disappeared, and average buying power increased a bit for virually all French men and women in work. François Mitterrand took advantage of these favorable figures to pose a picture of France divided politically into two camps, the rich versus the poor, the dismantlers of the welfare state versus the protectors of it. Typical of this line of attack was the president's 15 December 1985 explanation on French television of what his program had accomplished. After outlining all of the advantages that average French men and women had gained from his government, he warned them: "Listen, do what you want to do in three months' time, but at least protect what you have gained." After attacking the right for threatening the social security system, he concluded with a pledge to preserve the system intact.[72]

Mitterrand continued his confrontational rhetoric up to the middle of February, at which point he withdrew from the campaign to preserve a sense of presidential decorum and to keep open the possibility of *cohabitation* with the right. Socialist fortunes improved dramatically as the result of his involvement. Polls showed the party approaching the 30 percent mark, enough to prevent a serious defeat in March. The Communist voters, in particular, were attracted to the president's position. Socialist polls indicated that half of the Communist electorate had a favorable opinion of the government's record and that 30 percent were considering voting for Socialist candidates. The slogan, "Vote utile, vote Socialiste," gained support in Communist strongholds as the result of the president's confrontational style and his popularity among the PCF faithful.[73]

Meanwhile, Lionel Jospin assumed the role of the conciliator in the campaign, without totally forsaking his own taste for confrontation. Jospin had the difficult task of keeping intact the militant support that

Mitterrand helped bring back into the fold and reaching out to the center. Such words as "consensus" and "modernize" became commonplace in Jospin's vocabulary, alongside his denuniciations of the right. On one occasion of particular interest for lovers of dialectical thinking, he outlined a number of changes that the left had implemented, labeled them changes in the name of consensus, and concluded that the left favored consensus and the right confrontation.[74] On another occasion he denounced the right for its "liberalmania" that threatened the welfare state and the nation's independence, while praising the Socialist left for its modernity: "Modernity of decentralization, of the liberation of audiovisual communications, of Badinter's policy of dusting off the penal code, of the important role accorded to science and culture. . . . In short, the modern image is on the side of the left."[75] But, when Jospin was asked by his interviewers at *Le Point* to define the Socialist program for the 1986 elections he was hard pressed to offer much of anything:

> *Q.*: In spite of everything, your program does not define the future as it did in 1981.
> *R.*: We were committed to the propositions of François Mitterrand. In the Fifth Republic the President is the decisive political element. 1986 did not offer a good opportunity to elaborate completely a new political contract. It is a stage in the *septennat*."[76]

In contrast, the right attempted to present its program as a revolution, a break with the past. However, there were limits on how far this kind of rhetoric could be permitted. Too much of a break would confirm the Socialist position that the right threatened the welfare state and the security of the French. On the other hand, to accept the notion that the Socialists were on the true path, with their program of modernity and consensus, would make the right indistinguishable from its opponents. As a result, the right's election campaign was a bizarre mixture of consensus and confrontation. For example, Raymond Barre came out totally opposed to any form of *cohabitation* with the Socialists after the March elections, but the same Raymond Barre argued persuasively that the Socialists had been on the right track, economically, since 1983 and that the problems the nation faced were primarily structural, not conjunctural, which should have made Barre into a supporter of *cohabitation*. On the other hand, Giscard d'Estaing, who supported *cohabitation*, offered blistering critiques of the left and called the right's program revolutionary, a challenge to the post-1945 consensus. In the end, however, Jacques Chirac emerged as the standard-bearer of the right and his conciliatory gestures in the direction of *cohabitation* prevailed. As the election approached, Chirac changed direction, going from a Reaganite program to a modified form of statism. Although Chirac still criticized the Socialist government, he qualified his criticisms with calls for consensus.[77]

The growing inevitability of consensus and *cohabitation* did not appeal to everyone. The unions were universally skeptical of the direction that the political parties had taken. No union publicly supported any political party, not even the CFDT, which had backed the Socialists since 1970. In turn, the increasingly marginalized Communist party and the new radical rightist National Front remained outside of the consensus. Both believed that the major parties had ruined the nation, with the Communists maintaining that all three were nothing more than capitalist front organizations for the destruction of the proletariat and the National Front viewing them as pro-immigrant, anti-French organizations that had destroyed the prosperity of the French people through their internationalist policies. Both parties, as one might expect, appealed to those who felt marginalized by the mainstream consensus, or about 20 percent of the population, roughly equal to the level of support for extremist parties since 1945. Of the two, however, the National Front posed the greatest threat to consensus by 1986. Polls indicated that Le Pen's views on immigrants had gained increased support since 1984, when Le Penism was barely known: between May 1984 and October 1985 those who agreed with Le Pen's views on immigrants increased from 28 to 31 percent in a SOFRES poll. While the Communists had been fairly well contained by the Socialists, the right's great fear was that the National Front would steal the election from them. As Chirac never ceased to say, "Voter Front National, c'est voter Mitterrand."[78]

Given the apathetic consensus, the slight reprise of the economy, and the appeal of extremists outside of the consensus, the March 16 election results were not surprising. In general, France voted for *cohabitation*, with some reservations. The Socialists achieved their objective of winning more than 30 percent of the vote, as they garnered 31.04 percent with their Radical partners, or 35.88 percent of the seats. This marked their best showing in a national election since 1981, when they totalled 37.5 percent of the vote on the first round of the legislative elections, and it marked their second-best total in a legislative election held under the Fifth Republic, reaffirming their standing as the largest party in France. But the remainder of the left did miserably. The Communists gained only 9.78 percent of the vote, for 6.06 percent of the seats, or the same total that the National Front received. The March elections clearly confirmed the long-term political decline of the PCF that had accelerated greatly with the 1981 elections, when the party slipped to around 16 percent of the vote in both the presidential and the legislative contests.

The combined leftist vote equaled a little over 43 percent of the total, which was the worst result for the left since 1968. For the Socialists to gain power again, it would be necessary to win 40 percent of the vote, as the Communists could no longer be relied upon for support. The March elections reconfirmed the new course that the Socialists had taken: victory would be won at the center in the future, not through any union of the left.

Yet, despite the clear defeat of the left in the legislative elections, which was even more crushing in the regional elections that were held simultaneously (the left won control of only two of twenty-two regions), the traditional right did not win an overwhelming victory. The total RPR-UDF vote, with various dissident rightists included, came to 44.88 percent, roughly the same as in 1981, or 50.43 percent of the seats in the new assembly. Such a narrow victory made *cohabitation* much more likely, especially since Jacques Chirac's RPR emerged as the dominant party on the right. If the right was committed to its preelection pledge not to unite with the National Front, which gained 9.65 percent of the vote, it would have to choose compromise and consensus rather than confrontation.[79]

With 84 percent of the seats in the new legislature going to the three major parties, proportional representation did not lead the nation down the slippery slope of political fragmentation, as its critics had argued it would. Quite the opposite: the 1986 legislative elections marked the first time in the history of the Fifth Republic that only three political parties dominated the stage. Of course, proportional representation had nothing to do with this outcome, which evolved from the long history of the left and the actions of the Socialist governments during the 1980s. The 1986 legislative elections confirmed the end of an era in French politics, not the beginning of increased political confrontation due to electoral technicalities. The old left had died in the process and in its place had emerged a polyglot, a cross between the American Democratic party, social democracy, and the old French Radical tradition, all contained within the Socialist party. In place of the old left, which emphasized the rupture with capitalism, a new one had emerged around such slogans as "*moderniser et rassembler*" and such words as realism and pragmatism. The March electoral results reinforced this evolution, proving that such a political monster as the new Socialist party could gain the support of a broad spectrum of French voters. Whether, however, this meant that the party had lost its soul in the pursuit of electoral success is another matter, one for the theologians to debate.

Conclusion

After almost five years in power, the longest that any Socialist government had experienced in the history of France, the Socialist party gave up control over the legislative branch with a sigh of relief. No recriminations poured forth from the various currents within the party, no massive rethinking of Socialist strategy occurred in the wake of the March defeat. Yet, during those five years in power, the Socialist government had turned socialist theory upside down. *Autogestion*, the agenda of the *dexuième gauche*, the much-vaunted "rupture with capitalism," and all the other catchwords of the left had been buried by the exercise of power. The party had been transformed from a utopian post-1968 construct into a party of *alternance*. The generally good showing in the March 1986 legislative elections reinforced this realistic, pragmatic trend.

Why had this occurred in such a short period of time? The easy answer to this question is that the Socialists had never been a party of revolution. From the days of Jean Jaurès through the mid-1980s the party had remained staunchly within the democratic tradition, appealing ultimately to the electorate for power. But the peculiar history of the French left and French politics under the Third and Fourth Republics conspired to create the image of a Socialist party intent on destroying the foundations of capitalism and French democracy as it existed. The Socialists found it necessary to compete with the discourse of the Communist party in order to win votes from the far left, which remained a major political force until the 1981 elections. This meant creating a rhetoric that was revolutionary, while forging a reformist program that captured votes to the right of the Communists. Since various factions within the party, from CERES to the old political bosses of the Nord and the Bouches-du-Rhône, reflected these divergent trends, the internal cohesion of the party was also dependent on the creation of such a dual representation. Furthermore, until the victories of 1981, the presence of a strong Communist party, capturing a significant proportion of leftist votes, combined with the relative electoral weakness of the Socialists, prevented the party from forming effective, long-lasting governments in which it could implement its program without serious opposition from either the left or the right. This was true of the Cartel des Gauches in the 1920s, the Popular Front of the 1930s, and the various coalition governments of the 1940s and 1950s, all of which were loose combinations of the Socialists and several unreliable partners who undermined most leftist reforms or, in the case of the Communists, attacked the Socialists for lack of revolutionary zeal. Paradoxically, the Fifth Republic created the conditions for the ultimate electoral and governmental success of the Socialist party by forcing left and right to form electoral coalitions if they wanted to govern and by concentrating power in the executive branch at the expense of the legislature. Since no Communist leader could ever gain election to the presidency, unless the party were totally transformed into a reformist organization, and since any leftist presidential candidate would have to appeal, in part, to the center of the electorate, it was only a matter of time before a Socialist presidential candidate would be able to win victory on a program that offered reform, with certain revolutionary overtones to appease the far left, and that guaranteed that the Communists would have minimal influence on governmental decisions.

François Mitterrand proved to be the man who carried out this formidable task of undercutting the Communists and revolutionary socialism. He did it by making the party accept, at least tacitly, the institutions of the Fifth Republic. This meant that the party aimed at winning control of the presidency, which translated into the acceptance of Mitterrand's leadership and dominance in the 1981 electoral campaign, which after victory translated into Mitterrand's control over the government's agenda. In the process, the party became increasingly irrelevant and the president became the driving force behind party and governmental decisions. The ideology of the party, consequently, took a distant second place to the overarching objective of governing and maintaining power. In short, the Socialist party capitulated to the Socialist executive branch on ideological matters because no major Communist threat existed to move the party to the left after 1981 and because the party had no viable alternatives to the government's pragmatic, realist position. Electoral success took precedence over ideological purity, especially given the disastrous results that such purity brought to the Communist party in the 1980s.

The acquiescence of the party in Mitterrand's agenda was not purely opportunistic or even cynical in nature. Nor did such acquiescence cause internal problems of any consequence. This is remarkable, given the seeming volatility of the party prior to 1981, but this volatility has to be placed in context: no group in the party ever threatened or thought of breaking from it to join the Communists, the center, or the right. CERES, which was closest to the Communist party in ideology, agreed completely with Mitterrand's agenda of undercutting the Communists, although CERES believed that the way to eliminate the Communist threat was through embracing the vast majority of Communist programs as Socialist ones. When Mitterrand proved that this was not necessary, CERES lost its trump card as the leftist alternative in the party, leaving it with no other choice than to accept the course of events, which Jean-Pierre Chevènement proceeded to do with enthusiasm as minister of education. CERES had nowhere to go outside of the Socialist party—at least as long as the Fifth Republic existed. And the same was true of other currents within the party, most of which were more amenable to reformism and pragmatism than CERES was.

— Yet all of these explanations seem to leave out the major factor in the Socialist conversion to pragmatism, namely the economic crisis that affected the western capitalist democracies during the early 1980s. There are good reasons, however, for not counting this crisis as the major cause of change within the party and the government. Most important, the economic crisis by itself would not have caused the move to the right within the government without the existence of the political factors previously outlined. If the Communists had been a major electoral force in 1981, and thus a major player in the Mitterrand government, the impact of the CERES current on that government would have been greater, which would have meant, *at the very least*, that the government would have pursued a protectionist path in March 1983, pulling out of the European monetary system and most of the free trade rules of the Common Market. In short, the economic crisis was secondary to the ideological and political structures that existed during Socialist rule. Those structures determined, or at least played the major role in, the reaction of the government to the crisis, and not the other way around.

Which brings us back to 1981 or before in explaining why the Socialists retreated so rapidly from *autogestion* to accept a reformist, social democratic position. Lack of a clear ideological program in 1981 played a key role here. Such a lack was not fortuitous; it was due to the imperatives of gaining power under the Fifth Republic. Like Molière's bourgeois gentleman, the Socialists were speaking pragmatism and reform before they ever knew it. Jean-Pierre Chevènement was correct in stating that the party had no ideological direction when it came to power, although he was wrong in believing that such direction was the sine qua non of Socialist success. Socialist success could only occur in the context of ideological muddle, for a clear-cut ideological position would have split the party into warring factions, similar to the situation that had emerged on the right by 1986, with the National Front contesting bitterly the consensus that had existed between Gaullists and liberals. Therefore, lack of an ideology was a clear advantage, if one accepts that the Socialist party was always a democratic party, intent on winning elections and gaining power. Of course, as we have pointed out before, the party could have forsaken this heritage for ideological purity and powerlessness, but instead it refused to take the Communist route. In so doing, the party virtually condemned itself to the centrist position that it took by 1986, leading to a consensus between it and the classical right on a number of issues, which formed the basis for *cohabitation*.

Does all of this mean that socialism is doomed in France? Hardly. Although radical change did not occur as the result of the Socialist program of the 1980s, significant reforms did take place in a number of areas, including culture, decentralization of government, worker rights, and new liberties for oppressed groups. True, in many of these cases the government retreated from its 1981 plans and by 1984 it had accepted the more modest program of *"moderniser et rassembler,"* moving away from equality toward liberty, but at no point did the Socialists totally reverse their commitment to solidarity with the poorest nor did they give in to rightist demands to repeal these somewhat modest reforms. The Socialists became social democrats in the course of their wanderings, but they did not embrace laissez-faire or the worst excesses of neoliberalism in their search for consensus. Liberty might have taken precedence over equality by 1986, but it was liberty with a human face, tempered by a welfare state that had been kept intact by the Socialists in the face of a massive attack upon it from the neoliberals and their allies. Only if one assumes that socialism must be Marxist and only Marxist can one conclude that socialism in France was doomed by 1986.

Still, the socialism of 1986 tended to place much more emphasis on concepts and institutions that had been formerly disdained: the entrepreneur, the market, the *économie mixte*, and the liberal/second-left concept of the primacy of civil society over the state. Had the neoliberals and the second left won out in the end, converting the Socialists to their ideas in creating *cohabitation* and consensus? Although the Socialists would continue to insist that their emphasis on liberty differed profoundly from the classical right's, in reality the Socialists and the right agreed with each other on most of the major issues, creating a sort of apathetic consensus of 80 percent of the nation behind a centrist course. For the most part, the experience of *cohabitation* would confirm and extend the experience of the post-1984 Fabius government. Continuity, not confrontation, has been the legacy of the Socialist government, as left and right have agreed tacitly that modernization and liberty are the keys to French success in the world. Ideology, consequently, seems to be dead, except for the wounded Communist giant and the xenophobic National Front. Whether they will be able to challenge the Socialist legacy of *cohabitation* and consensus remains to be seen, as well as the degree to which such a legacy is a solution to the political and governmental problems of the Fifth Republic.

Notes

Chapter 1.
Victory! *Pour quoi faire*?

1. On 1981 as a significant shift, see Jérôme Jaffré, "De Valéry Giscard d'Estaing à François Mitterrand: France de gauche vote à gauche," *Pouvoirs* 20 (1982): 5–27. Tony Judt, *Marxism and the French Left: Studies on Labour and Politics in France, 1830–1981* (Oxford: Oxford University Press, 1986), 290, views the electoral significance in terms of the balance of power on the left. See also the interpretation of Gérard Grunberg, "Causes et fragilités de la victoire socialiste de 1981," in *1981: Les élections de l' alternance*, ed. Alain Lancelot (Paris: Fondation Nationale des Sciences Politiques, 1986), 23–67.

2. On the Communists, see M. Adereth, *The French Communist Party: A Critical History (1920–1984)* (Manchester: Manchester University Press, 1984), 255–65; Jean Baudouin, "L'échec communiste de juin 1981: Recul électoral ou crise hégémonique?" *Pouvoirs* 20 (1982): 45–53.

3. *Le Monde*, 21–22 June 1981.

4. Ibid., 16 April 1981.

5. Olivier Duhamel and Jean-Luc Parodi, "L'évolution des intentions de vote, contribution à l'exploration de l'élection présidentielle de 1981," *Pouvoirs* 18 (1981): 171.

6. Howard Machin and Vincent Wright, "Why Mitterrand Won: The French Presidential Elections of April–May 1981," *West European Politics* 5, no. 1 (January 1982): 15. For other polls on nationalization, see Jack Hayward, *The State and the Market Economy: Industrial Patriotism and Economic Intervention in France* (New York: New University Press, 1986), 228.

7. *Le Monde*, 2 June 1981.

8. See François Goguel, "Encore un regard sur les élections législatives de juin 1981," *Pouvoirs* 23 (1982): 134–43. See also the rejoinder by Jérôme Jaffré, "En réponse à François Goguel: Retour sur les élections du printemps 1981," *Pouvoirs* 24 (1983): 159–68.

9. Jaffre, "En réponse."

10. Alain Peyrefitte, *Quand la rose se fanera...Du malentendu à l'espoir* (Paris: Plon, 1983), chap. 3. See Claude Estier, *Mitterrand président: Le journal d'une victoire* (Paris: Stock, 1981), 34, for Mitterrand's 9 November 1980 speech at Carmaux. See also pp. 71–73, 116, and 130.

11. Estier, *Mitterrand président*, xiv–xv is the main source here; D. S. Bell and Byron Criddle, *The French Socialist Party: Resurgence and Victory* (Oxford: Oxford University Press, 1984), 82, 111.

12. Lionel Stoleru, *La France à deux vitesses* (Paris: Flammarion, 1982), 44 and 47ff.

13. See Estier, *Mitterrand président*, 108–9 on the "positive" image; see also Alain Duhamel, *La République de M. Mitterrand* (Paris: Bernard Grasset, 1982), 49.

14. Dominique Labbé, *François Mitterrand: Essai sur le discours* (Grenoble: Pensée sauvage, 1983), 177.

15. Estier, *Mitterrand président*, 220–21; see François Mitterrand, *Politique 2, 1977–1981* (Paris: Fayard, 1981), 257, for the *Courrier de l'Oise* article. See pp.

245–94 for the entire election campaign, which Mitterrand presents in terms of the issue of unemployment and the need to *rassembler* the nation.

16. *Le Monde,* 2, 10 April 1981; on Barre's *relance,* see Alain Fonteneau and Pierre-Alain Muet, *La gauche face à la crise* (Paris: Fondation Nationale des Sciences Politiques, 1985), 95.

17. *Le Monde,* 5–6 April 1981 on Mitterrand's program. For the entire campaign, see also *Le Monde, L'élection présidentielle 26 avril–10 mai 1981* (Paris: *Le Monde,* 1981).

18. *Le Monde*, 2, 7 May 1981. See Machin and Wright, "Why Mitterrand Won," 30–31.

19. *Le Monde*, 10–11 May 1981.

20. The composition of the first Mauroy government can be found in *Pouvoirs* 20 (1982): 146–47. See also in that issue Jean-Louis Quermonne, "Un gouvernement présidentiel ou un gouvernement partisan?" 67–86. Hubert Landier, *Demain, quels syndicats?* (Paris: Librairie Générale Française, 1981), 10.

21. Quoted in Quermonne, "Un gouvernement présidentiel," 72.

22. The main source for the June elections is *Le Monde.* For Mauroy's statements, see the edition of 19 June 1981.

23. See the gloomy prognostications in such popular well-known works as Jean Fourastié, *Les trente glorieuses,* rev. ed (Paris: Fayard, 1979; Pluriel, 1980), esp. the third part, and Christian Stoffaës, *La grande menace industrielle* (Paris: Calmann-Lévy, 1978; Pluriel, 1979). Fourastié's title became a cliché, used by every French observer as shorthand for the period 1945–75 and as a sort of nostalgic reference to the "good old days" that were no more.

24. Keith Reader, *Intellectuals and the Left in France since 1968* (New York: St. Martin's Press, 1987), chap. 2.

25. See Luc Ferry and Alain Renaut, *La pensée 68: Essai sur l'anti-humanisme contemporain* (Paris: Gallimard, 1985). See also Allan Megill, *Prophets of Extremity* (Berkeley: University of California Press, 1985), on Foucault and Derrida, and Pascal Ory, *L'entre-deux-mai: Histoire culturelle de la France, mai 1968–mai 1981* (Paris: Éditions du Seuil, 1983), esp. 244–49, where Ory argues that 1968 marked the end of the enlightenment and the beginning of "decadence" and the "quest for cultural identity."

26. On this liberal, antistatist environment, see J. Chevallier, "La fin de l'État-providence," *Projet* 143 (March 1980): 267–71. Chevallier thought that this environment was essentially rightist and that right-wing politicians would benefit most from it. But see also Jean-Pierre Cot, "Actualité et ambiguités du libéralisme," *Commentaire* 9, no. 35 (Autumn 1986): 403–11. Cot agreed that liberalism returned with 1968, but he saw the Socialists as the "true" liberals, as opposed to the Orleanist right.

27. On the role of such journals in shaping opinion, and on the role of the media in general, see Hervé Hamon and Patrick Rotman, *Les Intellocrates: Expédition en haute intelligentsia* (Paris: Ramsay, 1981), 229ff.

28. On the new left in general, see Bernard E. Brown, *Socialism of a Different Kind: Reshaping the Left in France* (Westport, Conn.: Greenwood Press, 1982), and Arthur Hirsch, *The French Left: A History and Overview* (Montreal: Black Rose Books, 1982). On Rocard and the PSU, see Charles Hauss, *The New Left in France* (Westport, Conn.: Greenwood Press, 1978). On 1968, see Raymond Aron, *The Elusive Revolution: Anatomy of a Student Revolt* (New York: Praeger, 1969); Daniel Cohn-Bendit, *Obsolete Communism: The Left-Wing Alternative* (New York: McGraw-Hill, 1968); Richard Johnson, *The French Communist Party versus the Students* (New Haven: Yale University Press, 1972).

29. See Hirsch, *The French Left*, chaps. 4 and 5. The quote is in Hirsch, p. 131. See also Henri Lefebvre, *Everyday Life in the Modern World* (New York: Harper Torchbooks, 1971).

30. Jacques Julliard, *Contre la politique professionnelle* (Paris: Éditions du Seuil, 1977), 102.

31. Ibid., 135.

32. Ibid., 150.

33. Ibid., 157.

34. Pierre Rosanvallon, *L'âge de l'autogestion* (Paris: Éditions du Seuil, 1976), 42.

35. Ibid., 45.

36. Ibid., 173. See also Pierre Rosanvallon and P. Viveret, *Pour une nouvelle culture politique* (Paris: Éditions du Seuil, 1977), 83–84, which is much more critical of Marxism.

37. Judt, *Marxism and the French Left,* 218.

38. Hirsch, *The French Left,* 221–33.

39. See André Gorz, *Strategy for Labor* (New York: Beacon Press, 1967), on these views.

40. André Gorz, *Adieux au prolétariat* (Paris: Éditions Galilée, 1980; Points, 1981), 35.

41. Ibid., 64.

42. Ibid., 98.

43. Ibid., 170–71.

44. On politics, the state, and civil society, see ibid., 156–76.

45. Jean-Marie Domenach, *Enquête sur les idées contemporaines* (Paris: Éditions du Seuil, 1981), 55–64, for a good brief analysis.

46. On the political debate about the *nouveaux philosophes*, see Sylvie Boucasse and Denis Bourgeois, eds. *Faut-il brûler les nouveaux philosophes?* (Paris: Oswald, 1978), and the hostile work of François Aubral and Xavier Delacourt, *Contre la nouvelle philosophie* (Paris: Gallimard, 1977).

47. See Bernard-Henri Lévy, *Barbarism with a Human Face* (New York: Harper and Row, 1979), 195 for the quote.

48. On his 1968 reflections, see André Glucksmann, *1968: Stratégie et révolution en France* (Paris: Christian Bourgois, 1968), esp. chap. 1 but also pp. 56–60 and 121–22. The quote is from André Glucksmann, *La cuisinière et le mangeur d'hommes* (Paris: Éditions du Seuil, 1975), 219.

49. Boucasse and Bourgeois, *Faut-il brûler*, 50.

50. Michel Le Bris, *L'Homme aux semelles de vent* (Paris: Bernard Grasset, 1977), 12–55.

51. Ibid., 211–74.

52. Jean-Paul Dollé, *L'Odeur de la France* (Paris: Bernard Grasset, 1977), 84.

53. Ibid., 90. See also the biographical information in Boucasse and Bourgeois, *Faut-il brûler*, 29

54. Boucasse and Bourgeois, *Faut-il brûler*, 39.

55. Jean-Marie Benoist, *Les Nouveaux Primaires* (Paris: Hallier, 1978), 9–15.

56. Ibid., 72.

57. Jean-Marie Benoist, *Un Singulier Programme: Le carnaval du Programme commun* (Paris: Presses universitaires de France, 1978), 89–105.

58. Benoist, *Les Nouveaux Primaires*, 185–86, 218–19.

59. On this particular speech, see Albert du Roy and Robert Schneider, *Le Roman de la rose: D'Épinay à l'Élysée, l'aventure des socialistes* (Paris: Éditions du Seuil, 1982), 72–73.

60. Historians of French socialism have differed over the degree to which ideology

should be taken seriously. Hugues Portelli, *Le socialisme français tel qu'il est* (Paris: Presses universitaires de France, 1980), 158–60 argues that the party's ideas were tied to which current prevailed and were mainly developed prior to 1968, but he places key emphasis on *autogestion*, especially up to 1978. Yves Roucaute, *Le Parti socialiste* (Paris: B. Huisman, 1983), gives more weight to action in the party, claiming that ideas have not had much effect on socialism (see pp. 6–8). For a concrete application of the threefold strategy, see Parti socialiste, *Changer la vie: Programme de gouvernement du Parti socialiste* (Paris: Flammarion, 1972), esp. the presentation by François Mitterrand.

61. Portelli, *Le socialisme français*, 161–63 has argued this quite persuasively, only to conclude that after 1978 *autogestion* declined in importance and the party resorted to using ideology in a negative sense, to define currents in relation to other currents, for the purpose of gaining dominance.

62. See Alain Meyer, "Pourquoi le Front de classe?" *La nouvelle revue socialiste* 29 (1977): 33–40. Meyer became editor of the *Revue* in 1978, replacing Lionel Jospin.

63. See Portelli, *Le socialisme français*, 124–26.

64. See the accounts in R. W. Johnson, *The Long March of the French Left* (New York: St. Martin's Press, 1981), 254–64, and Bell and Criddle, *The French Socialist Party*, 84–108.

65. See especially the excellent analysis of Portelli, *Le socialisme français*, 197–202. Portelli argues that Mitterrandism and Rocardism are not very far apart. Both are very comfortable with the radical, Mendès-France tradition in the PS. For more traditional views, see Roucaute, *Le Parti socialiste*, 120–25, and Johnson, *The Long March*, 254–64.

66. Mitterrand, *Politique 2*, 216.

67. Ibid., 228.

68. Ibid., 227.

69. Alain Myer, "Les socialistes et les pensées de crise de la fin des années 70," *La nouvelle revue socialiste* 42 (1979): 61–65.

70. See, in particular, Alain Meyer, "Nouveaux philosophes et nouvelle droite. De l'ange à la bête. I) Bernard-Henri Lévy ou la passion du dégagement," *La nouvelle revue socialiste* 43 (September–October 1979): 59–63, and "II) Surhomme ou bête: la nouvelle droite," *La nouvelle revue socialiste* 44 (November–December 1979): 75. See also Alain Meyer, "Requiem pour le socialisme. Célébrant: Alain Touraine," *La nouvelle revue socialiste* 50 (September–November 1980): 87–95.

71. *Feux croisés sur le Stalinisme. Colloque organisé par l'Institut socialiste d'études et de recherche* (Paris: Collection de la Revue Politique et Parlementaire, 1980), 173.

72. Ibid., 174–76.

73. Ibid., 178.

74. Ibid., 181.

75. Ibid., 186–87.

76. Ibid., 187.

77. Ibid. See also Jean-Pierre Chevènement's attack on the new philosophers, the *gauche américaine*, and the irrationalists in *Être socialiste aujourd'hui* (Paris: Cana, 1979). Chevènement feared that the left had already lost the battle against these forces (see p. 78).

78. See Parti socialiste, *Assises du socialisme* (Paris: Stock, 1974). For an overview, see du Roy and Schneider, *Le Roman de la rose*, 89–93, 160–62. A good introduction to *autogestion* is Brown, *Socialism of a Different Kind*.

79. As noted previously, Portelli saw *autogestion* as the only Socialist ideology, although he doubted if the party ever possessed a clear-cut ideology of its own and

was certain that it did not after 1978. On the other hand, Michael Keating and Paul Hainsworth, *Decentralisation and Change in Contemporary France* (Aldershot: Gower, 1986) place considerable emphasis on *autogestion* and decentralization as the center of Socialist ideology throughout the 1970s and into the 1980s.

80. M. Charzat, J. P. Chevènement, and G. Toutain, *Le Ceres: Un combat pour le socialisme* (Paris: Calmann-Lévy, 1975), 178.

81. Ibid., 180–83.

82. Ibid., 187–200, 225–32.

83. Jean-Pierre Chevènement, *Le Vieux, la Crise, le Neuf* (Paris: Flammarion, 1974), 126.

84. Quoted in ibid., 159.

85. Ibid., chap. 14, 192–208, 247. See also David Hanley, "CERES," in *The Left in France: Towards the Socialist Republic,* ed. D. S. Bell and Eric Shaw (Nottingham: Nottingham University Press, 1983).

86. Charzat, Chevènement, and Toutain, *Le Ceres,* 247.

87. H. Hamon and P. Rotman, *La Deuxième Gauche: Histoire intellectuelle et politique de la CFDT* (Paris: Éditions du Seuil, 1984), 273–77.

88. Edmond Marie, *Demain l'autogestion* (Paris: Seghers, 1976), 117.

89. Ibid., 135.

90. Ibid., 146. For a different perspective on Maire's form of *autogestion,* see Hubert Landier, *Demain quels syndicats?* 282–86.

91. On the Rocardians, see Hervé Hamon and Patrick Rotman, *L'Effet Rocard* (Paris: Stock, 1980), 336–51.

92. See Michel Rocard, *Parler vrai* (Paris: Éditions du Seuil, 1979), 76–84.

93. Ibid., 97–101.

94. Ibid., 96, 167.

95. Ibid., 169.

96. Hamon and Rotman, *L'Effet Rocard.* See also Rocard's contribution "La social-démocratie et nous," in *Qu'est-ce que la social-démocratie?* ed. Michel Rocard, et al. (Paris: Faire, 1979), 11–26.

97. See Peter Alexis Gourevitch, *Paris and the Provinces: The Politics of Local Government Reform in France* (London: George Allen and Unwin, 1980).

98. Robert Lafont, *La Révolution régionaliste* (Paris: Gallimard, 1967), 153, 158, 181.

99. Of course, Rocard and Philipponneau were not the only major regionalist thinkers in the 1960s. For other examples, see Michel Philipponneau, *La grande affaire: Décentralisation et régionalisation* (Paris: Calmann-Lévy, 1981), chaps. 1 and 2.

100. Robert Lafont, *Autonomie: De la région à l'autogestion* (Paris: Gallimard, 1976), 94.

101. Ibid., 120–69.

102. This is what Keating and Hainsworth, *Decentralisation and Change,* 63, argue.

103. Parti socialiste, *La France au pluriel* (Paris: Éditions Entente, 1981), 59.

104. Ibid., 25–30, 73–83, 106–10.

105. An outpouring of articles on *autogestion* appeared at this time, 1974–77, in the Socialist party's review, *La nouvelle revue socialiste.*

106. "Les socialistes et le débat idéologique, un colloque de l'ISER," *La nouvelle revue socialiste* 26 (1977).

107. "L'expérimentation sociale," *La nouvelle revue socialiste* 37 (January, 1979): 8–9.

108. Ibid., 17.

109. Ibid., 25.

110. Parti socialiste, *Projet socialiste pour la France des années 80* (Paris: Club Socialiste du Livre, 1981), 62. On the reception of the *Projet* in the party, see Johnson, *The Long March*, 263–64.

111. Parti socialite, *Project socialiste,* 110.

112. Ibid., 121, 131.

113. Ibid., 146, 153.

114. Ibid., 252.

115. Ibid., 280, 311.

116. Ibid., 159–70, 361–71.

117. See Claude Manceron and Bernard Pingaud, *François Mitterrand: L'homme, les idées, le programme* (Paris: Flammarion, 1981), for the 110 propositions.

118. For the quote, see ibid., 114. On Mitterrand's opportunism, see Catherine Nay, *Le Noir et le Rouge ou l'histoire d'une ambition* (Paris: Bernard Grasset, 1984).

119. Manceron and Pingaud, *François Mitterrand*, 111–30.

120. François Mitterrand, *Ici et maintenant: Conversations avec Guy Claisse* (Paris: Fayard, 1980), 45.

121. This was the advice of Jean François Bizot in *La nouvelle revue socialiste* (February–March 1981): 4.

122. Jean-Pierre Chevènement, *Le pari sur l'intelligence* (Paris: Flammarion, 1985), 68–69. Before 1981, Chevènement had made similar statements.

Chapter 2.
"The Rupture with Capitalism," 1981–1983:
Utopia and Reality

1. According to Alain Duhamel, *La République de Monsieur Mitterrand* (Paris: Bernard Grasset, 1982), 72.

2. D. S. Bell and Byron Criddle, *The French Socialist Party: Resurgence and Victory* (Oxford: Oxford University Press, 1984), 199–203.

3. Annie Collovald, "La République du militant: Recrutement et filières de la carrière politique des deputés socialistes en 1981," in *Les élites socialistes au pouvoir, 1981–1985,* ed. Pierre Birnbaum (Paris: Presses universitaires de France, 1985), 46–51.

4. Brigitte Gaiti, " 'Politique d'abord': Le chemin de la réussite ministérielle dans la France contemporaine," in ibid., 54–57, 70; Bell and Criddle, *The French Socialist Party*, 197–216.

5. Duhamel, *La République*, 105; Jack Hayward, *Governing France: The One and Indivisible Republic*, 2d ed. (New York: Norton, 1983), 104, 128–29; Daniele Lochak, "La Haute Administration à l'épreuve de l'alternance," in Birnbaum, *Les élites socialistes*, 165; *L'Express*, 22 January 1982. Michel Crozier sees the Socialists increasing the power of the Grandes Écoles elite by carrying out massive nationalization. See Crozier, *On ne change pas la société par décret*, rev. ed. (Paris: Bernard Grasset, 1979; Pluriel, 1982), 167.

6. Roger Quillot, *Sur le pavois ou la recherche de l'équilibre* (Paris: Collection de la Revue Politique et Parlementaire, 1985), 21–22, 33, 36–37, 54–55.

7. Yvette Roudy, *À cause d'elles* (Paris: Albin Michel, 1985), parts I and II; see Defferre's preface to Michel Philipponneau, *La grande affaire: Décentralisation et régionalisation* (Paris: Calmann–Lévy, 1981), 7–11; Thierry Pfister, *La vie quotidienne à Matignon au temps de l'union de la gauche* (Paris: Hachette, 1985), 22–42 (quotation from 39–40).

8. Howard Machin and Vincent Wright, "Economic Policy under the Mitterrand Presidency, 1981–1984: An Introduction," in *Economic Policy and Policy-Making under the Mitterrand Presidency,* ed. Howard Machin and Vincent Wright (London: Frances Pinter, 1985), 9–11.

9. Jack Hayward, *The State and the Market Economy: Industrial Patriotism and Economic Intervention in France* (New York: New York University Press, 1986), 231, on the jumble in industrial planning.

10. Philip Cerny, "Economic Policy: Crisis Management, Structural Reform and Socialist Politics," in *Socialism in France from Jaurès to Mitterrand* ed. Stuart Williams (London: Frances Pinter, 1983), 102–6.

11. See *Le Monde*, 12 June 1981 and Delors's later defense of the relance in Philippe Alexandre and Jacques Delors, *En sortir ou pas* (Paris: Bernard Grasset, 1985), 71–75.

12. *Le Monde*, 12 June 1981.

13. Ibid., 19 June 1981.

14. Ibid., 24 June 1981; see also André Donneur, *L'alliance fragile: Socialistes et communistes françaises (1922–1983)* (Montréal: Nouvelle Optique, 1984), 296–97.

15. Ibid., 25 July 1981.

16. Pierre Mauroy, *C'est ici le chemin* (Paris: Flammarion, 1982), 31–33.

17. *L'Express*, 12 June 1981.

18. Alexandre and Delors, *En sortir*, 21, 71–79. Rocard would later claim that he had opposed the *relance*. There is no evidence at this point in time that he voiced objections in the government, except to argue for a different kind of *relance*. See also Philippe Bauchard, *La Guerre des deux roses: Du rêve à la réalité, 1981–1985*, (Paris: Bernard Grasset, 1986), 33, on Chevènement's protectionism.

19. Stéphane Denis, *La Leçon d'automme* (Paris: Albin Michel, 1983), 42–43; *Le Monde,* 2, 6 October 1981. On Fabius's role as the author of the budget and on the issues surrounding devaluation, see Bauchard, *La Guerre*, 52–57; see also Gabriel Milesi, *Jacques Delors* (Paris: Belfond, 1985), 159, on Delors's role in the devaluation.

20. Quoted in Bauchard, *La Guerre*, 17.

21. Denis, *La Leçon,* 45–46. See also *Le Monde*, 29 September and 17 October 1981, on the PSU position and divisions on the left, respectively.

22. Quoted in Jean Gabriel Fredet and Denis Pingaud, *Les patrons face à la gauche* (Paris: Ramsay, 1982), 36.

23. *Le Monde*, 15 September, 25–26, 27 October 1981. See also Pierre Mauroy, *À gauche* (Paris: Albin Michel, 1985), 42, for his speech at Valence.

24. *Le Monde*, 4 November 1981.

25. Mauroy, *À gauche*, 117–22.

26. *Le Monde*, 1 December 1981.

27. Ibid.

28. Pfister, *La vie quotidienne*, 213, "Rigueur n'est pas synonyme de pause."

29. *Le Monde,* 2 December 1981. Chevènement expressed his support of Delors and Paul Quilès expressed his backing for the grand synthesis that French socialism was, implicitly accepting at least some of what Delors had said. See Fredet and Pingaud, *Les patrons*, 45, on Mitterrand's support of reform.

30. See Yves Morvan, "Industrial Policy," in Machin and Wright, *Economic Policy*, 129–30.

31. *Le Monde,* 16 September 1981.

32. Ibid., 17 September 1981, for Jean-Pierre Dumont's article on the subject. See also Pierre-Alain Muet, "Economic Management and the International Environment, 1981–1983," in Machin and Wright, *Economic Policy,* 75.

33. Fredet and Pingaud, *Les patrons*, 18–20, 24–25, 39–40; Suzanne Berger,

"The Socialists and the *patronat*: The Dilemma of Co-existence in a Mixed Economy," in Machin and Wright, *Economic Policy*, 225–28, 231.

34. *Le Monde*, 4 November 1981.

35. Ibid., 18 November 1981.

36. Michel Noblecourt, "Le pouvoir syndicale en France depuis mai 1981," *Pouvoirs* 26 (1983): 101–8.

37. André Bergeron, *1500 jours, 1980–1984* (Paris: Flammarion, 1984).

38. Ibid., 16–20; see also pp. 52, 57, for FO's reservations on SMIC increases and other aspects of the second left's program.

39. *Le Monde,* 13, 14 November 1981.

40. According to J. Brémond and G. Brémond, *L'économie française face aux défis mondiaux* (Paris: Hatier, 1985), 84, profits reached their lowest point in the postwar period in 1981.

41. *Le Monde,* 3, 12 November 1981; Gary Freeman, "Socialism and Social Security," in *The French Socialist Experiment*, ed. John S. Ambler (Philadelphia: Institute for the Study of Human Issues, 1985), 104–6.

42. See the historical background in Charles Millon, *L'extravagante histoire des nationalisations* (Paris: Plon, 1984), 36–37, 60–71, and Pierre Rosanvallon, *Misère de l'économie* (Paris: Éditions du Seuil, 1983), 70–82.

43. The argument is Richard Holton's in his article "Industrial Politics in France: Nationalization under Mitterrand," *West European Politics* 9, no. 1 (January 1986): 70–71.

44. Quoted in Millon, *L'extravagante histoire*, 78.

45. Lionel Zinzou, *Le fer de lance: Essai sur les nationalisations industrielles* (Paris: Olivier Orban, 1985), 72–73; and Holton, "Industrial Politics," 73–74.

46. *Le Monde*, 17 July 1981.

47. Ibid., 22 September 1981.

48. Mauroy, *À gauche*, 111–14. The best work on the 1982 nationalizations, André G. Delion and Michel Durupty, *Les nationalisations 1982* (Paris: Economica, 1982), notes this move from the Common Program toward realism while pointing also to some attempts to preserve parts of the original program, usually with little success. See pp. 6–7, 9–10, and 79–81.

49. Zinsou, *Le fer de lance,* 34–36.

50. Pfister, *La vie quotidienne,* 158–64, 170–72. On Delors's position regarding nationalization, see Milesi, *Jacques Delors*, 165–66.

51. Delion and Durupty, *Les nationalisations,* 207; Revue politique et parlementaire, *Gauche: Premier bilan* (Paris: Collection de la Revue Politique et Parlementaire, 1985), 152–53.

52. *Le Monde*, 19 February 1982.

53. Ibid., 7, 14 August 1981, for the disillusionment of ecologists with the government over nuclear policy and 7, 9 October and 26 November 1981 on the government's nuclear policy.

54. Ibid., 19 June and 1, 14 July 1981.

55. François Mitterrand, *Réflexions sur la politique extérieur de la France* (Paris: Fayard, 1986), 16.

56. See ibid., 321–34 in particular on Franco-Algerian relations; *Le Monde,* 4 November, 2 December 1981 and 3 February, 1982; *Le Point,* 8 February 1982. For a summary of Socialist policies in the Third World, see Stéphane Hessel, "Mitterrand's France and the Third World," in *The Mitterrand Experiment: Continuity and Change in Modern France,* ed. George Ross, Stanley Hoffmann, and Sylvia Malzacher (New York: Oxford University Press, 1987), 324–37.

57. *Le Monde,* 5 January 1982.

58. Ibid., 11 July 1981; Henri Claude, *Mitterrand ou l'atlantisme masquée* (Paris: Messidor, 1986), 149–50.

59. See Michel Rocard, *Plan intérimaire: Stratégie pour deux ans, 1982/1983* (Paris: Flammarion, 1982). See also Peter Holmes, "Broken Dreams: Economic Policy in Mitterrand's France," in *Mitterrand's France,* ed. Sonia Mazey and Michael Newman (London: Croom Helm 1987), 44–45.

60. Pierre Sadran, "Les socialistes et la région," *Pouvoirs* 19 (1981): 141–44; Catherine Grémion, "Decentralization in France: A Historical Perspective," in Ross, Hoffmann, and Malzacher, *The Mitterrand Experiment,* 237–41.

61. Jean-Émile Vié, *La décentralisation sans illusion* (Paris: Presses universitaires de France, 1982), 92.

62. Pierre Mauroy, *C'est ici,* 95; Yves Mény, "Decentralisation in Socialist France: The Politics of Pragmatism," *West European Politics* 7, no. 1 (January 1984): 73.

63. *Le Monde,* 7 October 1981.

64. See also the penetrating critique of Vincent Wright, "Questions d'un jacobin anglais aux régionalistes français," *Pouvoirs* 19 (1981): 119–30.

65. Georges Gontcharoff and Serge Milano, *La décentralisation.* Vol. 2: *Le transfert des compétences* (Paris: ADELS et Syros, 1984), 12–16.

66. Philipponneau, *La grande affaire,* 104–11.

67. Georges Gontcharoff and Serge Milano, *La décentralisation.* Vol. 1: *Nouveaux pouvoirs, nouveaux enjeux* (Paris: ADELS et Syros, 1983), 13–15.

68. *Le Monde,* 17 June 1982.

69. Quoted in Mark Kesselman, "The Tranquil Revolution in Clochemerle: Socialist Decentralization in France," in *Socialism, the State and Public Policy in France,* ed. Philip G. Cerny and Martin A. Schain (London: Methuen, 1985), 180.

70. Gontcharoff and Milano, *La décentralisation,* 1:76–78, 81–83.

71. Ibid., 132ff.

72. Georges Gontcharoff and Serge Milano, *La décentralisation.* Vol. 3: *Les compétences transferées en 1983* (Paris: ADELS et Syros, 1984), 12–15, 55–65, 69–71, 91–93, 99–100.

73. Gontcharoff and Milano, *La décentralisation,* 2:103.

74. Mény, "Decentralisation," 77. Such negative evaluations of decentralization were common among French academics. See François Dupuy and Jean-Claude Thoenig, "La loi du 2 mars 1982 sur la décentralisation. De l'analyse des textes à l'observation des premiers pas," *Revue française de science politique* 33, no. 6 (December 1983): 962–86; Xavier Frégé, *La décentralisation* (Paris: Éditions La Découverte, 1986), esp. the critical final chapter, pp. 101–22. American academics, in contrast, tend to be more optimistic about decentralization. See Kesselman, "The Tranquil Revolution," 181, and Douglas Ashford, "Reconstructing the French 'État': Progress of the *Loi Defferre,*" *West European Politics* 6, no. 3 (July 1983): 263–70. See also Michael Keating and Paul Hainsworth, *Decentralisation and Change in Contemporary France* (Aldershot: Gower, 1986) 129–30, who concluded that decentralization brought very few structural changes to the system.

75. *L'Express,* 31 July 1981.

76. *Le Monde,* 20 May 1982.

77. Vié, *La décentralisation,* 134–38.

78. Philipponneau, *La grande affaire,* 224–36.

79. See esp. *Le Monde,* 11 January 1983; see also *Le Monde,* 24 December 1981 for the Council of Ministers' decision on the Corsican statute. Thierry Michalon, "Sur la question Corse: Dualisme et utopie," *Revue française de science politique,* 35, no.

5 (October 1985): 892–907, sees the consumer revolution and not autonomy as the main reason for the destruction of *la Corse profonde* and the independence movement.

80. *Le Monde*, 26 May 1982. Later, some support was given to language study, but it was minor.

81. John Loughlin, "A New Deal for France's Regions and Linguistic Minorities," *West European Politics* 8, no. 3 (July 1985): 108–9 points out that Gaston Defferre feared that creation of a Basque department would lead to Basque independence from France.

82. *Le Monde*, 13 August, 22, 23, 30 September 1981; 16 January, 18, 26 June 1982.

83. Quoted in Catherine Clément, *Rêver chacun pour l'autre: Sur la politique culturelle* (Paris: Fayard, 1982), 295.

84. *Le Monde*, 7 August 1982. For a hostile account of Jack Lang's cultural positions, see Diana Pinto, "The Left, the Intellectuals and Culture," in Ross, Hoffmann, and Malzacher, *The Mitterrand Experiment*, 217–27.

85. Pfister, *La vie quotidienne*, 135–38. See Quillot, *Sur le pavois,* 65–66, on Mitterrand's control over the cultural budget.

86. *1981–1986, le bilan de la VIIe législature* (Paris: Syros, 1986), 55–57.

87. Clément, *Rêver chacun*, 303ff.; *Le Monde*, 5 September 1981.

88. *Le Monde*, 13 February 1983.

89. See ibid., 13 March 1986, for the impressive *bilan* of the Lang years. See also Clément, *Rêver chacun*, 70.

90. *Le bilan*, 161, and Clément, *Rêver chacun*, 144–46, 160–63.

91. Mauroy, *À gauche*, 212–14; *Le Monde*, 15 June 1983. For a critical view of Lang's tenure, see Jill Forbes, "Cultural Policy: The Soul of Man under Socialism," in Mazey and Newman, *Mitterrand's France*, 140–41, 152–57. Forbes maintains that Lang's policies were elitist, Parisian, and wasteful. The evidence does not seem to support these conclusions, if the Lang years are compared with what came before.

92. Bauchard, *La Guerre*, 79–83.

93. Jean Auroux, *Les droits des travailleurs* (Paris: La Documentation Française, 1981), 3–5. See also George Ross, "From One Left to Another: *Le Social* in Mitterrand's France," in Ross, Hoffmann, and Malzacher, *The Mitterrand Experiment,* 203–4, 213.

94. See Charlotte Laurent-Atthalin, ed., *Les nouveaux droits des travailleurs* (Paris: Éditions La Découverte et Journal *Le Monde*, 1983), 32–33, 78–80, 101–3.

95. Ibid., chap. 7, pp. 152–56; Duncan Gallie, "*Les lois Auroux*: The Reform of French Industrial Relations?" in Machin and Wright, *Economic Policy*, 208.

96. Loughlin, "New Deal," 109.

97. *Le Monde*, 18 November, 9 December 1981; Fredet and Pingaud, *Les patrons*, 46–48.

98. *Le Monde*, 7 January, 10, 19 February 1982; Fredet and Pingaud, *Les patrons*, 49–50, 134.

99. *Le Monde*, 19 April 1982; Fredet and Pingaud, *Les patrons*, 64–65.

100. Numerous sources claim that as early as February the Socialists realized that a new devaluation would be necessary. See for example, Revue politique et parlementaire, *Premier bilan*, 119.

101. *Le Monde*, 17–18 January, 9, 10 February 1982; Bergeron, *1500 jours*, 57.

102. *Le Monde*, 19 February 1982; *Le Point,* 18 January 1982; Fredet and Pingaud, *Les patrons*, 51–52, 58.

103. *Le Monde*, 16, 24 March 1982; *Le Point*, 15 March 1982.

104. Michel Debatisse, *Le projet paysan* (Paris: Éditions du Seuil, 1983), 129, saw

the peasant demonstrations as apolitical, but this is highly questionable. See Cerny and Schain, *Socialism*, 28, on Debré's statement. See also *Le Monde*, 24 March, 27 April, 18, 19, 25, 26 May 1982.

105. Mauroy, *À gauche*, 44–45; *Le Monde*, 25 March, 20, 25–26, 27 April 1982.

106. Olivier Duhamel and Jean-Luc Parodi, "Images syndicales," *Pouvoirs* 26 (1983): 157–59; *Le Monde*, 16–17, 25, 29 May 1982.

107. *Le Monde*, 20, 21, 26, 30–31 May 1982.

108. Ibid., 18–19, 27 April, 16–17, 20 May, 4, 15 June 1982.

109. Ibid., 19 June 1982.

110. Ibid., 26 May, 1, 4 June 1982.

111. Ibid., 16–27, 25, 27 May, 5 June 1982. See also Brémond, *L'économie française*, 186–88, on the machine tool industry.

112. Bauchard, *La Guerre*, 88–89.

113. *Le Monde*, 21, 22, 23–24, 25 May 1982.

114. Ibid., 25, 29 May, 2, 5 June 1982; *Le Nouvel Observateur,* 5 June 1982.

115. Bauchard, *La Guerre*, 102–5.

116. *Le Monde,* 17, 22, 24 June 1982; Bauchard, *La Guerre,* 82.

117. Fredet and Pingaud, *Les patrons*, 71–72.

118. For Questiaux's comments on social security, see *Le Monde*, 9 June 1982; Bauchard, *La Guerre*, 107–8; *L'Express*, 7 July 1982.

119. For the Socialists, see the results of the *convention socialiste* in *Le Monde*, 22 June 1982. For the invective of the right, see *Le Monde*, 27 July 1982 and *Le Figaro*, 4 August 1982. But see also the harsh criticism of the opposition for failing to offer an alternative to the Socialist government's policies in *L'Express*, 8 October, 19 November 1982, esp. the 8 October issue in which the journal's chief political correspondent, Noël-Jean Bergeroux, offered his critique.

120. *Le Monde*, 10, 22 July, 5, 6, 20 October 1982; Freeman, "Socialism and Social Security," in Ambler, *French Socialist Experiment*, 107.

121. *Le Monde*, 24 June, 6 July, 10–11 October, 5 November 1982; *L'Express,* 19 November 1982, also expressed approval of the government's realism.

122. *Le Monde*, 2, 3 September 1982. But see also the revisions in *Le Monde*, 26 October 1982.

123. *L'Express*, 17, 24 September 1982.

124. Michel Rocard, *À l'épreuve des faits: Textes politiques 1979–1985* (Paris: Éditions du Seuil, 1986), 65–74.

125. *Le Monde*, 16 September, 8 October, 6 November 1982.

126. Ibid., 24 July 1982.

127. Morvan, "Industrial Policy," in Machin and Wright, *Economic Policy*, 124–26.

128. *Le Monde*, 30 July, 5 August 1982; Pascal Petit, "Defining the New French Industrial Policy: The Burden of the Past," in *Socialism in France from Jaurès to Mitterrand*, ed. Stuart Williams (London: Frances Pinter, 1983), 86–87. See also Jean-Louis Moynot, "The Left, Industrial Policy and the *Filière électronique*," in Ross, Hoffmann, and Malzacher, *The Mitterrand Experiment*, 263–76.

129. Petit, "French Industrial Policy," in Williams, *Socialism in France*, 82–84; *Le Monde*, 16 October 1982, on coal policy.

130. *Le Monde,* 2 September 1982.

131. Ministre de la Recherche et de l'Industrie, *Une politique industrielle pour la France. Actes des journées de travail des 15 et 16 novembre 1982* (Paris: La Documentation Française, 1982), 3–32.

132. Ibid., 104–7, 191–94, 199, 281–82.

133. Pfister, *La vie quotidienne*, 143–44, on the Mauroy–Delors relationship. See Paul Fabra's article on the *dirigisme* of the government in *Le Monde*, 9 July 1982.

134. *Le Monde*, 7 September 1982.

135. Ibid., 13 October 1982, from Mauroy's remarks to *Le Matin de Paris*.

136. Ibid., 21, 27, 31 October–1 November, 16 November 1982; *Le Nouvel Observateur*, 30 October 1982; see Delors's observations on the need to devalue for a third time in Alexandre and Delors, *En sortir*, 76–79.

137. The arguments in the party during November and December were reported in *Le Monde*, 18, 23 November, 5–6, 14 December; see also *Le Nouvel Observateur*, 14 December 1982.

138. See *L'Express*, 19 November 1982, for the Gallup poll results.

139. Denis, *La Leçon*, 115–16; *Le Monde*, 2–3, 4 January 1983.

140. *Le Monde*, 15 January 1983.

141. Denis, *La Leçon*, 118.

142. Ibid., 120.

143. Ibid.; *Le Monde*, 2 February 1983; Bauchard, *La Guerre*, 126.

144. Bergeron, *1500 jours*, 113; *Le Monde*, 3, 5, 8, 12 February 1983.

145. Mauroy, *À gauche*, 90–91.

146. *Le Monde*, 19 February 1983.

147. Ibid., 27–28 February 1983.

148. Ibid., 2, 4 March 1983.

149. Badinter spoke of this fear as existential, "Un jour je vous parlerai de la justice... Entretien avec Robert Badinter," *Le débat* 33 (January 1985): 10–11.

150. Paul Oriol, *Les immigrés: Métèques ou citoyens?* (Paris: Syros, 1985), 90.

151. Ibid., 92–95; *Le Monde*, 20 April 1982.

152. Oriol, *Les immigrés*, 101–4; Gilles Verbunt, "Immigrés et associations," *Les temps modernes* 452–54 (March–May 1984): 2063; *Le Monde*, 13, 14 August 1981; Françoise Gaspard and Claude Servan-Schreiber, *La fin des immigrés* (Paris: Éditions du Seuil, 1984), 207–8.

153. Gaspard and Servan-Schreiber, *La fin des immigrés*, 65–66.

154. Edwy Plenel and Alain Rollat, *L'effet Le Pen* (Paris: Le Monde, 1984), 199–200; Étienne Balibar, "Sujets ou citoyens?" *Les temps modernes* 452–54 (March–May 1984): 1727–29; *Le Monde*, 9 April, 17 November 1982, and 7 January, 20–21 March 1983.

155. *Le Monde*, 13, 29 January, 9, 10 February 1983; see also Balibar, "Sujets ou citoyens?" 1727–29.

156. Gaspard and Servan-Schreiber, *La fin des immigrés*, 60–64; Plenel and Rollat, *L'effet Le Pen*, 199; Sami Nadir, "Marseille: Chronique des années de lèpre," *Les temps modernes* 452–54 (March–May 1984): 1593; *Le Monde*, 8 February 1983. See also the special *L'Express*, 4 February 1983, edition on immigrants.

157. Jérôme Jaffré, "Les élections municipales de mars 1983: Les trois changements du paysage électoral," *Pouvoirs* 27 (1983): 143–58; *Le Monde*, 16–17 March, 12–13 June 1983.

158. These accounts are supported by a number of journalists who may or may not have known all of the participants. See esp. Pfister, *La vie quotidienne*, 236–37, 251–52, 255, 257–58. But also see Bauchard, *La Guerre*, 141ff.; Serge July, *Les années Mitterrand* (Paris: Bernard Grasset, 1986), 83–84; and Jean-Marie Colombani, *Portrait du Président* (Paris: Gallimard, 1985), 65–66.

159. Alexandre and Delors, *En sortir*, 80–83.

Chapter 3.
"Rigueur encore une fois!": From the Municipal Elections
of March 1983 to the Fabius Government of July 1984

1. Philippe Bauchard, *La Guerre des deux roses: Du rêve à la réalité, 1981–1985* (Paris: Bernard Grasset, 1986), 148.

2. *Le Monde*, 24, 26 March 1983; Serge July, *Les années Mitterrand* (Paris: Bernard Grasset, 1986), 95–100; Gabriel Milesi, *Jacques Delors* (Paris: Belfond, 1985), 212–17.

3. *L'Express*, 1, 8 April 1983; *Le Monde*, 27–28 March 1983; *Le Nouvel Observateur*, 8 April 1983.

4. Quoted in Bauchard, *La Guerre*, 162. See also *Le Monde*, 29, 30 March 1983; André Bergeron, *1500 jours, 1980–1984* (Paris: Flammarion, 1984), 124; and Edmond Maire's criticisms in Pierre Nora, ed., *La C.F.D.T. en questions* (Paris: Gallimard, 1984), 241–45.

5. See *Le Monde*, 1, 2 and (esp.) 7 April 1983.

6. Ibid., 12, 13 April 1983.

7. Ibid., 28 April 1983.

8. Ibid., see the almost daily accounts in the paper during April and early May; Thierry Pfister, *La vie quotidienne à Matignon au temps de l'union de la gauche* (Paris: Hachette, 1985), 211, on the tourist issue; John S. Ambler, "Equality and the Politics of Education," in *The French Socialist Experiment*, ed. John S. Ambler (Philadelphia: Institute for the Study of Human Issues, 1985), 135.

9. *Le Monde*, 29, 30 April, 2, 3, 4, 7 May 1983.

10. Ibid., 10, 29 June 1983; Serge July, *Les années Mitterrand*, 100–11, had doubts on this score; see Bauchard, *La Guerre*, 175, on the September press conference; *Le Nouvel Observateur*, 23 September 1983.

11. See the poll results in *Le Nouvel Observateur*, 23 September, 1 October 1983.

12. *Le Monde*, 10, 29–30, 31 May 1983.

13. Ibid., 1 June 1983; *Le Nouvel Observateur*, 8 July 1983.

14. Jean-Marie Colombani, *Portrait du Président* (Paris: Gallimard, 1985), 124–25; *Le Monde*, 21 October 1983; *L'Express*, 28 October, 11 November 1983.

15. *Le Monde*, 16 September 1983; *L'Express*, 23, 30 September 1983; *Le Nouvel Observateur*, 23 September 1983.

16. *Le Monde*, 18 February, 18 April, 18 May 1984; *1981–1986, le bilan de la VIIe législature* (Paris: Syros, 1986), 73–77.

17. See *Le Monde*, 24 August 1983, for the UNEDIC study on the matter.

18. Ibid., 12 January 1984.

19. Ibid., 4 February 1983; Pfister, *La vie quotidienne*, 141–42.

20. *Le Monde*, 13 April 1983.

21. Richard Holton, "Industrial Politics in France: Nationalization under Mitterrand," *West European Politics* 9, no. 1 (January 1986): 76–77; Lionel Zinsou, *Le fer de lance: Essai sur les nationalisations industrielles* (Paris: Olivier Orban, 1985), 40–44.

22. Laurent Fabius, *Le coeur du futur* (Paris: Calmann-Lévy, 1985), 184. The entire speech is contained on pp. 171–206.

23. Ibid., 187.

24. Ibid., 190.

25. Ibid., 205.

26. Jean Le Garrec, *Demain la France: Les choix du IXe Plan, 1984–1988* (Paris: Éditions La Découverte, 1984), 14.

27. See *Le Nouvel Observateur*, 22 July 1983, article on energy.

28. See Jack Hayward, *The State and the Market Economy: Industrial Patriotism and Economic Intervention in France* (New York: New York University Press, 1986), 98–100; *Le Monde*, 29 September, 22 December 1983 and 11 January 1984.

29. *Le Monde*, 29–30 May, 11 June 1983 and 24 May 1984; *Le Nouvel Observateur*, 23 September 1983; J. Brémond and G. Brémond, *L'économie française face aux défis mondiaux* (Paris: Hatier, 1985), 182–83, 186–88.

30. Jean-Yves Potel, *L'état de la France et de ses habitants* (Paris: Éditions La Découverte, 1985), 380–81; *Le Monde*, 14 July, 13 October, 20, 28 December 1983, and 7 January 1984; *Le Nouvel Observateur,* 22 July 1983.

31. *Le Monde*, 13–14, 20–21 May 1984; *L'Express*, 27 April, 25 May 1984; *Le Nouvel Observateur*, 31 August 1984.

32. Quoted in *L'Express*, 29 June 1984. See also *Le Monde*, 28 September, 4 October 1983; *Le Point*, 30 April 1984.

33. Quoted in *L'Express*, 13 July 1984; see also Brémond, *L'économie française*, 189–90.

34. Bauchard, *La Guerre*, 243; *Le Monde*, 24, January, 8, 9, 10 February, 2, 3 March 1984.

35. *Le Monde*, 31 March 1984.

36. *Le Point,* 2 April 1984.

37. Ibid., 9 April 1984; *Le Monde*, 30 March 1984; *L'Express*, 13 April 1984. See also Bauchard, *La Guerre*, 194–201.

38. *La Monde*, 1–2, 3, 4 April 1984; Bergeron, *1500 jours*, 184–85, 190.

39. *Le Monde*, 5 April 1984.

40. For examples of this, see Bauchard, *La Guerre*, 194–201; July, *Les années Mitterrand*, 160–65; and Pierre Rosanvallon's analysis in *Le Point*, 9 April 1984.

41. *Le Monde*, 12 April 1984; *L'Express*, 20 April 1984.

42. *Le Monde*, 13 April 1984.

43. Ibid., 15–16, 21, 29–30 April 1984.

44. Ibid., 11 May 1984; Colombani, *Portrait du Président*, 202.

45. On the profs and the Socialists, see Hervé Hamon and Patrick Rotman, *Tant qu'il y aura des profs* (Paris: Éditions du Seuil, 1984; Points, 1986), 233–34, 257–59.

46. Alain Savary, *En toute liberté* (Paris: Hachette, 1985), 11.

47. Ibid., 54; *Le bilan,* 139.

48. Hamon and Rotman, *Des profs*, 318–19, 327–28.

49. See esp. ibid., 223, 233–34, 244–45, which is very critical of the corporatist, privileged professoriat. See also Alain Savary, "Entretien avec Mona Ozouf," *Le débat* 32 (November 1984): 9–12; Ambler, *Socialist Experiment*, 124–25, 127–29; *Le Monde*, 20 January, 22 June 1983.

50. Ambler, *Socialist Experiment*, 132–33; *Le Monde*, 14, 21 October 1983 and 26 January 1984; *Le Nouvel Observateur*, 21 October 1983.

51. Hamon and Rotman, *Des profs*, 233–34; *L'Express,* 2 September 1983.

52. Savary, *En toute liberté*, 36–39.

53. Ibid., 16, 19, 103, 118–19; *Le Nouvel Observateur*, 21 October 1983; *Le Monde*, 13 June 1984.

54. See Savary, *En toute liberté*, 90, 96–97; and the succinct article by Antoine Prost, "The Educational Maelstrom," in *The Mitterrand Experiment: Continuity and Change in Modern France,* ed. George Ross, Stanley Hoffmann, and Sylvia Malzacher (New York: Oxford University Press, 1987), 229–36.

55. *Le Point*, 30 April 1984; *Le Monde*, 24 April 1984.

56. See the IFOP-*Matin* poll in *Le Matin,* 30 May 1984. An IFOP poll taken in November 1983 showed at that early date that 71 percent of the French favored the existence of private education. See *Le Monde*, 13 December 1983.

57. See Jospin's statement that domestic policy would be irrelevant in the June elections in *Le Monde*, 27 March 1984.

58. Ibid., 7 June 1984.

59. Ibid., 9 June 1984.

60. Ibid., 23 May 1984.

61. Ibid., 19, 30 June 1984; *Le Nouvel Observateur*, 6 July 1984; Jérôme Jaffré, "Les élections européennes en France: L'ultime avertissement du corps électoral," *Pouvoirs* 31 (1984): 123–47.

62. Edwy Plenel and Alain Rollat, *L'effet Le Pen* (Paris: Le Monde), 45–47.

63. There are numerous indications of the inability of the left to create a coherent policy on immigration and the traditional right's willingness to capitalize on that. See *Le Monde*, 15 July 1983, for Chirac's policy; *Le Monde*, 3 August 1983, for Georgina Dufoix's views on a tighter policy regarding immigrants; *Le Nouvel Observateur,* 22 July 1983. See also *Le Monde*, 4 November 1983, on the new *contrôles d'identité* policy inaugurated by the government; Paul Oriol, *Les immigrés: Métèques ou citoyens?* (Paris: Syros, 1985), 113–14, for polls on immigrants; and *Les temps modernes* 452–54 (March–May 1984); 2092–94, 2098 on immigrant workers.

64. *Le Monde*, 19 June 1984; Plenel and Rollat, *L'effet Le Pen*, 116–30.

65. *L'Express*, 30 September 1983.

66. Plenel and Rollat, *L'effet Le Pen,* 40.

67. *Le Monde*, 16 March 1984; see Oriol, *Les immigrés*, 125, on Islam as the second religion of France and of the French.

68. *Le Monde*, 5 June 1984, for Cardinal Lustiger's interview.

69. Ibid., 21, 23 June 1984.

70. Pierre Mauroy, *À gauche* (Paris: Albin Michel, 1985), 279–84. Mauroy even made an appeal to the pope on the educational issue. See Savary, *En toute liberté,* 168–69. See also *Le Monde, 24–25,* 26 June 1984.

71. *L'Express*, 13 July 1984; *Le Monde*, 27 June, 1–2, 7, 8–9, 10, 12 July 1984; *Le Nouvel Observateur*, 6 July 1984.

72. *Le Monde*, 14 July 1984.

73. Ibid., 19, 21, 25 July 1984; *Le Point*, 23 July 1984; see also Terry Pfister, *La vie quotidienne*, 290–92, for Mauroy's resignation. Savary actually wanted to resign in May: see Savary, *En toute liberté*, 165–67. But see also Stanley Hoffmann, "Conclusion," in Ross, Hoffmann, and Malzacher, *The Mitterrand Experiment*, 347. He sees no "benefit for the President" in these referendum maneuvers. Hoffmann offers no evidence to support his conclusion.

Chapter 4.
Changing Ideological Contours: The Critique of Socialism in Power

1. Alain Peyrefitte, *Quand la rose se fanera... Du malentendu à l'espoir* (Paris: Plon, 1983), xiii, 10–31, 232–36.

2. Ibid., 73–86, 105–17, 176–84, 209, and chaps. 19–23.

3. Ibid., see chaps. 15–16.

4. Ibid., see chaps. 24–30.

5. Ibid., 305.

6. Ibid., 309–49.

7. Michel Massenet, ed., *La France socialiste* (Paris: Hachette, 1983), preface, 15–17, 25–26, 44, 46–53; Jean Féricelli, "Les logiques de l'État socialiste," in ibid., 74–78; Jose Frèches, "L'État socialiste," in ibid., 460; Annie Kriegel, "Le socialisme est derrière nous," in ibid., 472–73, 476–79.

8. See Pierre Biacabe, "Les mésaventures du franc," in ibid., 131–34; Roland Granier, "Expérience socialiste, emploi, chômage," in ibid., 284–93. See also Béatrice Bazil, "L'irrésistible logique de la socialisation," in ibid., 303–06, on the welfare state.

9. Caton, *De la reconquête* (Paris: Fayard, 1983), 18–21, 41–44.

10. Ibid., 52–55, 79–85.

11. Ibid., 181.

12. Ibid., 209–10.

13. Ibid., 232–34.

14. Guy Sorman, *La solution libérale* (Paris: Fayard, 1984; Pluriel, 1984), 13, 23–24, 31–33, 60–63, 67.

15. Ibid., the preface and 102–4, 108–10, 127–28, 158.

16. Ibid., 178.

17. *L'Express*, 24 May 1985, for a lengthy article on this little-known club.

18. Michel Prigent, ed., *La liberté à refaire* (Paris: Hachette, 1984).

19. Ibid., 390–91.

20. Michel Massenet, "Le reste du chemin," in ibid., 464, 479.

21. See Charles Millon, *L'extravagante histoire des nationalisations* (Paris: Plon, 1984); Bertrand Jacquillat, *Désétatiser* (Paris: Robert Laffont, 1985); Jean Loyrette, *Dénationaliser: Comment réussir la privatisation* (Paris: Dunod, 1986).

22. Jacquillat, *Désétatiser*, 27.

23. Ibid., 23, 30–46.

24. Ibid., 91.

25. Ibid., 138–40, 144–47, 154.

26. Ibid., 198–99, 201–3, 211, 266–71, 279, and chap. 10.

27. Ibid., 293–94.

28. See Raymond Barre, *Réflexions pour demain* (Paris: Hachette, 1984), 36–38, 42, and Valéry Giscard d'Estaing, *Deux Français sur trois*, 2d ed. (Paris: Flammarion, 1984; Le Livre de Poche, 1985), 141–68.

29. Barre, *Réflexions*, 111.

30. Ibid., 174–78, 184, 275–93, 435.

31. Giscard d'Estaing, *Deux Français*, 77–79, 117–40, 141–52.

32. Ibid., 153–85, 213–21, 223–59.

33. Ibid., 288–89, 295–97.

34. Pierre Pascallon, ed., *Pour sortir la France de la crise* (Paris: Éditions Cujas, 1986), 234–43.

35. Ibid., 295–97, 335–40.

36. Jean-Marie Benoist, *Le devoir d'opposition* (Paris: Robert Laffont, 1982), 9–10, 16–17, 21, 81, 97–101, 140–41, 266.

37. Ibid., 27–29.

38. Bernard-Henri Lévy, *Questions de principe* (Paris: Editions Denoël, 1983), 26–27, 28, 30–33, 34–36. See also Lévy's earlier work, *L'Idéologie française* (Paris: Bernard Grasset, 1981), in which he identified France as the first racist nation in Europe.

39. Lévy, *Questions*, 328.

40. Ibid., 269.

41. Émile Malet, ed., *Socrate et la rose: Les Intellectuels face au pouvoir socialiste* (Paris: Éditions du Quotidien, 1983), 85–98.

42. Jean-Paul Dollé, *Monsieur le Président, il faut que je vous dise...* (Paris: Lieu Commun, 1983), 21–25.

43. Ibid., 150.

44. Ibid., 51.

45. Jean-Marie Domenach, *Lettre à mes ennemis de classe* (Paris: Éditions du Seuil, 1984), 26.

46. Ibid., 84–87, 118–21.

47. Ibid., 44.

48. Ibid., 136.

49. Ibid., 138–42, 185, 188.

50. Pierre Rosanvallon, *La crise de l'État providence,* 2d ed. (Paris: Éditions du Seuil, 1981; Points, 1984), 7–18.

51. Ibid., 20–32.

52. Ibid., 33–37, 41–48.

53. Ibid., 63–96.

54. Ibid., 98, 103.

55. Ibid., 112–23.

56. Ibid., 132–36. The quotation is from p. 136.

57. Pierre Rosanvallon, *Misère de l'économie* (Paris: Éditions du Seuil, 1983), 25–28, 32, 38, 140–41.

58. André Gorz, *Les chemins du Paradis* (Paris: Éditions Galilée, 1983), 23.

59. Ibid., 38–40, 72, 76, 78, 85–86.

60. Ibid., 98–99, 102, 118.

61. Ibid., 140.

62. Ibid., 150.

63. Ibid., 249.

64. Robert Lafont, *Le dénouement français* (Paris: Jean-Jacques Pauvert aux Éditions Suger, 1985), 12–13, 19–20, 30–37, 133–39, 159.

65. Ibid., 99–100, 108, 123.

66. Ibid., 159–164.

67. Ibid., 182–83, 193, 202, 212–13, 232–33.

68. Les Gracques, *Pour réussir à gauche* (Paris: Syros, 1983), 26–27, 29, 67–70, 80–83, 93–101.

69. Ibid., 29–31, 168–70, 178.

70. Ibid., 119.

71. Ibid., 138, 140ff.

72. Alain Lipietz, *L'audace ou l'enlisement: Sur les politiques économiques de la gauche* (Paris: Éditions La Découverte, 1984), 21, 25ff., 46–53, 56–64, 181–87.

73. Ibid., 80–83, 87–92, 116–17, 157, 212–13, 219–20.

74. Ibid., 252–66, 305–15, 322–25, 336–37.

75. Anicet Le Pors, *L'État efficace* (Paris: Robert Laffont, 1985), 26, 32, 39–40, 71, 82–84, 97–100.

76. Ibid., 159.

77. Ibid., 162, 170, 176–80, 188–89.

78. Ibid., 194–95, 203–4, 215.

79. Ibid., 230.

80. Pierre Juquin, *Autocritiques* (Paris: Bernard Grasset, 1985), esp. the final chapter.

81. See Alain Minc, *L'après-crise est commencé* (Paris: Gallimard, 1982), esp. the last chapter. See also François de Closets, *Toujours plus!* (Paris: Bernard Grasset, 1982); Michel Crozier, *On ne change pas la société par décret,* rev. ed. (Paris: Bernard Grasset,

1979; Pluriel, 1982); and Michel Albert, *Le pari français*, 2d ed. (Paris: Éditions du Seuil, 1985). All of these authors are pragmatic realists, in the so-called Anglo-Saxon tradition, but with a profound understanding of French history and society. They represent the enlightened center and center left.

82. Some examples of the shallowness of Socialist responses to the crisis that the party faced would include Louis Mermaz, *L'autre volonté* (Paris: Robert Laffont, 1984); Max Gallo, *La troisième alliance pour un nouvel individualisme* (Paris: Fayard, 1984); Olivier Todd, *Une légère gueule de bois* (Paris: Bernard Grasset, 1983); and everything that Pierre Mauroy wrote. None of these works is worth summarizing; all of them deal in shallow political rationalizations of Socialist policy. It is significant that François Mitterrand wrote only on foreign affairs, totally avoiding the domestic crisis that the party faced.

83. Jacques Mandrin, *Le socialisme et la France* (Paris: Sycomore, 1983), 57.

84. Ibid., 227–31, for a summary of the argument for the CERES form of socialism. See also the defensive, anti-second-left position of Jean Poperen, *Le nouveau contrat socialiste: Socialistes et libertés* (Paris: Ramsay, 1985).

85. See *La nouvelle revue socialiste* (September–October 1984), an issue devoted to the topic "Liberalisme et socialisme."

86. Ibid., (March–April 1984), "Enquête sur la modernité."

87. Paul Quilès, *La politique n'est pas ce que vous croyez* (Paris: Robert Laffont, 1985), 133 for the quotation.

Chapter 5.
"Moderniser et Rassembler": The Long March toward *Cohabitation*, July 1984–March 1986

1. Thierry Pfister, *La vie quotidienne à Matignon au temps de l'union de la gauche* (Paris: Hachette, 1985), 290–92.

2. Similar arguments on the Mitterrand–Mauroy rift were made by Serge July, *Les années Mitterrand* (Paris: Bernard Grasset, 1986), 160–65, and Jean-Marie Colombani, *Portrait du Président* (Paris: Gallimard, 1985), 116–18.

3. See Olivier Duhamel's analysis in *Le Monde*, 20 July 1984.

4. *L'Express*, 27 July 1984.

5. On Fabius, see ibid., and *Le Monde*, 26 October 1985; *Le Point,* 23 July 1984.

6. See Jacques Mandrin, *Le socialisme et la France* (Paris: Sycomore, 1983), 10ff.

7. *Le Point,* 23 July 1984; *Le Monde*, 21 July 1984; July, *Les années Mitterrand*, 186–88.

8. See Laurent Fabius, *Le coeur du futur* (Paris: Calmann-Lévy, 1985), 49–62.

9. *L'Express,* 3 August 1984.

10. *Le Nouvel Observateur,* 31 August 1984.

11. These quotations from leading Socialists were presented in *Le Monde,* 7 December 1984.

12. See *L'Express,* 27 July 1984; *Le Monde,* 14 September 1984; *Le Point,* 17 September 1984.

13. See ibid., and Philippe Bauchard, *La Guerre des deux roses: Du rêve à la réalité, 1981–1985* (Paris: Bernard Grasset, 1986), 290–94.

14. On the 1986 budget, see *Le Monde,* 27 June, 26 July, 19 September 1985, and *Le Nouvel Observateur,* 20 September 1985.

15. For the quotation, see *Le Nouvel Observateur,* 20 September 1985; see also *Le Monde,* 21 June, 26 July 1985.

16. Colombani, *Portrait du Président,* 90.

17. *Le Nouvel Observateur,* 31 August 1984; *Le Monde,* 28 September 1984, and 18 February 1985; Bauchard, *La Guerre,* 297–99.

18. *Le Monde,* 6 February, 18 April, 18 July, 19 December 1985.

19. Ibid., 28 September 1984, and 24 December 1985.

20. Ibid., 21, 22 February, 18, 28 November 1985; *Le Nouvel Observateur,* 15 November 1985; *L'Express,* 24 January 1986; Bernard Moss, "After the Auroux Laws: Employers, Industrial Relations and the Right in France," *West European Politics* 11, no. 1 (January 1988): 77.

21. On the declining image of the unions, see Olivier Duhamel and Jean-Luc Parodi, "Images syndicales," *Pouvoirs* 26 (1983): 153–63. On strikes, see *Le Monde,* 21 February 1986. On *comités d'entreprise,* see *Le Monde,* 1 August 1985. On CFDT membership, see *L'Express,* 6 July 1984. For Maire's and Krasucki's comments, see *Le Monde,* 12 June 1985, and *Le Point,* 9 September 1985. See also Edmond Maire's comments on the social security elections of 1983 in Pierre Nora, ed., *La C.F.D.T. en questions* (Paris: Gallimard, 1984), 239; and on the unions under the Socialists, see George Ross, "Labor and the Left in Power: Commissions, Omissions, and Unintended Consequences," in *The French Socialists in Power, 1981–1986,* ed. Patrick McCarthy (New York: Greenwood Press, 1987), 118–21. The anti-union attitude is surpisingly reflected in the very hostile book by François de Closets, *Tous ensembles* (Paris: Editions du Seuil, 1985), which appeared in the fall of 1985. *Le Figaro Magazine,* 12 October 1985, interviewed Closets with obvious pleasure.

22. For the general thrust of the argument, see the articles on privatization in *Le Monde,* 1 October 1985.

23. Ibid., 4 October 1985, for the Senate report on nationalized industries; *L'Express,* 22 February, 13 December 1985.

24. *L'Express,* 5 October 1984; *Le Monde,* 6 December 1984, 20 March 1985. See also Lionel Zinsou, *Le fer de lance: Essai sur les nationalisations industrielles* (Paris: Olivier Orban, 1985).

25. Zinsou, *Le fer de lance,* 129–51, 249–50; *Le Monde,* 18 September, 1 October 1985.

26. On coal, see *Le Monde,* 13 March 1985; on steel, see *Le Monde,* 7 December 1984, 15 February, 25 July, 1 August 1985; *L'Express,* 9 August 1985. On shipbuilding, see *Le Monde,* 13 March, 17 July 1985.

27. Bauchard, *La Guerre,* 303–5; *Le Monde* 4 February, 11 May, 17 October 1985; *L'Express,* 28 June, 13 September, 4, 25 October 1985; *Le Point,* 14 October 1985.

28. Philippe Alexandre and Jacques Delors, *En sortir ou pas* (Paris: Bernard Grasset, 1985), 112–17, 122 (for the quotation).

29. On inflation, see *Le Monde,* 15 January 1986; on foreign trade, see *Le Monde,* 22 January, 27 February 1986, and *L'Express,* 31 January 1986; on investment and productivity increases, see *L'Express,* 10 August 1984, and *Le Monde,* 14 August 1985 (the OECD report). See also Peter A. Hall, "The Evolution of Economic Policy under Mitterrand," in *The Mitterrand Experiment: Continuity and Change in Modern France,* ed. George Ross, Stanley Hoffmann and Syliva Malzacher (New York: Oxford University Press, 1987), 61.

30. *Le Monde,* 28 June, 22 October 1985, and esp. 5 February 1986; *1981–1986, le bilan de la VIIe législature* (Paris: Syros, 1986), 77.

31. *Le Point,* 14 October 1985. The journal measured total government debt, local and national. For France it was 32 percent of gross national product, for West Germany

41 percent, for the United States 41.3 percent, for Great Britain 56.4 percent, and for Japan 54.7 percent in 1984. See also Jean-Yves Potel, *L'état de la France et de ses habitants* (Paris: Éditions La Découverte, 1985), 350–60.

32. *Le Monde*, 22 January, 4 March, 31 August 1985, and 26 January 1986 (a report of the plan on foreign trade). See also Christian Stoffaës, *La grande menace industrielle* (Paris: Calmann-Lévy, 1978; Pluriel, 1979) for an indication of the long-term structural problems that the French economy faced. Other popular works, such as Jean Fourastié's *Les trente glorieuses*, rev. ed. (Paris: Fayard, 1979; Pluriel, 1980), indicated that the age of economic prosperity had ended by the mid-1970s.

33. J. Brémond and G. Brémond, *L'économie française face aux défis mondiaux* (Paris: Hatier, 1985), 84, 113, 118, 133; Potel, *L'état de la France*, 239–375, on the regions of France. Even the *pôles de conversion* failed to dent the surface. Few jobs had been created in them by the end of 1985. See *Le Monde*, 28 November 1985. For a good analysis of Socialist economic policies, see Alain Fontenau and Pierre-Alain Muet, *La gauche face à la crise* (Paris: Fondation Nationale des Sciences Politiques, 1985).

34. *Le bilan*, 54–57.

35. Ibid., 58–61.

36. *Le Monde*, 16 March 1986.

37. Jean-Pierre Chevènement, *Apprendre pour entreprendre* (Paris: Librairie Générale Française, 1985), 190–96; *Le Monde*, 28, 30, 31 July, 31 August 1984.

38. Chevènement, *Apprendre*, 9.

39. Ibid., 28–29.

40. Ibid., 44–47, 111–12, 145–59, 229 (for the quotation).

41 *Le Monde*, 10 September 1985 and 8 January 1986.

42. Ibid., 27, 28 June 1985, and 21 February 1986; *Le Point,* 9 September 1985; *Le Nouvel Observateur,* 9 August 1985; James G. Shields, "Politics and Populism: The French Far Right in the Ascendant," *Contemporary French Civilization* 11, no. 1 (Fall–Winter 1987): 48.

43. *Le Monde*, 17 July 1985.

44. See Wayne Northcutt and Jeffra Flaite, "Women, Politics and the French Socialist Government," *West European Studies* 8, no. 4 (October 1985): 58–63; Yvette Roudy, *À cause d'elles* (Paris: Albin Michel, 1985).

45. *Le Monde*, 21 June, 14 December 1985.

46. On the Basques, see ibid., 14–15 October 1984 and *L'Express,* 3 August, 4 October 1984. On the Corsicans, see esp. *Le Monde,* 14 August 1984, and 12 June, 13 August 1985.

47. *Le Monde*, 7 November 1985; but see also the articles on the Antilles in *L'Express* 26 July 1985, and the viewpoint of an Antilles nationalist, Guy Numa, *Avenir des Antilles-Guyane: Des solutions existent* (Paris: L'Harmatton, 1986). Numa offers no real solutions, despite the title of his book.

48. See esp. *Le Monde dossiers et documents,* no. 120 (March 1985), on New Caledonia, and Miriam Darnoy, *Politics in New Caledonia* (Adelaide: Sydney University Press, 1984), 267.

49. *Le Monde dossiers et documents; Le Nouvel Observateur,* 30 November 1984.

50. The Council of Ministers decision was announced in *Le Monde,* 23 April 1985. But see also *Le Point,* 7 October 1985, on the new constitution, and *Le Monde,* 12 October 1985, for Pisani's reform agenda.

51. But see Robert Ramsay, *The Corsican Time Bomb* (Manchester: Manchester University Press, 1983). Ramsay believes the Corsican problem will inevitably equal the problem of Northern Ireland. See also Numa, *Avenir des Antilles*, on the Antilles.

52. *Le Monde,* 18 September 1985; Claude Lecomte, *Coulez le Rainbow Warrior!* (Paris: Messidor, 1985), 103–4.

53. Ibid., 29 August, 24, 25 September 1985; *L'Express,* 4, 11 October 1985; *Le Point,* 23 September 1985.

54. François Mitterrand, *Réflexions sur la politique extérieur de la France* (Paris: Fayard, 1986), 29, 31–32.

55. Ibid., 90–91, 95, 100–1.

56. *Le Monde,* 16–17, 20, 21, 27 June 1985; *Le Nouvel Observateur,* 21 June 1985.

57. *Le Monde,* 10, 17, 25 July 1985; *L'Express,* 12 July 1985; *Le Nouvel Observateur,* 5 July 1985.

58. *L'Express,* 5 April 1985; *Le Monde,* 6 April, 15 June 1985.

59. *L'Express,* 6 September 1985.

60. Ibid.

61. *Le Monde,* 10, 24 September, 8 October 1985.

62. See Rocard's speech in Michel Rocard, *À l'épreuve des faits: Textes politiques, 1979–1985* (Paris: Éditions du Seuil, 1986), 37–49; *Le Monde,* 13–14, 15 October 1985; *Le Nouvel Observateur,* 18 October 1985; *L'Express,* 25 October 1985.

63. *Le Monde,* 29, 31 October, 12 November, 11 December 1985; *Le Point,* 4 November 1985; *Le Nouvel Observateur,* 15 November 1985; see also July, *Les années Mitterrand,* 259, 269.

64. The right's program was outlined in *Le Monde,* 18 January 1986.

65. See Zinsou, *Le fer de lance.*

66. Sofres, *Opinion publique 1986* (Paris: Gallimard, 1986), 68.

67. *L'Express,* 9 August 1985.

68. Ibid., 1 November 1985.

69. *Le Nouvel Observateur,* 21 February 1986.

70. Ibid., and 18 October 1985, on Le Pen's supporters.

71. *Le Point,* 20 January 1986.

72. Ibid., 13 January 1986; *Le Monde,* 17 December 1985, and 20 January 1986; *L'Express,* 20 December 1985.

73. *Le Point,* 20 January 1986; *L'Express,* 24 January 1986.

74. *Le Monde,* 13 March 1986.

75. *Le Nouvel Observateur,* 28 February 1986.

76. *Le Point,* 13 January 1986.

77. See Barre's comments in *Le Monde,* 1 February 1986, and *L'Express,* 7 March 1986. For Giscard, see his remarks in *L'Express,* 21 February 1986.

78. *Le Monde,* 17 October 1985, 14 March 1986; *L'Express,* 28 February 1986; see also Jérôme Jaffré. "Front national: la relève protestataire," in *Mars 1986: La drôle de défaite de la gauche,* ed. Élisabeth Dupoirier and Gérard Grunberg (Paris: Presses universitaires de France, 1986), 222–29. Joffré found evidence that National Front voters were more in favor of the Socialists than the RPR–UDF, but most important, he found the FN supporters to be protest voters, not a new radical right.

79. *Le Monde,* 18 March 1985; Andrew Knapp, "Proportional but Bipolar: France's Electoral System in 1986," *West European Politics* 10, no. 1 (January 1987): 103–6; see also Dupoirier and Grunberg, *Mars 1986.*

Bibliography

Books

Adereth, M. *The French Communist Party: A Critical History (1920–1984)*. Manchester: Manchester University Press, 1984.

Albert, Michel. *Le pari français*. 2d ed. Paris: Éditions du Seuil, 1985.

Alexandre, Philippe, and Jacques Delors. *En sortir ou pas*. Paris: Bernard Grasset, 1985.

Ambler, John S., ed. *The French Socialist Experiment*. Philadelphia: Institute for the Study of Human Issues, 1985.

Aron, Raymond. *The Elusive Revolution: Anatomy of a Student Revolt*. New York: Praeger, 1969.

Aubral, François, and Xavier Delcourt. *Contre la nouvelle philosophie*. Paris: Gallimard, 1977.

Auroux, Jean. *Les droits des travailleurs*. Paris: La Documentation Française, 1981.

Barre, Raymond. *Réflexions pour demain*. Paris: Hachette, 1984.

Bauchard, Philippe. *La Guerre des deux roses: Du rêve à la réalité, 1981–1985*. Paris: Bernard Grasset, 1986.

Baudrillard, Jean. *A l'ombre des majorités silencieuse ou la fin du social*. Paris: Denoël, 1982.

Bell, D. S., and Byron Criddle. *The French Socialist Party: Resurgence and Victory*. Oxford: Oxford University Press, 1984.

Bell, D. S., and Eric Shaw, eds. *The Left in France: Towards the Socialist Republic*. Nottingham: Nottingham University Press, 1983.

Benoist, Jean-Marie. *Le devoir d'opposition*. Paris: Robert Laffont, 1982.

――――. *Les Nouveaux Primaires*. Paris: Hallier, 1978.

――――. *Un Singulier Programme: Le carnaval du Programme commun*. Paris: Presses universitaires de France, 1978.

Bergeron, André. *1500 jours, 1980–1984*. Paris: Flammarion, 1984.

Birnbaum, Pierre, ed. *Les élites socialistes au pouvoir, 1981–1985*. Paris: Presses universitaires de France, 1985.

Boucasse, Sylvie, and Denis Bourgeois, eds. *Faut-il brûler les nouveaux philosophes?* Paris: Oswald, 1978.

Brémond, J., and G. Brémond. *L'économie française face aux défis mondiaux*. Paris: Hatier, 1985.

Brown, Bernard E. *Socialism of a Different Kind: Reshaping the Left in France*. Westport, Conn.: Greenwood Press, 1982.

Caton. *De la reconquête*. Paris: Fayard, 1983.

Cerny, Philip G., and Martin Schain, eds. *Socialism, the State and Public Policy in France*. London: Methuen, 1985.

Charzat, M., J. P. Chevènement, and G. Toutain. *Le Ceres: Un combat pour le socialisme.* Paris: Calmann-Lévy, 1975.

Chevènement, Jean-Pierre. *Apprendre pour entreprendre.* Paris: Librairie Générale Française, 1985.

_____. *Être socialiste aujourd'hui.* Paris: Cana, 1979.

_____. *Le pari sui l'intelligence.* Paris: Flammarion, 1985.

_____. *Le Vieux, la Crise, le Neuf.* Paris: Flammarion, 1974.

Claude, Henri. *Mitterrand ou l'atlantisme masquée.* Paris: Messidor, 1986.

Clément, Catherine. *Rêver chacun pour l'autre: Sur la politique culturelle.* Paris: Fayard, 1982.

Closets, François de. *Toujours plus!* Paris: Bernard Grasset, 1982.

_____. *Tous ensembles.* Paris: Éditions du Seuil, 1985.

Cohen-Solal, Annie. *Sartre 1905–1980.* Paris: Gallimard, 1985.

Cohn-Bendit, Daniel. *Obsolete Communism: The Left-Wing Alternative.* New York: McGraw-Hill, 1968.

Colombani, Jean-Marie. *Portrait du Président.* Paris: Gallimard, 1985.

Crozier, Michel. *On ne change pas la société par décret.* Rev. ed. Paris: Bernard Grasset, 1979; Pluriel, 1982.

Darnoy, Miriam. *Politics in New Caledonia.* Adelaide: Sydney University Press, 1984.

Debatisse, Michel. *Le projet paysan.* Paris: Éditions du Seuil, 1983.

Delion, André, and Michel Durupty. *Les nationalisations 1982.* Paris: Economica, 1982.

Denis, Stéphane. *La Leçon d'automme.* Paris: Albin Michel, 1983.

Dollé, Jean-Paul. *Monsieur le Président, il faut que je vous dise....* Paris: Lieu Commun, 1983.

_____. *L'Odeur de la France.* Paris: Bernard Grasset, 1977.

Domenach, Jean-Marie. *Enquête sur les idées contemporaines.* Paris: Éditions du Seuil, 1981.

_____. *Lettre à mes ennemis de classe.* Paris: Éditions du Seuil, 1983.

Donneur, André. *L'alliance fragile: Socialistes et communistes françaises (1922–1983).* Montréal: Nouvelle Optique, 1984.

Duhamel, Alain. *La République de M. Mitterrand.* Paris: Bernard Grasset, 1982.

Dupoirier, Élisabeth, and Gérard Grunberg, eds. *Mars 1986: La drôle de défaite de la gauche.* Paris: Presses universitaires de France, 1986.

Estier, Claude. *Mitterrand président; Le journal d'une victoire.* Paris: Stock, 1981.

Fabius, Laurent. *Le coeur du futur.* Paris: Calmann-Lévy, 1985.

Ferry, Luc, and Alain Renaut. *La pensée 68: Essai sur l'anti-humanisme contemporain.* Paris: Gallimard, 1985.

Feux croisés sur le Stalinisme. Colloque organisé par l'Institut socialiste d'études et de recherche. Paris: Collection de la Revue Politique et Parlementaire, 1980.

Fonteneau, Alain, and Pierre-Alain Muet. *La gauche face à la crise.* Paris: Fondation Nationale des Sciences Politiques, 1985.

Fourastié, Jean. *Les trente glorieuses.* Rev. ed. Paris: Fayard, 1979; Pluriel, 1980.

Fredet, Jean Gabriel, and Denis Pingaud. *Les patrons face à la gauche.* Paris: Ramsay, 1982.

Frégé, Xavier. *La décentralisation.* Paris: Éditions La Découverte, 1986.

Gallo, Max. *La troisième alliance pour un nouvel individualisme.* Paris: Fayard, 1984.

Gaspard, Françoise, and Claude Servan-Schreiber. *La fin des immigrés*. Paris: Éditions du Seuil, 1984.

Giscard d'Estaing, Valéry. *Deux Français sur trois*. 2d ed. Paris: Flammarion, 1984; Le Livre de Poche, 1985.

Glucksmann, André. *La cuisinière et le mangeur d'hommes*. Paris: Éditions du Seuil, 1975.

_____. *1968: Stratégie et révolution en France*. Paris: Christian Bourgois, 1968.

Gontcharoff, Georges, and Serge Milano. *Le décentralisation*. Vol. 1: *Nouveaux pouvoirs, nouveaux enjeux*. Paris: ADELS et Syros, 1983.

_____. *La décentralisation*. Vol. 2: *Le transfert des compétences*. Paris: ADELS et Syros, 1984.

_____. *La décentralisation*. Vol. 3: *Les compétences transferées en 1983*. Paris: ADELS et Syros, 1984.

Gorz, André. *Adieux au prolétariat*. Paris: Éditions Galilée, 1980; Points, 1981.

_____. *Les chemins du Paradis*. Paris: Éditions Galilée, 1983.

_____. *Strategy for Labor*. New York: Beacon Press, 1967.

Gourevitch, Peter Alexis. *Paris and the Provinces: The Politics of Local Government Reform in France*. London: George Allen and Unwin, 1980.

Gracques, Les. *Pour réussir à gauche*. Paris: Syros, 1983.

Hall, Peter. *Governing the Economy: The Politics of State Intervention in Britain and France*. Cambridge: Polity Press, 1986.

Hamon, Hervé and Patrick Rotman. *La Deuxième Gauche: Histoire intellectuelle et politique de la CFDT*. Paris: Éditions du Seuil, 1984.

_____. *L'Effet Rocard*. Paris: Stock, 1980.

_____. *Les Intellocrates: Expédition en haute intelligentsia*. Paris: Ramsay, 1981.

_____. *Tant qu'il y aura des profs*. Paris: Éditions du Seuil, 1984; Points, 1986.

Hauss, Charles. *The New Left in France*. Westport, Conn.: Greenwood Press, 1978.

Hayward, Jack. *Governing France: The One and Indivisible Republic*. 2d ed. New York: Norton, 1983.

_____. *The State and the Market Economy: Industrial Patriotism and Economic Intervention in France*. New York: New York University Press, 1986.

Hirsch, Arthur. *The French Left: A History and Overview*. Montreal: Black Rose Books, 1982.

Jacquillat, Bertrand. *Désétatiser*. Paris: Robert Laffont, 1985.

Johnson, Richard. *The French Communist Party versus the Students*. New Haven: Yale University Press, 1972.

Johnson, R. W. *The Long March of the French Left*. New York: St. Martin's Press, 1981.

Judt, Tony. *Marxism and the French Left: Studies on Labour and Politics in France, 1830–1981*. Oxford: Oxford University Press, 1986.

Julliard, Jacques. *Contre la politique professionnelle*. Paris: Éditions du Seuil, 1977.

July, Serge. *Les années Mitterrand*. Paris: Bernard Grasset, 1986.

Juquin, Pierre. *Autocritiques*. Paris: Bernard Grasset, 1985.

Keating, Michael, and Paul Hainsworth. *Decentralisation and Change in Contemporary France*. Aldershot: Gower, 1986.

Labbé, Dominique. *François Mitterrand: Essai sur le discours*. Grenoble: Pensée sauvage, 1983.

Lafont, Robert. *Autonomie: De la région à l'autogestion*. Paris: Gallimard, 1976.

_____. *Le dénouement français*. Paris: Jean-Jacques Pauvert aux Éditions Suger, 1985.

_____. *La Révolution régionaliste*. Paris: Gallimard, 1967.

Lancelot, Alain, ed. *1981: Les élections de l'alternance*. Paris: Fondation Nationale des Sciences Politiques, 1986.

Landier, Hubert. *Demain, quels syndicats?* Paris: Librairie Générale Française, 1981.

Laurent-Atthalin, Charlotte, ed. *Les nouveuax droits des travailleurs*. Paris: Éditions la Découverte et Journal *Le Monde,* 1983.

Le Bris, Michel. *L'Homme aux semelles de vent*. Paris: Bernard Grasset, 1977.

Lecomte, Claude. *Coulez le Rainbow Warrior!* Paris: Messidor, 1985.

Lefebvre, Henri. *Everyday Life in the Modern World*. New York: Harper Torchbooks, 1971.

Le Garrec, Jean. *Demain la France: Les choix du IXe Plan, 1984–1988*. Paris: Éditions La Découverte, 1984.

Le Pors, Anicet. *L'État efficace*. Paris: Robert Laffont, 1985.

Lévy, Bernard-Henri. *Barbarism with a Human Face*. New York: Harper and Row, 1979.

_____. *L'Idéologie française*. Paris: Bernard Grasset, 1981.

_____. *Questions de principe*. Paris: Éditions Denoël, 1983.

Lipietz, Alain. *L'audace ou l'enlisement: Sur les politiques économiques de la gauche*. Paris: Éditions La Découverte, 1984.

Loyrette, Jean. *Dénationaliser: Comment réussir la privatisation*. Paris: Dunod, 1986.

Machin, Howard, and Vincent Wright, eds. *Economic Policy and Policy-Making under the Mitterrand Presidency*. London: Frances Pinter, 1985.

Maire, Edmond. *Demain l'autogestion*. Paris: Seghers, 1976.

Malet, Émile, ed. *Socrate et la rose: Les Intellectuels face au pouvoir socialiste*. Paris: Éditions du Quotidien, 1983.

Manceron, Claude, and Bernard Pingaud. *François Mitterrand: L'homme, les idées, le programme*. Paris: Flammarion, 1981.

Mandrin, Jacques. *Le socialisme et la France*. Paris: Sycomore, 1983.

Massenet, Michel, ed. *La France socialiste*. Paris: Hachette, 1983.

Mauroy, Pierre. *C'est ici le chemin*. Paris: Flammarion, 1982.

_____. *À gauche*. Paris: Albin Michel, 1985.

Mazey, Sonia, and Michael Newman, eds. *Mitterrand's France*. London: Croom Helm, 1987.

McCarthy, Patrick, ed. *The French Socialists in Power, 1981–1986*. New York: Greenwood Press, 1987.

Megill, Allan. *Prophets of Extremity*. Berkeley: University of California Press, 1985.

Mermaz, Louis. *L'autre volonté*. Paris: Robert Laffont, 1984.

Milesi, Gabriel. *Jacques Delors*. Paris: Belfond, 1985.

Millon, Charles. *L'extravagante histoire des nationalisations*. Paris: Plon, 1984.

Minc, Alain. *L'après-crise est commencé*. Paris: Gallimard, 1982.

Ministre de la Recherche et de l'Industrie. *Une politique industrielle pour la France. Actes des journées de travail des 15 et 16 novembre 1982*. Paris: La Documentation Française, 1982.

Mitterrand, François. *Ici et maintenant: Conversations avec Guy Claisse*. Paris: Fayard, 1981.

————. *Politique 2, 1977–1981.* Paris: Fayard, 1981.

————. *Réflexions sur la politique extérieur de la France.* Paris: Fayard, 1986.

Le Monde. Dossiers et documents. No. 120, March 1985.

————. *L'élection présidentielle 26 avril–10 mai 1981.* Paris: *Le Monde,* 1981.

Nay, Catherine. *Le Noir et le Rouge ou l'histoire d'une ambition.* Paris: Bernard Grasset, 1984.

1981–1986, le bilan de la VIIe législature. Paris: Syros, 1986.

Nora, Pierre, ed. *La C.F.D.T. en questions.* Paris: Gallimard, 1984.

Numa, Guy. *Avenir des Antilles-Guyane: Des solutions existent.* Paris: L'Harmattan, 1986.

Oriol, Paul. *Les immigrés: Métèques ou citoyens?* Paris: Syros, 1985.

Ory, Pascal. *L'entre deux-mai: Histoire culturelle de la France, mai 1968–mai 1981.* Paris: Éditions du Seuil, 1983.

Parti socialiste. *Assises du socialisme.* Paris: Stock, 1974.

————. *Changer la vie: Programme de gouvernement du Parti socialiste.* Paris: Flammarion, 1972.

————. *La France au pluriel.* Paris: Éditions Entente, 1981.

————. *Projet socialiste pour la France des années 80.* Paris: Club Socialiste du Livre, 1981.

Pascallon, Pierre, ed. *Pour sortir la France de la crise.* Paris: Éditions Cujas, 1986.

Peyrefitte, Alain. *Quand la rose se fanera... Du malentendu à l'espoir.* Paris: Plon, 1983.

Pfister, Thierry. *La vie quotidienne à Matignon au temps de l'union de la gauche.* Paris: Hachette, 1985.

Philipponneau, Michel. *La grande affaire: Décentralisation et régionalisation.* Paris: Calmann-Lévy, 1981.

Plenel, Edwy, and Alain Rollat. *L'effet Le Pen.* Paris: *Le Monde,* 1984.

Poperen, Jean. *Le nouveau contrat socialiste: Socialistes et libertés.* Paris: Ramsay, 1985.

Portelli, Hugues. *Le socialisme français tel qu'il est.* Paris: Presses universitaires de France, 1980.

Potel, Jean-Yves. *L'état de la France et de ses habitants.* Paris: Éditions La Découverte, 1985.

Prigent, Michel, ed. *La liberté à refaire.* Paris: Hachette, 1984.

Quilès, Paul. *La politique n'est pas ce que vous croyez.* Paris: Robert Laffont, 1985.

Quillot, Roger. *Sur le pavois ou la recherche de l'équilibre.* Paris: Collection de la Revue Politique et Parlementaire, 1985.

Ramsay, Robert. *The Corsican Time Bomb.* Manchester: Manchester University Press, 1983.

Reader, Keith. *Intellectuals and the Left in France since 1968.* New York: St. Martin's Press, 1987.

Revue politique et parlementaire. *Gauche: Premier bilan.* Paris: Collection de la Revue Politique et Parlementaire, 1985.

Rocard, Michel. *À l'épreuve des faits: Textes politiques 1979–1985.* Paris: Éditions du Seuil, 1986.

————. *Parler vrai.* Paris: Éditions du Seuil, 1979.

_____. *Plan intérimaire: Stratégie pour deux ans, 1982/1983*. Paris: Flammarion, 1982.

Rocard, Michel, et. al. *Qu'est-ce que la social-démocratie?* Paris: Faire, 1979.

Rosanvallon, Pierre. *L'âge de l'autogestion*. Paris: Éditions du Seuil, 1976.

_____. *La crise de l'État providence*. 2d ed. Paris: Éditions du Seuil, 1981; Points, 1984.

_____. *Misère de l'économie*. Paris: Éditions du Seuil, 1983.

Rosanvallon, Pierre, and P. Viveret, *Pour une nouvelle culture politique*. Paris: Éditions du Seuil, 1977.

Ross, George, Stanley Hoffmann, and Sylvia Malzacher, eds. *The Mitterrand Experiment: Continuity and Change in Modern France*. New York: Oxford University Press, 1987.

Roucaute, Yves. *Le Parti socialiste*. Paris: B. Huisman, 1983.

Roudy, Yvette. *À cause d'elles*. Paris: Albin Michel, 1985.

Roy, Albert du, and Robert Schneider. *Le Roman de la rose: D'Épinay a l'Elysée, l'aventure des socialistes*. Paris: Éditions du Seuil, 1982.

Savary, Alain. *En toute liberté*. Paris: Hachette, 1985.

Sofres. *Opinion publique 1986*. Paris: Gallimard, 1986.

Sorman, Guy. *La solution libérale*. Paris: Fayard, 1984; Pluriel, 1984.

Stoffaës, Christian. *La grande menace industrielle*. Paris: Calmann-Lévy, 1978; Pluriel, 1979.

Stoleru, Lionel. *La France à deux vitesses*. Paris: Flammarion, 1982.

Todd, Olivier. *Un légère gueule de bois*. Paris: Bernard Grasset, 1983.

Vié, Jean-Émile. *La décentralisation sans illusion*. Paris: Presses universitaires de France, 1982.

Williams, Stuart, ed. *Socialism in France from Jaurès to Mitterrand*. London: Frances Pinter, 1983.

Zinzou, Lionel. *Le fer de lance: Essai sur les nationalisations industrielles*. Paris: Olivier Orban, 1985.

Articles

Ashford, Douglas. "Reconstructing the French 'État': Progress of the *Loi Defferre*." *West European Politics* 6, no. 3 (July 1983): 263–70.

Badinter, Robert. "Un jour je vous parlerai de la justice... Entretien avec Robert Badinter," *Le débat* 33 (January 1985): 4–23.

Balibar, Étienne, "Sujets ou citoyens?" *Les temps modernes* 452–54 (March–May 1984): 1726–53.

Baudouin, Jean. "L'échec communiste de juin 1981: Recul électoral ou crise hégémonique?" *Pouvoirs* 20 (1982): 45–53.

Chevalier, J. "La fin de l'État-providence." *Projet* 143 (March 1980): 262–73.

Cot, Jean-Pierre. "Actualité et ambiguités du libéralisme." *Commentaires* 9, no. 35 (Autumn 1986): 403–11.

Duhamel, Olivier and Jean-Luc Parodi. "L'évolution des intentions de vote, contribution à l'exploration de l'élection présidentielle de 1981." *Pouvoirs* 18 (1981): 159–74.

————. "Images syndicales." *Pouvoirs* 26 (1983): 153–63.

Dupuy, François, and Jean-Claude Thoenig. "La loi du 2 mars 1982 sur la décentralisation. De l'analyse des textes à l'observation des premiers pas." *Revue française de science politique* 33, no. 6 (December 1983): 962–86.

Goguel, François. "Encore un regard sur les élections législatives de juin 1981." *Pouvoirs* 23 (1982): 134–43.

Holton, Richard. "Industrial Politics in France: Nationalization under Mitterrand." *West Europèan Politics* 9, no. 1 (January 1986): 67–80.

Jaffré, Jérôme. "De Valéry Giscard d'Estaing à François Mitterrand: France de gauche vote à gauche." *Pouvoirs* 20 (1982): 5–27.

————. "Les élections européennes en France: L'ultime avertissement du corps électoral." *Pouvoirs* 31 (1984): 123–47.

————. "Les élections municipales de mars 1983: Les trois changements du paysage électoral." *Pouvoirs* 27 (1983): 143–58.

————. "En réponse à François Goguel: Retour sur les élections du printemps 1981." *Pouvoirs* 24 (1983): 159–68.

Knapp, Andrew. "Proportional but Bipolar: France's Electoral System in 1986." *West European Politics* 10, no. 1 (January 1987): 89–114.

Loughlin, John. "A New Deal for France's Regions and Linguistic Minorities." *West European Politics* 8, no. 3 (July 1985): 101–13.

Machin, Howard, and Vincent Wright. "Why Mitterrand Won: The French Presidential Elections of April–May 1981." *West European Politics* 5, no. 1 (January 1982): 5–35.

Mény, Yves. "Decentralisation in Socialist France: The Politics of Pragmatism." *West European Politics* 7, no. 1 (January 1984): 65–79.

Michalon, Thierry. "Sur la question Corse: Dualisme et utopie." *Revue française de science politique* 35, no. 5 (October 1985): 892–907.

Moss, Bernard. "After the Auroux Laws: Employers, Industrial Relations and the Right in France," *West European Politics* 11, no. 1 (January 1988): 68–80.

Nadir, Sami. "Marseille: Chronique des années de lèpre." *Les temps modernes* 452–54 (March–May 1984): 1591–1615.

Noblecourt, Michel. "Le pouvoir syndicale en France depuis mai 1981." *Pouvoirs* 26 (1983): 101–8.

Northcutt, Wayne, and Jeffra Flaite. "Women, Politics and the French Socialist Government." *West European Studies* 8, no. 4 (October 1985): 50–70.

Quermonne, Jean-Louis. "Un gouvernement présidentiel ou un gouvernement partisan?" *Pouvoirs* 20 (1982): 67–86.

Revue politique et parlementaire no. 927 (January–February 1987): 50–68.

Sadran, Pierre. "Les socialistes et la région." *Pouvoirs* 19 (1981): 139–47.

Savary, Alain. "Entretien avec Mona Ozouf." *Le débat* 32 (November 1984): 4–26.

Shields, James G. "Politics and Populism: The French Far Right in the Ascendant." *Contemporary French Civilization* 11, no. 1 (Fall–Winter 1987): 39–52.

Verbunt, Gilles. "Immigrés et associations." *Les temps modernes* 452–54 (March–May 1984): 2053–64.

Wright, Vincent. "Questions d'un jacobin anglais aux régionalistes français." *Pouvoirs* 19 (1981): 119–30.

Newspapers and Magazines

Le Figaro, 1981–86, occasional issues.
Le Matin de Paris, 1981–86, occasional issues.
Le Monde, 1981–86.
Libération, 1981–86, occasional issues.

L'Express, 1981–86.
Le Nouvel Observateur, 1981–86.
La Nouvelle Revue Socialiste, 1975–85.
Le Point, 1981–86.

Index

263